PENNINE VALLEY

The Authors

Geoffrey Binns
Leslie Goldthorp
Lawrence Greenwood
Lillian Greenwood
Fred Helliwell
Freda Heywood

Malcolm Heywood
Bernard Jennings *editor*
Colin Spencer
Bella Travis
Sheila Wade
Edward Watson

PENNINE VALLEY

A HISTORY OF UPPER CALDERDALE

Hebden Bridge WEA
Local History Group

edited by Bernard Jennings

First published in 1992 by Smith Settle Ltd, Otley

Reprinted with corrections 1994

Reprinted in 2011 with the kind permission of the authors and the previous publishers by

Hebden Bridge Local History Society
The Birchcliffe Centre
Birchcliffe Road
Hebden Bridge
HX78DG
www.hebdenbridgehistory.org.uk

This 2011 reprint contains some minor corrections and digitally enhanced images

ISBN 978-0-9537217-4-0

Printed by The Amadeus Press, Cleckheaton, BD19 4TQ

Contents

Acknowledgments

We would like to express our thanks to the owners and custodians of the records listed in the Bibliography and References for the use of their material, and also, for information and advice, to David Fletcher and his colleagues at Pennine Heritage, Colum Giles and Dr Ian Goodall of the Royal Commission on Historical Monuments, Julian Harber, Mrs Joan Helliwell, Dr George Ingle, Dr D T Jenkins, David Michelmore, and all the people in upper Calderdale who have assisted members of the group with their researches. Librarians, archivists and local newspapers have been most helpful, and we are particularly indebted to the archivists of Calderdale, Leeds City, the Borthwick Institute of Historical Research and the Yorkshire Archaeological Society. Extracts from probate records and from documents in the Public Record Office appear by permission of the Keeper of the Public Records.

We are grateful for the support of members of staff of the University of Hull: Professor Gwyn Harries-Jenkins, Director of Adult Education, for assistance with research costs; Mrs Carol Bucknall, Mrs Karen Buttle, Mrs Diane Daddy and Mrs Hilary Drysdale for work on typesetting and lettering; Keith Scurr for drawing maps and Dr Trevor Wild for permission to base the map of canals and railways on a similar map which appeared in an article by Dr Wild and G Shaw in the *Journal of Historical Geography* Vol 1, No 2, 1975.

We acknowledge with gratitude permission to use photographs as follows:

Aerofilms, pp9, 50; R Birch & Todmorden Photographic Society, p65; Bill Breakell & Pennine Heritage, p4; F Brierley & Todmorden Photographic Society, p106; Fielden Brothers, p112*t*; Peter Garnett of Messrs Calverts, p112; *Halifax Evening Courier*, pp8, 30, 55, 101, 118, 140, 159, 205; Hebden Bridge Local History Section, pp174, 176, 189, 190; Brian Lomax, p93; Keith Parkinson, pp127, 133; Pennine Heritage, pp81, 126, 135, 149, 195, 197; Royal Commission on the Historical Monuments of England, p200; W Sutcliffe & Todmorden Photographic Society, p204; *The Times*, pp17, 21, 121, 165, 167; Martin Wade, pp24, 33, 41, 131, 164, 168, 187, 198*t*, 201; Simon Warner, pp11, 12, 61, 63, 113, 115, 117.

The remaining photographs and drawings are the work of the authors. The drawings of houses are by Lawrence Greenwood.

Preface

Upper Calderdale is defined for the purposes of this book as the nine townships west of the modern town of Halifax: Sowerby, Warley, Midgley, Erringden, Wadsworth, Heptonstall, Stansfield, Langfield, and Todmorden with Walsden. The last-named was in Lancashire, the others in Yorkshire. Soyland, which was sometimes treated as part of Sowerby and at other times as a separate unit, is included in the medieval section. The Cornholme area of Cliviger township (Lancashire), which was absorbed into the modern town of Todmorden in the late nineteenth century and is physically part of the upper Calder Valley, is brought into the account of nineteenth century history. The survey of economic development before the Industrial Revolution embraces Halifax, and there are references to the town in other chapters, especially those dealing with religious life and social movements. The book is, however, concerned essentially with the nine townships listed above.

The book had its origins in the research undertaken by a WEA/Leeds University tutorial class which met in Hebden Bridge, with members drawn from the area between Todmorden and Halifax, from 1966 to 1974. We were able to build upon a strong tradition of local historical studies; for example, one important source is the work of a member of the first tutorial class in Hebden Bridge, which began in 1909. A lifetime's research by another tutorial class student, Abraham Newell of Todmorden, went into the book, *A Hillside View of Industrial History* (Todmorden, 1925). The books by W B Crump and T W Hanson, listed in the References, and the publications of the Halifax Antiquarian Society were of considerable value. The work of the class was, however, based mainly upon a rich collection of primary sources, including the court rolls and other records of the manor of Wakefield; the Savile estate papers; wills and inventories; township records; census returns; local newspapers; and a wide range of industrial records, including the insurance policies of textile mills.

From the first meeting, the class was a co-operative learning enterprise. The initial intention was to make a systematic study of the history of upper Calderdale for its own sake, but after a few years the conviction grew that the knowledge gained should be shared with the people living in, or otherwise interested in, our distinctive Pennine valley. A plan was therefore drawn up for a comprehensive economic and social history of the area, treated as a whole and not as a collection of histories of separate towns or villages. This turned out to be an ambitious undertaking, partly because the valley is so well documented.

There was still a considerable amount of ground to be covered when, in October 1974, I moved from the Department of Adult Education at Leeds University to become Professor of Adult Education at the University of Hull. Because of preoccupations there, which included creating the first-ever undergraduate degree in regional and local history, I was able to give only intermittent support to the Hebden Bridge group. I am grateful for their patience and tolerance during the periods when the work was held up for this reason. We kept in touch, however, and the members carried on working, some of them publishing articles or books on particular topics, or contributing material to large-scale research projects on industrial building and vernacular housing.

When we had finally completed a comprehensive account, we had a typescript more than twice the length of the present book. It was too long for publication at a reasonable price; and the whole point of the enterprise would be lost if it reached only a limited specialist readership. On the other hand, in the processes of drafting and editing, the treatment of some well-documented topics, especially industrial history, religious life and social movements, had already been excessively curtailed. The draft was therefore, from different perspectives, both too long and too short. A solution was provided when Smith Settle agreed to publish a more concise version, and the group decided to use the royalties to fund the production, in limited editions, of much fuller accounts of selected topics. By this means the reader is provided with a general survey of the history of upper Calderdale of a convenient length, but future historians will be able to build on our detailed researches without having to repeat them.

This book has been written primarily for people interested in the history of upper Calderdale in particular and the Pennines in general. It also makes a contribution to the history of the north of England, but we have deliberately emphasised internal rather than external connections, considering how a particular development has influenced the historical evolution of upper Calderdale, rather than fitting that development into the framework of a detailed regional comparison. The external connections will be explored more fully in another book by Bernard Jennings and Cheryl Keen, *A History of Yorkshire*, now in preparation. In pursuit of the same objective, to make the book coherent and accessible, we have avoided using technical terms wherever possible, and have provided explanations in the text, and a glossary, for medieval terms and concepts which may be unfamiliar.

Amounts of money are given in the original pre-decimal currency, twelve (old) pence (d) making one shilling (s), with twenty shillings to the pound (£). It seems to us to be less trouble to learn the old values than to deal with odd figures such as 1.67p as the annual rent of an acre of land, or to wade through a text cluttered by the alternative formulation, eg '4d (1.67p)'.

In addition to the authors listed elsewhere, the other members of the Hebden Bridge tutorial class, who contributed to the research in a variety of ways, were Mary Bryant, Bessie Callin, John Cockcroft, Sheila Greenwood, Harold Hemm, Frank Horsfall, Kathleen Lever, Ethel Riley, Irene Tetlaw and Nancy Travis.

Bernard Jennings
Department of Adult Education
University of Hull
August 1992

I

Man and the Landscape

For the study of local history, one of the richest sources is the landscape itself. The 'bones' of the landscape – the rocks, hills and valleys – are the work of nature. The 'flesh' – fields, farms, villages, roads and mills – has been created by man within the framework provided by nature, and therefore provides a unique record of human effort in clearing, cultivating and building, and in economic and social organisation. This is true of any locality, but in upper Calderdale the topography is bolder, and the interaction between landscape and human activity closer, than in most areas. The local landscape is therefore more than a harmonious or dramatic composition of form and colour. It is a document, the record of a thousand years of human endeavour, which can be used to supplement and illustrate the written record.

The rocks of the upper Calder Valley belong to the Millstone Grit, or Namurian, series, alternating bands of gritstone, finer sandstones and shales, laid down when the area formed the estuary of a great river, flowing from the north.[1] Grits are coarse sandstones, in which the grains are visible to the naked eye. Their suitability for making millstones to grind corn gave the series its traditional name. In the course of time the estuary silted up and became a swamp, which was covered with dense tropical vegetation. Periodic changes in the sea level brought further layers of sand and silt, separating the plant beds which were compressed into coal seams. This series of rocks, known as the Coal Measures or Westphalian, can be seen on the east side of Halifax and in the Burnley Valley. From Halifax to Todmorden, however, these deposits have been removed by erosion, leaving the strata of the Upper Grits to cap the highest hills.

A succession of earth movements after the Coal Measures period pushed up the rocks into a fold or anticline which we know as the Pennines. In the upper Calder Valley the anticline is markedly asymmetrical. West of its axis, which runs from Gorple south to the western edge of Stansfield Moor, and then south-east across Langfield Common to Blackstone Edge, the strata dip steeply on the Lancashire side. On the Yorkshire side the beds are nearly horizontal, although the geology is complicated by a series of faults. Natural erosion over a long period, during which the climate ranged between tropical and arctic, produced a rolling plateau surface at an elevation (in terms of the present landscape) of 1,200 to 1,400 feet. The streams draining the plateau were tributaries of the River Calder, which flowed at a much higher level than at present.

At the end of the last phase of glaciation the configuration of the valley was dramatically changed. A tongue of ice from the Ribble glacier pushed south along the Burnley Valley and down the Calder Valley to Eastwood, where it deposited some rocks which had been carried from the Lake District. It may have been reinforced by an ice flow down the Walsden Valley, but the higher land seems to have been left uncovered. As the ice melted, the water from the local ice was augmented by a flood

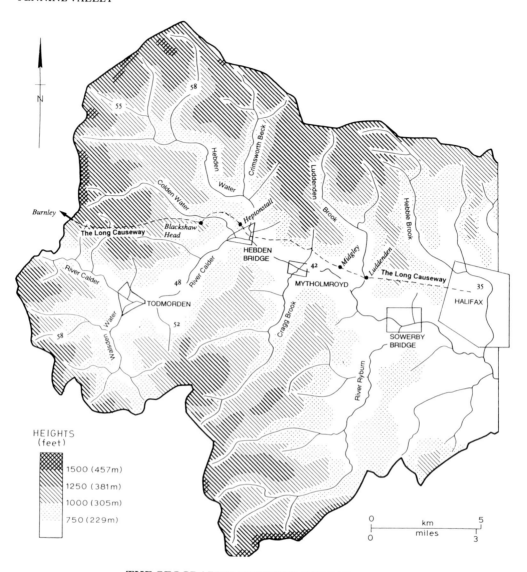

THE GEOGRAPHY OF UPPER CALDERDALE.
Annual rainfall figures: 58.
Modern towns: TODMORDEN.

of water down the Walsden Valley from a lake formed on the Rochdale side, and a similar torrent coming down the Burnley Valley. The swollen Calder carved out a steep-sided valley, several hundred feet deeper than previously. For a time its eastward flow was obstructed by a moraine at Mirfield, filling the Calder Valley with a great lake as far west as Mytholmroyd, where a deposit of gravel about eight feet thick marks the point at which the upper course of the river reached the lake. The tributary valleys, left 'hanging' above the main valley, were gradually deepened as their streams cut down from the old level of the Calder to the new one hundreds of feet below.

Above Sowerby Bridge the main valley has a gorge-like character, which is particularly marked to the west of a fault crossing the valley about three-quarters of a mile below Hebden Bridge. This throws the beds up to the west, creating the massive crags of coarse Kinderscout Grit which overhang the valley and exposing on the lower slopes the Pendleside Beds, the instability of which has given rise to frequent landslips.

The land rises relatively gently above the Calder gorge to form broad terraces at heights of 700 to 900 feet, on the shales overlying the grits which form the lip of the gorge. These terraces continue, although narrowing, along the sides of the tributary valleys. Several of the latter have gorges of their own, giving rise to magnificent scenery such as Hardcastle Crags in the Hebden Valley. From the main terraces the land sweeps up, in places to higher terraces, and then to the moorland plateau at heights rising to over 1,500 feet. The moorland surface is bleak, its most striking feature being the gritstone outcrops, some of which have been carved into weird shapes by the 'sand blasting' action of the constant winds. The rainfall is high, evaporation is low and the rocks are impermeable. As a result extensive peat bogs have been formed, averaging four feet in depth but reaching fifteen feet in places. In a few areas of better drainage, heather and crowberry offer a pleasant change from the ubiquitous cotton grass, the characteristic plant of wet, acid moorland.

The contrasting landscapes of the main gorge, the tributary valleys, the terraces and the moor create great scenic variety and seemingly endless visual delights. At the same time they provide the key to the understanding of local history. On a clear day the view from the moorland heights on the north side is rewarding. The moors themselves show little trace of human activity except for the occasional boundary wall, but the terraces below are criss-crossed with an intricate pattern of drystone walls, farmsteads, roads and trackways. From many of the vantage points which give a good view of the terraces, however, the main Calder gorge is invisible. At the same time the less observant traveller going along the valley bottom by rail or by road may be quite unaware of the life above on the terraces, which for long stretches are completely cut off from view by the crags overhanging the gorge.

The visual relationship between gorge and terrace, with the two often seeming to belong to different worlds, is paralleled by an historical relationship which puts first one and then the other in the centre of the picture. For many centuries the deep gorge, with its narrow, ill-drained floor, was an obstacle to movement and generally unattractive to settlement. Some 4,500 years ago, before the axe and domesticated grazing animals had started their long war of attrition against the woodlands, the valley bottom would have been covered by alder and willow, with a dense undergrowth on the alluvial silt. The valley slopes, and the terraces up to a height of 1,200 feet or thereabouts, were occupied by dense woodlands, mainly oak with birch and pine on the higher ground. There was even some tree growth on parts of the moors. Tree stumps, mainly birch, have been found in the peat bogs, probably dating from a period when the climate was rather warmer and drier than at present.

Sculpture by sandblasting: the Rocking Pig Rock, Widdop.

The earliest traces of human activity in the area are the Mesolithic (middle stone age) implements found on or near the moor edge at Manshead in Soyland, on Saltonstall Moor and near Widdop Reservoir. These tools were used by hunters and food gatherers. The Neolithic (new stone age) peoples would be the first to create long-term settlements, probably on the better-drained southward-facing sites near the upper limit of the denser woodlands. It is safe to say that the main routeways which ran along the terraces, avoiding the Calder gorge but descending at intervals to cross the tributary valleys, are of great antiquity. Neolithic and Bronze Age artefacts and other remains have been discovered at Tower Hill in Warley, in Midgley and Wadsworth, at Blackheath in Stansfield, Mereclough and Worsthorne – all on the line of an ancient trackway later known as Long Causeway, which runs high on the hillsides, avoiding the deep valleys, to link the Halifax and Burnley areas. A Bronze Age occupation site was excavated in 1950 by the Burnley Historical Society at Mosley Height, only 150 yards from Long Causeway. Another line of finds along the route from Blackstone Edge down the Ryburn Valley to Sowerby Bridge points to the existence of another major prehistoric routeway.

About 500 BC, by which time iron tools were in use, climatic changes brought lower temperatures and a higher rainfall to the area. This resulted in the formation or extension of peat bogs. The combination of wet and cold conditions, acid soils, and the action of grazing animals in eating and trampling seedlings, caused a retreat of the woodlands on the upper slopes, giving the highest moors a mantle similar to that seen today.

The progress of development on the favoured terrace sites is uncertain until early medieval records provide a detailed picture of settlement and farming. It is clear, however, that until the late thirteenth century the great majority of the people lived on and farmed the terraces. The villages and farms were more numerous on the north side of the valley, which had the advantage of a southerly aspect, than on the south side, where settlement was concentrated in areas with an easterly or westerly aspect. By that period, because of population growth, there was little or no virgin land left on the terraces. The farmers had to turn to land previously regarded as unsuitable for agriculture, and they began to clear the steep and heavily-wooded slopes of the main valley. By about 1300 they were wrestling with problems of drainage in the valley bottom.

The centre of gravity of both population and economic life, however, remained on the terraces for another 500 years. The development of the textile industry from the later Middle Ages was facilitated by one of the natural resources of the area, abundant water – soft water for washing wool and water power to drive the fulling mills which were built along the Calder and its tributaries. The cloth trade was combined with farming to produce a flourishing 'dual economy', managed by a prosperous class of yeomen clothiers. Their legacy to us is an unrivalled collection of stone houses, most of them built or remodelled in the seventeenth century, which are strung out like jewels along the roads which traverse the terraces.

The wool and cloth of the textile industry were transported along the old hillside routeways. Their steep gradients, as much as one in four, made them unsuitable for wheeled vehicles and goods were carried by trains of packhorses. The main routes were paved with flagstones and traces of these 'causeys' (causeways) are not hard to find today.

A revolution in transport began in the middle of the eighteenth century which turned the main valley from an obstacle to movement into a multi-purpose highway. In 1761, work began on a turnpike road from Halifax to Todmorden, with branches to Rochdale and Burnley; between 1794 and 1804 the Rochdale Canal was constructed between Sowerby Bridge and Manchester, linking waterway networks in Yorkshire and Lancashire; and the same route was chosen for the first trans-Pennine railway in 1837-41.

This transport revolution broke down the relative isolation of the upper Calder Valley. The valley was now a major through route, open to economic influences from industrial Lancashire as well as from the West Riding. In the first phase of the industrial revolution, which developed locally in parallel to the transport revolution, cotton played a dominant part. Todmorden established and maintained closer economic links with Manchester than with Halifax.

The first textile mills were water-powered, most of them being built along the tributary valleys, eg Luddenden Dean and Cragg Vale. To secure an adequate flow of water in dry periods, dams and watercourses were constructed. Most of these survive as a feature of the present-day landscape, although often the mills which they powered have been pulled down, and the sites reclaimed by birch and sycamore.

The mechanisation of the textile industry was a gradual and uneven process. For several decades domestic and factory operations co-existed. Many families of hand workers, or hand and mill workers, were also farmers or smallholders. The persistence of this mixed economy increased the population of the hillside settlements – the terrace villages and the hamlets, scattered farms and cottages around and above them – to its maximum in the early nineteenth century. The farmland reached its greatest extent at about the same time. Piecemeal enclosure of land from the commons had gone on intermittently over the centuries, with the growth of population and of the dual economy of farming and textiles. During the Industrial Revolution some of the remaining commons were parcelled out in planned enclosures under Acts of Parliament, their rectangular shapes contrasting with the more irregular patterns of the older fields.

Steam power, using cheap coal brought by canal, began to spread from about 1800, although it did not overtake water power in the area as a whole for about forty years. Tall mill chimneys became a striking feature of the landscape, with the indirect effect of blackening the local buildings, drystone walls and gritstone outcrops with layers of soot. Industry and settlement began to concentrate in what were largely new valley-bottom towns, especially Todmorden, Hebden Bridge and Sowerby Bridge. Engineering industries grew up to support textiles. For a time the economic growth of the terrace and hillside settlements was merely halted. Then from the 1850s and 1860s, as most of the remaining hand processes were displaced and the smaller, more remote mills became uneconomic, the hillsides suffered a rapid depopulation. Small farms on marginal land, which could not be kept going without the support of some family income from industry, were abandoned. Walls crumbled and the moors reclaimed fields which had been cleared and improved with so much effort. Both industry and population drained down the hillsides to the towns below, which expanded across and along the valley floor. At Hebden Bridge the valley is so narrow that the town spread up the lower and often very steep slopes, with one house being built literally on top of another.

The migration of most of the local industry to the valley bottom has conferred one great blessing on the area. The old-established terrace villages, such as Heptonstall and Mankinholes, emerged with their pre-Industrial Revolution character largely intact. It is therefore much easier to revisit the past in the upper Calder Valley than

Beanhole Head.

Peel House, Warley (1598).

Heptonstall village, looking south-south-west over the 1764 octagonal Methodist chapel (centre foreground), and the medieval and Victorian churches. Mytholm (top left) and the Colden Valley are in the background.

in places where each phase of development has overlain the evidence of earlier ones.

The valley bottom is dominated by the products of the revolutions in transport and industry – the towns and villages, extended by long ribbons of industrial building and housing to make an almost continuous development from Sowerby Bridge to Todmorden; and by the arteries of communication, struggling for space in the narrow gorge. To accommodate the railway, coming last after river, road and canal, it was necessary to tunnel through projecting spurs of grit and build embankments, bridges and viaducts, which have become a distinctive feature of the landscape as well as recording a fine engineering achievement.

Road, river, canal and railway in the bottom of the Calder gorge, looking east-north-east to Hebden Bridge.

Looking south across the top of the Calder gorge between Todmorden and
Hebden Bridge.

Todmorden Edge, looking north over the mist-covered Burnley Valley to Bride
Stones on the skyline.

Lumb Falls and packhorse bridge, Crimsworth Dean.

Stoodley Pike (first built to celebrate the defeat of Napoleon in 1814) from
Stoodley Glen.

A study of the local landscape, as well as offering to the discerning eye an outline
of the history of the last six or seven centuries, can whet the appetite for more detailed
historical investigation. How did the medieval farmer cope with the problems of
cultivating land at heights of 700 to 900 feet in a cool and damp climate? What were
the causes of early industrial growth and of the emergence of the dual economy? Did
social institutions develop locally along different lines from those of the lowlands? Has
the character of the people of the valley been influenced by a long struggle with a
relatively hostile environment?

These questions are social as well as economic, because the topography, geology and
climate had indirect as well as direct effects. The medieval overlords had a hunting
lodge at Sowerby, but no castle – the area had neither strategic nor economic
importance. It was unattractive as a base for the leading landowners of the seventeenth
and eighteenth centuries, the Saviles, who built their great houses in gentler lowland
settings. Upper Calderdale never had any powerful resident lords. Until the fifteenth
century there was only one church in the valley above Halifax, and the local clergy
were men of humble status and limited influence. There was therefore no culture of
subservience to inhibit the yeoman clothiers.

At every stage of the historical investigation, the influence of the striking physical
setting should be borne in mind. A good local historian always has to be something of
a geographer. In upper Calderdale the two disciplines naturally go hand in hand.

2

The Early History of the Valley

The earliest documentary record of life in upper Calderdale is *Domesday Book* (1086), compiled twenty years after the Norman Conquest. There are no written records, as far as this this area is concerned, of the earlier conquests and migrations: by the English (Anglo-Saxons), who overcame the British tribes in West Yorkshire in the early seventh century; by the Danes, who conquered Yorkshire in AD 867 and settled their army on the land; and by the Norsemen, who came into the Yorkshire Pennines in the tenth century from older Viking colonies in Ireland and the Lake District, in a gradual and probably peaceful process. However, as we shall see, some light can be thrown on these developments by the study of place names.

The local *Domesday* entry reads:

In Wachefeld [Wakefield] with 9 berewicks, Sandala
[Sandal Magna], Sorebi [Sowerby], Werlafeslei
[Warley], Micleie [Midgley], Wadeswrde [Wadsworth],
Crumbetonestun [Cruttonstall in Erringden],
Langefelt [Langfield], Stanesfelt [Stansfield],
there are for geld 60 carucates of land and 3 $\frac{1}{3}$
bovates. 30 ploughs can plough this land. This
manor belonged to King Edward. Now they are in the
hands of the King [William]. There are 4 villani
there, and 3 priests and 2 churches and 7 sokemen
and 16 bordarii. Together they have 7 ploughs.
Pasturable woodland 6 leagues long and 4 leagues
broad. The whole 6 leagues long and 6 leagues broad.
In the time of King Edward it was worth £60; now £15.[1]

Allowing Cruttonstall to stand for Erringden, all of the Yorkshire townships of the upper Calder Valley are included in the above list, with the exception of Heptonstall. The latter township was, in the Middle Ages, part of the rectory manor of Halifax, which was in turn part of the greater manor of Wakefield. But Halifax is also missing from the account, probably the result of a simple clerical error; only eight berewicks are named.

'30 ploughs can plough this land'. The amount of land which could be cultivated in a year by one eight-ox plough team was known as a ploughland, made up of eight oxgangs or bovates. A ploughland is conventionally 120 acres, which would mean an oxgang of 15 acres. A survey of 1309 gives the size of the oxgang as 15 acres in Sowerby, 10 in Soyland and 18 in most of Warley.[2] If comparable figures were used in the rest of the manor of Wakefield, the total arable acreage of the lordship would have been of the order of 3-4,000. The term carucate, which can be used interchangeably with ploughland, here denotes a unit for the collection of a tax, the 'geld'. The carucage of the manor was just over twice the measurement of the ploughlands, suggesting that a good deal of its taxable capacity derived from pastoral farming. Two-thirds of the whole area of the manor (54 out of 81 square miles, a league being 1½ miles) was classed as pasturable woodland.

The landholders listed in the manor including its berewicks (outlying parts) were sokemen, free peasants who owed certain payments or services to the lord, and two classes of servile tenants. 'Bordarii' were smallholders, 'villani' held more land but owed more rents and services. Three priests took care of two churches. One of the latter may have been at Halifax, the centre of a huge parish.

The most striking feature of the local *Domesday* record is the decline of three-quarters in the value and agricultural activity of the manor and its berewicks since 1066. In addition only three of the fourteen dependent townships which made up the soke of Wakefield (around Wakefield and to the south-west, along the Holme Valley) had any tenants and plough teams in 1086, all three lying close to Wakefield. A comparative study of other large lordships which included Pennine tracts suggests that if fuller details had been given, most of the seven plough teams mentioned would have been found to be in Wakefield and Sandal Magna.

The value of Yorkshire as a whole showed a fall of about two-thirds between 1066 and 1086, with half of the townships described in *Domesday* as wholly or partly 'waste'. The main cause of this situation was the Norman devastation of Yorkshire in the winter of 1069-70, after a rebellion against William the Conqueror. Nearly all of the upper valleys and moor-edge settlements of the Yorkshire Pennines were completely 'waste' seventeen years later. It is, however, most unlikely that the Norman armies could have made a clean sweep of this extensive hill country, destroying all the farms and stock, in a midwinter campaign lasting for two or three months. None of the theories put forward to explain the distribution of 'waste' in 1086 is wholly convincing, but one partial explanation may be offered. Large 'waste' areas in the upland tracts of the great Yorkshire lordships were administered by the new Norman lords as hunting forests, some of which were extensions of pre-Conquest hunting grounds. It is possible that for some townships in these forests, the description 'waste' meant that the people no longer had to contribute to the geld or provide labour services, not that the area was totally depopulated.[3]

All but one of the berewicks of Wakefield formed a compact block in upper Calderdale, up to twenty-five miles distant from the headquarters of the manor. Although we have to wait until the thirteenth century for documentary evidence of what was then the Forest of Sowerbyshire, it is probable that the valley was used as a royal hunting forest and for the pasture of the king's livestock both before and after the Conquest.

The sole Lancashire township of the upper Calder Valley, Todmorden with Walsden, is not mentioned by name in *Domesday*. It was part of the manor of Rochdale, few details of which are recorded.

The early forms of place names often contain both linguistic and topographical information, telling us which language was spoken by the people who named the settlement or location and something about the local conditions in the early days of the settlement.[4] For example, Warley, Midgley and the other place names ending in 'ley' (Bentley, Chisley, Stoodley) are all English names which denote clearings or glades in wooded country.

N

WADSWORTH
Walshaw
HEPTONSTALL
Greenwood Lee
Shackleton(stall)
Crimsworth
Upper Heys
Upper Saltonstall
Lower Saltonstall
Heptonstall
Old Town
Chisley
? Fernside
Blackshaw
STANSFIELD
Hebden Bridge
MIDGLEY
Rawtonstall
Falling Royd
Shore
Wittonstall
Colden Mytholm
Cruttonstall
Redacre
Midgley
WARLEY
Greenhirst
Mytholmroyd
Luddenden
Warley Town
ERRINGDEN
Hathershelf
TODMORDEN
AND
WALSDEN
Todmorden
Stoodley
Bentley Royd
Stones
Snape
Swineshead
Mankinholes
Withens
SOWERBY
Sowerby Bridge
Sowerby Town
LANGFIELD
Walsden
Helm
Inchfield
? Nettletonstall
Soyland Town
SOYLAND

0   km   5
0   miles   3

EARLY PLACE NAMES.
Vaccaries: **_Cruttonstall_** (?=location uncertain).
Domesday names underlined.

Place-name evidence requires very careful use. In the list of twenty-eight names given below as recorded before 1300, half appear first in documents after about 1250. It is not always easy to put a date, even approximately, to the establishment of a settlement. For example the element 'ley' was used by the early English settlers in West Yorkshire from the seventh century to describe a clearing; and 'royd', from the Old English *rod* and meaning land cleared for cultivation, was in active use at the end of the thirteenth century. We do not know, however, when 'ley' was last used, or 'royd' used for the first time, in upper Calderdale.

Place names recorded before 1300
(*Domesday* names in capitals; medieval township names in italics)

Name	Early form if significantly different	Date of first reference	Meaning if not self-evident
WARLEY	Werlafsley	1086	Werlaf's clearing
Luddenden		1284	noisy stream – valley
Saltonstall		1196	sallow (willow) farmstead
SOWERBY		1086	sourland – farm/village
Bentley Royd		1275	bent grass – clearing – royd
Hathershelf		1274	heather – shelf
Marshaw		late 13C	mare – copse
MIDGLEY		1086	midge – clearing
Chisley	Chesewaldley	1296	cheese – well – clearing
WADSWORTH		1086	Wadda's enclosure
Old Town		13C	
Crimsworth	Crimblesworth	1275	small stream – enclosure
Falling Royd	Falgerode	c1250	?falling – royd
Heptonstall		1253	wild rose – farmstead
Shackleton	Shackletonstall	1219	shackle – farmstead
Walshaw		1277	copse of the Welsh
Greenwood		1275	
Rawtonstall	Ructonstall	1238	rough – farmstead
Erringden	Arikdene	1277	Eric's valley
CRUTTONSTALL	Cromtonstall	1086	crooked – farmstead
Stoodley		1238	stud – clearing
Mankinholes	Mankanholes	1275	Mancan's hollow
LANGFIELD		1086	long – field
STANSFIELD		1086	stone – field
Greenhirst		1274	green – copse
Todmorden	Tottmerden	1246	valley of Totta's marsh
Walsden		1235	valley of the Welsh

Nearly all of the above names are linguistically English. Two are Scandinavian, Sowerby and Mankinholes, and one Anglo-Scandinavian, Erringden – Eric's *dene*. These three names probably derive from Norse immigration from the west in the tenth century, rather than the Danish conquest in AD 867. Some of the Norse settlers from older Viking colonies in Ireland brought Irish personal names such as Mancan. The location of these few Scandinavian names on the bleak northward-facing side of the

The village of Midgley (top right) on a terrace above the steep wooded hillside which
was partially cleared for cultivation and settlement in the Middle Ages.

valley suggests that the more favoured southward-facing side was already well occupied
at the time of the Norse penetration.

Only three, or possibly four, of the local place names provide a link with the British
people who lived in the valley before the coming of the English. The River Calder has
a British name meaning 'violent stream', and the first element of Pennant Clough may
be *pen*, the British word for a hill, which is found in Pendle Hill. Two names, Walshaw
and Walsden, include references by English-speaking people to their 'Welsh'
neighbours – which is how they described the native British population. It is possible
that these were isolated British survivals in an area otherwise overrun by the English,
but there is evidence elsewhere in Yorkshire of British people still living in villages or
hamlets with English names.

Five of the listed names originally ended in 'tonstall', the special significance of
which will be discussed in Chapter 4. Eleven of the names refer to woodland (shaw,
hirst, wood) or clearings (ley, royd). Other name elements describe vegetation: willow,
heather, bent grass and the hip or wild rose, which forms the first part of both
Heptonstall and Hebden Bridge (first recorded in 1347 as Hepden Bridge).[5] Add to
these names others such as sourland farm (Sowerby), rough farmstead (Rawtonstall)
and boggy ground (Snape, first recorded in 1313), and the general impression is of the
gradual colonisation of rather wild hill country.

3

Land and Society in the Middle Ages

The manor of Wakefield, which included the whole of the upper Calder Valley except for Todmorden with Walsden, remained in the hands of the Crown until it was granted to William de Warenne, earl of Surrey, at some date before 1121. It descended to the eighth and last Warenne earl, John, who in 1318-19 conveyed it to Thomas, earl of Lancaster and lord of the Honour of Pontefract, for the term of John's life. On the execution of the earl of Lancaster for treason in 1322, the manor was confiscated by the Crown. It was re-granted in 1326 to John de Warenne, with reversion to the king. John died in 1347, without a legitimate heir, and the manor passed to King Edward III, who gave it to his son Edmund Langley. Joan de Bar, widow of John de Warenne, retained one third of the manor as her dower until 1359.

Edmund Langley was created duke of York by his nephew King Richard II. The manor of Wakefield descended to Edward, duke of York, who became king in 1461 as Edward IV. The manor subsequently belonged to the Crown (from 1554 as part of the Duchy of Lancaster) until the reign of Charles I.[1]

Only part of the upper Calder Valley was held directly by the lords of Wakefield, the rest being divided into a series of subordinate lordships and estates. The feudal structure in the late thirteenth century was as follows:

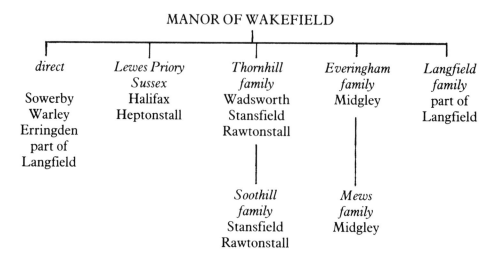

Halifax and Heptonstall townships, together with the parish church and the tithes of the vast parish of Halifax, were granted by the Warennes early in the twelfth century to Lewes Priory, a Cluniac house which they had founded. This estate was later known as the rectory manor of Halifax. In Langfield the family of the same name held the tenanted area, but extensive pastures were retained by the lords of Wakefield. Rawtonstall was part of Stansfield township, but there were at one stage separate sub-manors of Stansfield and Rawtonstall, the latter sometimes being called Rawtonstall with Blackshaw. There are records of courts being held for the sub-manors of Halifax-Heptonstall, Midgley, Wadsworth, Stansfield and Rawtonstall, but no indication of the existence of a sub-manor in Langfield.

From the late fourteenth century until 1480-1, Midgley was held by the Soothills. It then came into the possession of the Lacy family of Brearley, apparently by marriage. The Thornhill male line failed in 1369-70 and their property in upper Calderdale passed by marriage to Henry Savile of Thornhill. In the sixteenth century the Saviles acquired the Soothill interest through the marriage in 1533-4 of the Soothill heiress to Sir Henry Savile.[2]

Todmorden with Walsden lay within the manor of Rochdale. The latter was held, from some date before 1212, by the powerful Lacy family, who were lords also of the Honours of Clitheroe and Pontefract. On the death of Henry de Lacy, earl of Lincoln, in 1311, his estates passed by marriage to the house of Lancaster. Confiscated in 1322, they were not restored by the Crown until 1348. When Henry, duke of Lancaster, became king as Henry IV in 1399, Rochdale came back to the Crown again, to be so held until the reign of Charles I.

It is difficult to trace the early history of landholding in Todmorden with Walsden because it did not become a separate township until the 1660s. Before then it was part of the sprawling township of Hundersfield, which included Littleborough and Wardle. Records of land transactions often give just Hundersfield as the location.[3] In the later Middle Ages the two main subordinate lords were the Saviles of Thornhill, whose property included Inchfield, and the Radcliffe family, who from the thirteenth century built up an estate in Todmorden. In the fifteenth century the Saviles and Radcliffes claimed to hold Inchfield and Todmorden respectively as sub-manors. There is, however, no record of any manorial courts being held, and the authors of a survey of the manor of Rochdale in 1626 denied that there were any sub-manors in Todmorden with Walsden.[4]

The distinction between real and pretended sub-manors is not merely of antiquarian interest. When a subordinate lordship had its own manorial courts, there was a two-tier system of social control. Some matters were dealt with in the courts of the superior manor, and others by the sub-manors. Only fragments of medieval court rolls have survived for the inferior manors in the upper Calder Valley. The court of Wadsworth was used in the 1330s mainly to settle petty disputes between local people over debts, trespass of beasts, breaches of agreements about ploughing, and such matters.[5]

The courts of the manor of Wakefield had jurisdiction over the whole of Sowerbyshire, ie the Calder Valley from Halifax to the Lancashire border, in major criminal matters, commercial regulation and the general supervision of civil administration at township level. For these purposes, people in the sub-manors as well as in the main manor were answerable to the courts of the latter. For example, in 1336 Adam of Swineshead, from Langfield township, was hanged by order of the court of the manor of Wakefield for the theft of cattle at Heptonstall.[6] (Thieves in Sowerby and Warley in the early fourteenth century were beheaded.) In 1316 a fine of 40d was levied upon the constable and township of Midgley, and a similar sum upon the constable and township of Halifax, for refusing to lead prisoners to Wakefield prison.

In 1296 John the miller of Midgley was before the court for selling by a false

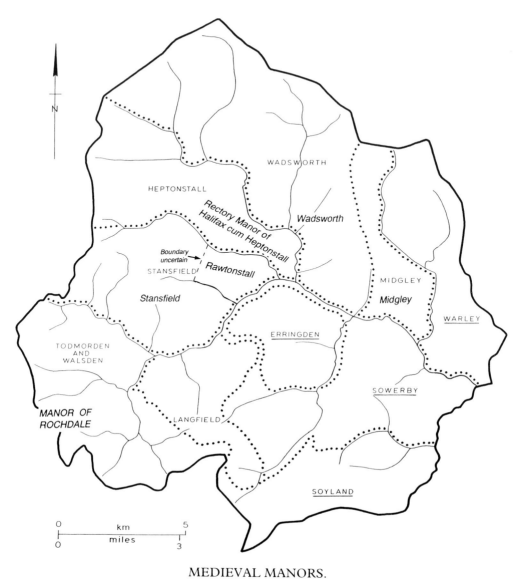

MEDIEVAL MANORS.
Sub-manors of the Manor of Wakefield: *Midgley*.
The townships underlined and part of Langfield were
integral parts of the Manor of Wakefield.

The hamlet of Lower Saltonstall.

measure. The township of Halifax was arraigned in 1337 for concealing forestallers, that is, people who bought up goods which should have been offered for sale in the market.[7] In 1308 the prior of Lewes was in trouble for appointing ale-tasters for Halifax and Heptonstall, which was the right of the lord of the manor of Wakefield.

Each township was required to have a constable. The office was apparently held for one year, and both freemen and bondmen were liable to serve. (The nature of 'bondage' is discussed later in this chapter.) Occasionally men paid 6d or 1s to be excused. The main responsibility of the post, which was described on one occasion as 'the constable of the peace', was the maintenance of law and order, including the arrest of suspected criminals. Collective punishments were imposed for neglect of duty by townships. In 1315 Stansfield was fined £4 for failing to 'raise the hue', ie organise the pursuit of malefactors, after burglaries at the houses of Amery of Hartley and Richard son of Roger of Stansfield. In 1316, when King Edward II ordered a general muster of able-bodied men to fight the Scots, who were threatening Yorkshire after their victory at Bannockburn (1314), it was recorded that 'no one of those elected [to arms] of the township of Heptonstall came, therefore the said township is fined 40d'. Two years earlier the township of Sowerby was indicted for failing to repair Sowerby Bridge, which it shared with Warley township. It is clear from the context of such cases that each township had some kind of assembly to manage its civil affairs, possibly the same body which regulated communal aspects of farming.

One feature of the overriding jurisdiction of the lords of Wakefield was their enjoyment, with minor exceptions, of all the hunting rights in the Forest of Sowerbyshire. 'Forest' in the Middle Ages was an administrative term, not a botanical one. It did not mean woodland, although every forest would contain some woodlands as well as tracts of open country. The term denoted an area subject to special laws for the preservation of wild beasts and their environment. A dispute in the 1230s between the earl and John of Thornhill was settled by an agreement allowing the latter limited hunting rights within his sub-manors.[8]

The lords of Wakefield would be very remote figures to the local people. The authority of the manor was personified by a group of officers. The most senior of the latter was the steward, who in the time of the Warennes was also responsible for the other estates of the earl in the north of England. They had deputies, who were in turn assisted by bailiffs. The administration of the forests within the manor was headed by the master forester, a post sometimes combined with that of constable of Sandal Castle. Responsible to him was the forester of Sowerbyshire, who was in turn assisted by under-foresters. Stock-keepers took care of the earl's livestock in the vaccaries and pastures.

The steward, bailiffs, foresters and stock-keepers were all servants of the earl, paid in money or in kind (although some at least of the foresters and stock-keepers in Sowerbyshire also farmed land). Another important office was that of the grave (in Latin, *praepositus* – 'fore-man'), who collected bondhold rents, received surrenders of bondhold land when a tenancy was being transferred, presented offenders in the manor court, kept an eye on the lord's property, and acted generally as a source of local information for the stewards and the manorial juries.

The graveship of Sowerby was originally co-extensive with Sowerbyshire, but most of the grave's business involved the integral parts of the manor, ie Soyland, Sowerby, Warley, Erringden Park and the moors in Langfield. In 1334 the graveship was divided into two, probably because there was too much work for one man. The townships on the north side of the River Calder from Halifax to Stansfield formed the graveship of Warley, leaving the rest of Sowerbyshire in the reduced graveship of Sowerby. The grave of Halifax mentioned in 1277 was presumably an officer of the sub-manor of Lewes Priory. The sub-manor of Wadsworth had two graves in the early fourteenth century, one for Shackleton, the other for the rest of Wadsworth.

In the manor of Wakefield, the obligation to serve the office of grave rested upon the tenants of bondhold land, whether or not they were personally bondmen. The graves were elected by the representatives of the graveship in the manor courts, presumably on the basis of some system of rotation, and served for one year. As compensation for the time devoted to official duties, they received an annual payment of 6s 8d, very roughly equivalent to about five weeks' pay for a skilled craftsman. The office was time-consuming, it could involve unpleasantness with neighbours, and any neglect of duty could bring down the wrath of the steward and the punishment of a fine. It is not surprising, therefore, that some men tried to avoid serving. In the autumn of 1314, Thomas of Wadsworth was elected grave of Sowerby in respect of a small amount of bondhold land which he held in Mytholmroyd and Blackwood. In the February following he paid 40s to be excused from that office and also from serving as a stock-keeper for life. John of Redacre and Thomas of Soyland were next in line, but each paid 13s 4d for postponement of office. (The reluctance of people to serve at this time may well have been related to the appalling weather and famine of 1314-16, described in Chapter 4.) In 1336 Thomas the mercer of Warley paid 40d to be excused from the office of grave of Warley, and it cost Thomas of Halifax 2s to secure the same privilege a year later.[9]

The courts of the manor of Wakefield had a wide range of judicial and administrative functions. The principal meetings, known as tourns and presided over by the steward, were held twice a year, in October or November and again after Easter, at four centres: Wakefield, Halifax, Brighouse or Rastrick, and Kirkburton. For the rest of the year, ordinary courts were held every three weeks at Wakefield, usually on Fridays, with a deputy steward normally in charge. There was a considerable overlap between the functions of the tourn and those of the ordinary courts, but serious criminal cases, breaches of the assizes of bread and ale (a system of price and quality control) and most matters relating to bondage were dealt with at the tourn.

Apart from criminal matters, the main classes of business were the management or leasing of the lord's mills, cattle stations and pastures (described in Chapter 4); offences against the lord; offences against the local community; disputes between individuals; and, the most important of all, transactions in bondhold land and questions relating to the status of tenants. For the last-named, and most minor disputes, the courts were concerned with the integral parts of the manor.

The most serious offence against the lord was poaching his deer, for which recorded fines ranged from 26s 8d to the £20 paid by the vicar of Rochdale in 1307. The latter was not the only cleric addicted to illegal hunting. The parson of Bury was accused of the same offence in 1361.[10] Examples of minor offences are:

William of Stoodley fined 6s 8d for allowing 14 cattle to stray into 'Ayrykdene Forest'. [Erringden Park, in 1277]

Seyr of Sowerby fined 6d for a mare straying and 1s for keeping a dog with which he guarded his corn, contrary to prohibition [1286]

The tenants had limited rights in the lord's woodlands. They could cut timber, under supervision, for the building and repair of their houses. For example:

One tree in Warley Wood is granted to John of Northend, the lord's tenant in Warley, for the repair of his house, to have it by view of the Forester. [1376][11]

The tenants could gather a limited amount of dry wood for fuel; and cut a certain amount of holly, a valuable winter feed for cattle, but not turn their stock loose to browse it. There were numerous fines for breaches of these regulations.

Even the nuts and bees in the woodlands belonged to the lord. Richard Walker of Sowerby was one of six people fined amounts of 2d to 1s in 1296 for gathering nuts in Sowerby Wood. In 1313 John Milner of Sowerby was fined 40d for 'cutting a swarm of bees from an oak in Luddenden', and had to pay a further 10d for the value of the bees. Tenants who turned their pigs into the woodland to feed on acorns and other fallen nuts, without paying for the privilege, were also fined.

The manorial courts were used to protect the interests of the community. Some collective punishments have already been mentioned. In 1336 two men were convicted of being common usurers – moneylenders, an offence against Church law as well as manorial rules. The fines were fixed by the jury at 20s each, later reduced by the steward to 13s 4d each.[12]

'Slatestones' (thin sandstone slabs) on the roof of the Lord Nelson Inn, Luddenden.

Customary farming practices were enforced through the courts, although it is probable that most problems were sorted out at township level. Fines were imposed for failure to fence arable land in the growing season, allowing animals to stray into the common meadows and obstructing rights of way 'in the open time', ie the period after harvest when the arable fields were thrown open to common pasture.

Co-operation between neighbouring farmers, eg in making up plough teams, was a practical necessity, but it sometimes led to unauthorised borrowing. John Milner sued John Pykeston in 1314 for 'putting one of his oxen to the yoke at night without his consent', (3d damages, 1s fine). A bolder piece of 'borrowing' took place in 1286 when William of Saltonstall was sued successfully by Richard Wood for lending Richard's mare to another man to go to 'Mamcestre' (Manchester) to fetch salt which had presumably come from the Cheshire salt mines.

Lawsuits over petty debts were common, eg for the sale of all manner of goods including arrows, for the use of grass, for the hire of an ox, and so on. In a few cases the debtor was the whole township. In 1335-6, Adam of Coventre sued the township of Warley for 3s 10d, for repairs he had carried out to Sowerby Bridge, and eventually collected 3s.[13]

If a dispute between neighbours or within the family led to violence, it was dealt with by the court as a minor criminal matter and the victim did not normally receive compensation. In many cases the violence was committed by a woman, although the fault was not always hers:

Juliana Wade shed the blood of William the Cowhird, her husband, fined 1s. [1308]

Eva, wife of Richard of Saltonstall, shed the blood of Adam the Wild in defending herself in her own house. Adam is therefore fined 1s for assaulting her. [1314]

Matthew the serving man of Henry of Saltonstall was fined only 2d in 1314 for shedding the blood of Adam the serving man of Ivo, possibly a reflection of their modest social status – the normal tariff was 1s.

Reference has been made to bondmen and bondhold land. The latter can be identified in the court rolls in three ways: by a direct description as bondhold or villein land; by a reference to land held 'by the rod' (after the grave's rod used in the ceremony of putting new bondhold tenants into possession); and by the imposition of a 'heriot', a death duty in respect of bondhold land which from the 1270s, if not earlier, was paid in money. The corresponding death duty for free land was known as a 'relief'. Nearly all of the land in Sowerby and Warley was bondhold, although a small part of it was held by people who were personally free. The tenants in the sub-manors of Stansfield and Rawtonstall were all freemen in 1266.[14] It is highly unlikely that their status subsequently changed. The status of people in the rest of the upper Calder Valley is unknown, although a heriot was paid in Langfield in 1316, when the Langfield family estate was in the hands of the earl following the death of Thomas of Langfield.

A freeman was allowed to hold bondhold land without losing his personal status, but otherwise he had to discharge all the obligations attached to the land including, as we have seen, service as grave. Bondmen were strictly forbidden, however, to hold free land, presumably because this might allow them or their descendants to claim the status of freemen at a later date. The tourn at Halifax heard in May 1275 that:

John the Smith of Staynesfeud [Stansfield] is the earl's bondman, and holds free land in Staynesfeud. He is to be distrained to answer how and wherefore he went out from bondage into freedom.

'Distraint' was the system of seizing some of an accused person's goods until he or she answered the charge.

In 1332 the grave of Sowerby was ordered to distrain John Culcus, 'the lord's born bondman', to answer for living on free land. Bondmen were not allowed to live outside the manor without licence. When permission was given a small annual payment, known as chevage, was levied so that the lord's interest in the person of the bondman was not forgotten.

The tenancy of bondhold land could be transferred by a surrender to the lord and a re-grant to a new tenant, recorded in the court rolls. Provided that the transfer was carried out in due form, the tenants could give away, sell or sub-let their land at will. The new tenant paid an entry fine to the lord, and assumed any obligations attached to it. The economic aspects of these transactions are discussed in Chapter 4.

Bondhold tenants could transfer the reversion of their land, that is, the right to the holding or part of it after their deaths, to one or more of their children. For example:

> Thomas of Connale surrenders to John his son . . . a messuage with toft and croft and 10 acres of land in Sowerby; John gives 12d fine for entry. Afterwards John surrenders the same to Thomas for life. [1307]

This method could be used to circumvent the manorial rule that land descended to the eldest son, the grant of a reversion making provision for younger sons. If a tenant left no sons, but two or more daughters, the land was divided between them.

Some of the common attributes of bondage applied in other parts of the manor of Wakefield, but not in Sowerbyshire. These included merchet, a payment to the lord by or on behalf of a bondgirl for licence to marry, and lecherwit, a fine for the loss of chastity. If we look for reasons why Sowerbyshire was treated differently, two factors stand out. In the first place, it was subject to forest rules, which imposed particular disciplines upon the local inhabitants, and may in consequence have had its own package of rights and obligations which did not correspond exactly with the customary procedures of the manor at large. Secondly, in Sowerbyshire there was no arable demesne (ie land held directly by the lord), and virtually no compulsory labour services. The survey of 1309, which lists the rents paid by the tenants in the graveship of Sowerby, does not mention labour services. The court rolls contain only a few casual references which suggest that some bondmen may have been required to beat for the hunt or do cartage services for the earl. There was no necessary connection between bondage and labour services, in that elsewhere in Yorkshire there were bondmen who owed no labour services and freemen who were obliged to work on their lord's land or send labourers to do so.

However, bondage put a powerful weapon into the hands of a manorial lord. In the event of any dispute about which services were due, and in particular if the lord demanded increased services, a free tenant could have recourse to law with the knowledge that he would probably win if custom was clearly on his side. A bondman could not sue his own lord, and had no redress against the latter if he called for extra labour services or indeed for higher rents. There is the further possibility that the pre-Conquest lordship of Wakefield had a variety of patterns of land tenure and personal status which were obscured without being completely obliterated by the uniformity of the Norman administration. Far from being a standard condition throughout the country, the nature of 'bondage' could vary even in the same lordship.

The absence of labour services conferred another benefit. When the basic peasant holding, the oxgang (18 acres in Warley, 15 in Sowerby) owed specific labour services eg so many days' ploughing and harvesting, manorial lords were often unwilling to allow the holding to be fragmented. There were no such restrictions in Warley and Sowerby, where a free market in bondhold land developed, stimulated by the clearance of new land described in Chapter 4.

The restrictions of forest law applied to free as well as to bond tenants. Both had obligations of service in the manorial courts (although free tenants often paid to be excused) and in the office of township constable, and individual and collective responsibilities in such matters as the maintenance of roads and bridges. The infrequent if irksome duty to serve as grave was attached to the occupation of bondhold land, some of which was held by free tenants, and not to the personal status of bondage.

To the modern mind 'bondage' implies either burdensome obligations or tiresome restrictions, or both. In fact only three things were forbidden to the bondmen: to hold free land, to live outside the manor without permission and to sue their lord in the king's courts. Most bondmen in upper Calderdale must have gone through life without the need or wish to do any of these things. The negative aspects of bondage status might be thought to compare favourably with patterns of 'bondage' known in the twentieth century, including compulsory military service, civilian conscription in wartime, and subtler forms such as the tied cottage system in agriculture. There is no record, however, of what the people of the area thought about bondage. Whether the head of a substantial peasant household in Warley or Sowerby, respected by his neighbours and active in community affairs, who was a bondman, felt demeaned by that status when he compared himself to someone of a similar economic standing and social role in Stansfield, who was a freeman, is beyond the reach of our knowledge.

4

Farming and the Medieval Landscape

The Forest of Sowerbyshire was, by definition, a hunting area, but its value to the lords of Wakefield was by no means limited to the wild beasts which it contained. Forest areas could be developed as pastoral demesnes, either by enclosing part of them as parks to provide pasture for horses and cattle as well as shelter for the deer, or by establishing 'vaccaries' – dairy cattle stations being the commonest meaning of the term. Vaccaries were numerous in the Pennine forests, eg Rossendale and Pendle.

Sowerbyshire had six vaccaries at the end of the thirteenth century: Upper Saltonstall, Fernside or Fernyside, Withens, Cruttonstall, Nettletonstall and Hathershelf. There were peasant settlements at Lower Saltonstall and part of Hathershelf. Fernside cannot be identified with certainty, but may be Ferny Lee, on the opposite side of Luddenden Dean from Saltonstall. Nettletonstall is 'lost', but as it was associated with the pastures of Marshaw and Baitings, it must have been on the south side of the main valley.

A survey of 1309 gives the capacity of five of the six vaccaries, based upon the number of stock which could be fed through the winter, using the hay produced on the vaccary, supplemented by holly. Upper Saltonstall, Fernside and Cruttonstall could each keep a bull, 30 cows and 20 calves. Nettletonstall and Hathershelf were smaller, and the capacity of Withens is not known. In summer the cattle were turned on to the open pastures. The herd from Cruttonstall went to Marshaw, the Nettletonstall cattle to Baitings, and the Withens stock (presumably) to Turley Moss and Mankinholes Moor.[1]

The output of vaccaries came in the form of butter, cheese, young stock and hides. No records of the delivery of dairy produce from the Sowerbyshire vaccaries have survived, but the court rolls for November 1274 give some incidental information about the other two items in an inquiry into irregularities in stock records and the sale of hides in 1270-4. These management problems may have been the reason for the letting off of three of the vaccaries on a stock-and-land lease in 1275, for a rent of £7 a year.[2]

The records of subsequent developments are fragmentary. £8 7s was realised by 'the sale of herbage' at four vaccaries and three pastures in 1308-9, and in 1315 Upper Saltonstall, Fernside and Cruttonstall were farmed out to three different men for a total of £13 14s a year. The latter two were still carrying the earl's cattle. If this was the case also at Upper Saltonstall, the situation did not last for long. At some time between 1317 and 1322 the vaccary was let off in equal parts to six tenants, most of them described as 'of Saltonstall' and therefore from the hamlet of Lower Saltonstall, for a total rent of £3 a year.

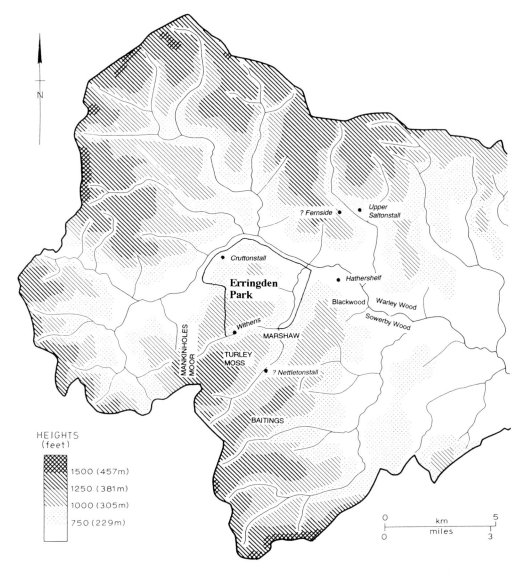

MEDIEVAL VACCARIES, PASTURES AND WOODLAND OF THE
MANOR OF WAKEFIELD.
Vaccaries: *Cruttonstall* (?=location uncertain).
Pastures: MARSHAW.
Woodlands: Blackwood.

Erringden Park

Marshaw Pasture

Cragg Vale from the south.

In November 1332 the six tenants jointly paid 3s 4d for leave to convert eighteen acres of the former meadow and pasture of the vaccary 'inside their hedge at Saltonstall' into arable land, 'namely, 3 acres for each of them'. In 1339 they secured permission, for a further 3s 4d, 'to assart [clear for cultivation] and plough the said land [ie all of the vaccary land] at will'. Whether this miniature 'common field' was merged with that of Lower Saltonstall is not known. Subsequently the shares of the former vaccary were bequeathed or conveyed, not under the usual description of so many oxgangs or acres, but as 'sixth parts' of Saltonstall. The land was subject to heriot, and so was presumably held on the same terms as bondage land.[3]

Withens, Turley Moss and Mankinholes Moor were all let off, for long terms, in the 1320s and 1330s.[4] The lords of Wakefield retained control of Erringden Park, which yielded profits in the form of fees for pasturing stock and the sale of wood as well as sheltering the deer. Although Erringden is mentioned, as 'Ayrykdene forest' in the 1277 court rolls, the palings are not recorded until 1330. It may be fortuitous that there is no earlier reference, but it is possible that the secure fencing of the area was made necessary by the clearance for cultivation, in the early fourteenth century, of land in Cragg Vale and along the northern fringe of Erringden in places such as Mytholmroyd. These clearances may explain the creation of 'Sowerby Ramble', a narrow strip of land running round the perimeter of the park, which remained part of the township of Sowerby even when Erringden attained township status.[5]

The names of three of the vaccaries mentioned above ended in 'tonstall', a name of Anglo-Saxon origin meaning farmstead. Four other places in upper Calderdale incorporated the same element: Shackletonstall (later known as Shackleton) in Wadsworth, Heptonstall, Rawtonstall and Wittonstall, near Shore in Stansfield. This pattern of place names has prompted the suggestion that 'tonstall' may have had locally the specific meaning of vaccary, and that the last four settlements may have emerged from the splitting up of vaccaries, as happened at Upper Saltonstall. The timescale argues against this, as the four were in sub-manors which had passed out of the control of the lords of Wakefield by the end of the twelfth century. It is more likely that the vaccaries were created by those lords in the expansion of demesne farming which began in the late twelfth century, in the case of most of them to exploit the bleak northward-facing side of the main valley between Langfield Edge and Hathershelf, which with a few exceptions was unattractive for peasant settlement. Most of the vaccaries in the adjacent Forest of Rossendale are thought to have been established in the thirteenth century.[6]

Until the end of the thirteenth century, most of the peasant settlements and cultivated lands were concentrated on the hillside terraces, at heights of 700-1,000 feet. Below them lay the steep, wooded sides of the main valley and its tributaries. Above the terraces the hills climbed to the bleak moorland plateau. The basic peasant holding was the oxgang, a variable measure which contained 15 acres in Sowerby, 15 acres in Lower Saltonstall in Warley (an estate sold by the Horbury family to their Warenne overlords in the 1290s), 18 in the rest of Warley, but only 10 acres in Soyland. As far as is known, the acre used in Warley and Sowerby was the statute acre of 4,840 square yards. As will be explained, the local acres in Wadsworth and Stansfield were larger.[7]

By the end of the thirteenth century the uniformity of oxgang holdings in Sowerby and Warley had been disturbed by sub-division and amalgamation. Some tenants held two oxgangs, others only a half. The two townships had between them about 700 acres of oxgang land, arable and meadow, dispersed in strips in the open fields. The arable strips were unfenced except for temporary fences during the growing season, and after the harvest they were thrown open for common pasture by the beasts of the occupiers of oxgang land. Some tenants were fined by the manor court for obstructing access to stock 'in the open time', others for failing to fence the ends of their strips adequately in the growing season.

When oxgang lands in Sowerby or Warley changed hands, they were often described in the Wakefield court rolls as 'lying in the field of Sowerby' or 'the field of Warley'. The term 'field' was reserved for open lands, permanently fenced areas being known as 'closes'. Several of the township fields can be located by using the evidence of the landscape itself, including surviving field and farm names, to fill out the scanty documentary record. The open arable lands of Warley stretched south and west from Warley Town and Hoyle Green. This area has no farms except for the significantly-named Field House, Old Field and Westfield, and lacks the network of lanes which criss-cross the hillsides elsewhere. How far the open fields extended up the east side of Luddenden Dean is uncertain. Lower Saltonstall had its own common field, which probably stretched from Field Head, just above the hamlet, to the edge of the terrace about 250 yards below. By the end of the thirteenth century, cultivation had extended for three-quarters of a mile up Luddenden Dean as far as Upper Heys, but whether as 'field' or 'close' is not known. The emergence of a mini-common-field at Upper Saltonstall has already been described.[8]

The 'field of Sowerby' occupied a terrace facing west and south-west over the Ryburn Valley, where part of its extent is indicated by such names as Longfield, Field House and Upper Field House.

Similar patterns can be identified in other parts of upper Calderdale. The open lands of Midgley stretched down the terrace towards the south-east as far as Mill Field, which was mentioned as part of the common arable fields in the sixteenth century.[9] If there was a parent settlement in Wadsworth it was probably Old Town, because of its location as well as its name. (In the Middle Ages, 'town' had a similar meaning to 'village' today.) It occupies a spur facing south and south-west at a height of 875-900 feet, which extends to the east as a terrace on which Chisley (800-875 feet) stands, to form the most extensive of the locations in the township favourable for agriculture. On the relatively gentle slope to the south of these two settlements is an apron of modern fields (created by the sub-division and enclosure of the former open fields) which have no farms except for Fearney Fields near the edge of Hebden Valley. There is a record from 1466-7 of 'three oxgangs and a plot of land called Pottercliff . . . in the fields of Oldton'.[10]

Crimsworth (900-925 feet), on the southward-facing slope of the upper Hebden Valley in Wadsworth township, had its own common arable field.[11] Some land at Walshaw, the most remote hamlet in Wadsworth township, lay in an open field in 1604, but this could have been created by subdivision during the population expansion of the late fifteenth and sixteenth centuries.[12] It is clear that, as one would expect from walking the ground, when hamlets in the upper reaches of the tributary valleys cultivated their land in open fields, these were small units separate from the principal township fields.

The hamlet of Shore-Wittonstall (975-1,000 feet), in Stansfield township, has in front of it an apron of modern fields on the Warley model, but no medieval documentation has survived. The purchase in 1364 by William Radcliffe of all the lands of Henry Ward of Stones which lay 'within the fences of the Ringge of Todmerdene' may indicate another common arable field.[13]

The lower hillside of Warley, cleared for cultivation in the early fourteenth century,
from Moor Bottom Lane, Sowerby.

The extension of the cultivated area, mainly by the clearing of the valley slopes below
the main terraces, can be traced in detail for Sowerby and Warley in the Wakefield
Manor records: the court rolls from 1274; a survey dated September 1309; and some
fifteenth century accounts.[14] (The survey, which survives only as a sixteenth century
copy, has some errors and omissions, but these can be corrected by correlation with
the court rolls.)

No 'assarts' – clearances of virgin land for cultivation – are recorded in the surviving
thirteenth century court rolls, which cover the years 1274-7, 1284-6 and 1296-8, except
for a few in 1298. Instead there is clear evidence of a retreat of cultivation, resulting
from soil exhaustion or a fall in population, or both. Whole oxgangs as well as smaller
holdings were abandoned. There is evidence of recovery in 1296-7 when six derelict
oxgangs, including three at Helm in Sowerby, and several smaller parcels of land were
re-occupied.

At some time between 1298 and 1306, when there is a gap in the court rolls, there
was a change of manorial policy over assarting. The annual rent was increased from
4d to 6d an acre. With the land market so sluggish as late as the middle 1290s, such
an increase could not have been achieved without some special incentive. This must
have been the release of hitherto preserved woodlands for assarting – many of the new
clearances are described as being in Warley Wood or Sowerby Wood. These woodlands
have left traces on the map, including Warley Wood Lane and Wood Lane in Sowerby,

and physical remains on slopes too steep to clear such as Hathershelf Scout. Another area of woodland which appears in the records of assarting was Blackwood, to the north and northwest of Boulder Clough in Sowerby. The incentives for the lord in releasing these lands were not only higher land rents but also greatly increased entry fines. The latter were not penalties, but payments made to the lord when land was cleared or tenancies changed hands.

The land cleared before the change of policy and rented at 4d an acre (45 acres in Sowerby and 29 in Warley) became known as 'old royd land', royd being the local name for assart. From the inauguration of the new policy to September 1309 nearly 200 acres in the two townships were cleared, two-thirds of this activity being concentrated in the years 1306-9. Another gap in the court rolls blanks out the evidence of the next four years, but in the period 1313-17, 84 acres were cleared in Sowerby and 20 in Warley. In addition 52 unauthorised clearances totalling 16½ acres, made during the previous 10 years, were reported to the manor court in June 1316.

The entry fines for assarts in the period 1307-9 were mainly 6d or 1s an acre. By 1314-17 they had increased sharply, none being less than 2s and some over 4s an acre. Exceptionally high entry charges were imposed for two valley-bottom clearances, 16s for 2½ acres near Mytholmroyd taken by John of Redacre, and 14s for 2 acres at 'Colden Mithum', opposite Eaves Bottom at the west end of the modern town of Hebden Bridge.[15]

The vigorous assarting activity of 1315-17 is all the more remarkable because it took place during a period of atrocious weather. After a poor summer in 1314, persistent heavy rains in 1315 and 1316 ruined harvests all over Europe north of the Alps. Oats, the dominant crop in upper Calderdale, could withstand these conditions better than other grains – on the Bolton Priory estates in Airedale and Wharfedale, wheat yields in 1315 were 30% of normal, oat yields 50-70% – but in November 1315 oats were selling in the Wakefield area for three and a half times the normal price.[16]

The story is again interrupted by a gap in the court rolls from August 1317 to April 1323, but accounts covering March to September 1322 record another misfortune for upper Calderdale. 'Nearly all of the animals of that district' had been killed by the cattle plague which broke out in the winter of 1319-20. Affected animals from the lord's herds had been moved to the pasture of the Withens in an attempt to contain the outbreak. Heavy losses of work animals must have halted assarting for several years. There was hardly any in the period April 1323-September 1326. During this period one messuage (farmhouse) and several parcels of land totalling eight acres, which had been abandoned, were reclaimed. An abandoned farm at Walsden was noted in the manor of Rochdale records.[17]

Assarting picked up again in 1326 and 1327, when forty acres were cleared, but continued subsequently at a declining rate. In May 1332 the rent for newly-cleared land was reduced from 6d to 4d an acre. The court rolls of the 1330s contain frequent references to land lying 'mold brest' (medieval English for 'soil-exhausted') and abandoned. There is other evidence of declining soil fertility. The entry fine for nine acres of low-lying land at Sowerby Bridge, bought in April 1336, was fixed at only 1s 6d 'because the whole township bears witness that the land is hardly worth anything'. In 1337-8 some 'molebristland' in Sowerby found new tenants at normal rents and with the usual entry fines, but in other cases the latter was reduced. A Luddenden man paid only 1s 6d as a heriot (10s would have been normal) to inherit a messuage and thirteen acres on the death of his father, 'and . . . no more because the land has lain waste'.[18]

It is clear that between 1274 and 1349 the stewards managed the licensing of assarts on the principle of charging what the market would bear. Rents moved from 4d to 6d an acre, and back to 4d. Entry fines were low in 1274-98, higher in 1307-8, very high in 1315-17 and lower after 1323. Fines for a transfer of tenancies followed a similar curve, reaching a peak of 1s-1s 3d per acre in 1315-17 and declining to 3d-6d an acre in 1343-49.

The trends in the colonisation process are shown in Table 1. Assarting had doubled the cultivated acreage of Sowerby, and increased that of Warley (excluding Upper Saltonstall) by about three-quarters. A substantial proportion of this colonising effort was concentrated in the first two decades of the fourteenth century, after which the pace slowed markedly and some land was abandoned. The climate became a little colder and a little wetter about the beginning of the fourteenth century, but that does not explain the abandoned holdings of the 1280s.

The underlying problem was that the upper Calder Valley as a whole, because of topography and climate, was not well suited to arable cultivation. References in the court rolls show that the dominant local crop was oats which, as noted above, could withstand cool and damp conditions better than other grains. As a bonus, oat straw provided a nutritious winter feed for stock. However, the yield was low, an average of 2½ bushels harvested for every one sown, judging by the experience of several Yorkshire estates for which relevant records circa 1300 exist. Wheat and barley ratios in the same period were normally in the range 3½-6.[19] The Calderdale farmers faced two related threats: declining soil fertility through cropping the land too frequently, a problem aggravated by the deterioration in the soil structure caused by heavy rainfall; and a run of bad seasons, leaving them without enough grain both to feed their households and sow as seed.

The 'royd' land, which by 1349 made up nearly half of the arable and meadow land of Sowerby and Warley, could be enclosed permanently, in contrast to the 'oxgang' land, which lay in open fields. The courts of the manor of Wakefield were not involved in regulating the cropping of the oxgang lands, which was dealt with at township level. It is probable, however, that the cropping plans were based upon the blocks of strips known as 'flatts', 'furlongs' or 'lands', rather than upon a single township system.

The manor court rolls provide some incidental information about stock, covering a wider area than Sowerby and Warley. Animals mentioned as grazing illegally, or seized for distraint, included substantial numbers of oxen, which were the normal plough beasts; cows and various kinds of young cattle; and flocks of up to fifty head of sheep. The stock of one holding was recorded because it was passed to the guardians of orphan heirs: 4 oxen, 7 cows, 4 steers and heifers, 23 sheep and lambs and 320 bushels of oats.[20] A random sample of stock and produce appears in a list of alleged burglaries reported at Easter 1317, after the hungry winter of 1316-17. The animals included sheep at Heptonstall and Saltonstall, and stirks (young cattle) at Greenwood Lee in Heptonstall township. Oats had been stolen at Shackleton, Midgley and Saltonstall, and vegetables at Warley.[21]

The troubles of 1315-22 had not faded from the memories of the older people when they found themselves facing a far worse visitation, the Black Death. This was the name given to a particularly virulent outbreak of plague which spread from the Far East across Europe to reach southern England in the summer of 1348. The plague bacillus was carried by fleas which lived on the black rat. The latter was fond of human habitations, and the fleas transferred their attention to people as the rats died.

	Oxgang land	old royd land	new royd land					extra land in 1347 survey	estimates for gaps in court rolls	total
			to Sept 1309	1313-17	1323-36	1336-40	1343-49			
Sowerby	355	45	109	84	52	3	6	22	65-80	741-756
Warley	333	29	85	20	45	5	3	19	40-50	579-589
total acres	688	74	194	104	97	8	9	41	105-130	1,320-1,345

Table I: THE ADVANCE OF CULTIVATION TO 1349. There are a few short gaps in the rolls for 1343-9. The 1347 survey produced a 'surplus of new land', apparently unauthorised small encroachments but possibly in part a paper increase resulting from more accurate surveying. The Warley figures do not include the land of the former vaccary of Upper Saltonstall, brought under the plough in 1330s. The estimates for gaps are given as a range of figures, to avoid a false picture of precise accuracy.

The plague reached York in May 1349. The three-weekly courts at Wakefield functioned normally until the 14th July. The next meeting should have followed on the 5th August, but was in fact convened in Horbury, some three miles away, on the 26th August. No business was transacted in Wakefield until the 20th October. For the rest of the year 1349-50 the courts were busy recording the deaths of tenants all over the manor.[22]

In Warley eight holdings, totalling 100 acres, were inherited from bondhold tenants who died during the plague year; and lands rented at 48s 2d a year were reported as abandoned in September 1350. The latter figure, allowing for the appropriate proportions of land rented at 4d and 6d an acre respectively, is equivalent to an acreage of about 132. The total of 232 acres is about forty per cent of the pre-plague acreage. The figures for Sowerby are 11 bond holdings and 2 cottages, with 95½ acres of land, passing by death; and 18 holdings totalling about 100 acres unoccupied in September 1350. Investigations of waste land recorded in the court rolls in 1350-2 show that the latter figures are incomplete.

The figures may include some land which was 'mold brest' in 1349. On the other hand, if a tenant held only a life interest having surrendered the reversion to his son, the land would not be recorded as vacated by death unless both men died. Secondly, an heir who was under twenty-one could delay 'answering for the holding', ie paying the heriot, until he came of age. The above calculations, therefore, probably understate the mortality.

In Warley only one of the eight holdings was inherited by a son of the deceased, and one by a daughter. The others went to more distant relatives. The deaths of whole families may have been less frequent in Sowerby. Five holdings passed to sons, three to daughters, and only three to other relatives. Conservative estimates of the death rates would be 40% in Warley and about 33% in Sowerby.

The Wakefield court rolls record heavy mortality and lists of abandoned holdings in other parts of the manor. In January 1350 the township of Shelf was described as 'dead', which presumably meant that its administration was no longer functioning. It was back in operation by June 1352. There are some comparative figures for Yorkshire: 45-50% of land in the Forest of Knaresborough vacated by death, and a 45% death rate amongst the rectors and vicars of the archdeaconry of the West Riding. The figure for the Pontefract deanery, which included Halifax parish, was 40%. Two successive vicars of Halifax died in the plague year.[23]

In an attempt to deal with the shortage of labour and rise in wages caused by the Black Death, the King's Council issued the Ordinance of Labourers in June 1349, ordering all wage labourers to accept service at the old rates and not move about in search of higher wages. In February 1351, Parliament passed the complementary Statute of Labourers, which appointed justices to regulate wages and prices. In June 1352 the court of the manor of Wakefield arraigned five women and one man from Sowerby and two men from Langfield for being servants 'who will not serve in the township or parish where they belong, but have gone away to work against the Ordinance'.[24]

Abandoned farms meant empty and neglected buildings. It was reported in the manor court in October 1351 that several men of Sowerby had taken advantage of gales which had blown down four timber-framed houses and removed the timbers for their own use. The culprits were fined amounts up to 3s 4d 'for wasting and destroying the lord's bondhold land there'. (It was the bondmen, not the lord, who erected farm buildings, but once built they passed with the title to the land.)[25]

Not surprisingly there was a marked downward trend in rents and entry fines after the Black Death. When the joint tenants of Upper Saltonstall vaccary renewed their lease in November 1351 for a term of ten years, the annual rent was cut from £3 to £2. When land previously rented at 6d an acre – the new royd land – had lain waste for some time, the rent was always reduced to 4d, in a few cases to 3d an acre, with relatively low entry fines, eg 1s 6d for 5 acres, 1s for 4¼ acres.

The plague returned in 1361-2, 1369 and 1375, but with much lower mortality rates. Subsequent waves of plague tended to be more localised, hitting some communities hard but missing others. Assarting resumed, spasmodically and on a very small scale, in the 1370s, mainly small plots which were probably wanted to round off earlier developments. It was not until the 1440s that the pace quickened, and even then there were several years mid-century with hardly any activity. In 1449-51, however, Erringden Park was 'disparked', and opened for settlement, initially by eight families. This marked the end of pastoral demesne farming by the lords of Wakefield in what had been the Forest of Sowerbyshire.[26]

5

The Beginnings of Industrial Growth

Until the expansion of the textile industry in the late Middle Ages, the industries of the upper Calder Valley were small in scale and were carried on primarily to meet local needs. The area was remote and difficult to reach, so that the stimulus to industrial growth which comes from commercial contact was lacking. Nor was the valley generously endowed with natural resources, with the single exception of water. The high rainfall and the topography, as described in Chapter 1, ensured an abundant supply of water for power; and the same water had the important advantage of being soft when it came to be used in processes such as washing wool.

Water wheels were first used in the valley for the grinding of corn. This was a manorial monopoly, a fact reflected in the distribution of corn mills. By the middle of the fourteenth century, mills were recorded for the sub-manors of Stansfield, Rawtonstall (Hudson Mill on Colden Water), Heptonstall (Hanging Royd Mill on Hebden Water), Wadsworth (Bridge Mill on the opposite bank of the same stream) and Midgley (Brearley Mill on the Calder). In the manor of Wakefield, the tenants of Sowerby and Warley had access to three mills: Soyland Mill on the Ryburn, Sowerby Bridge Mill on the Warley side of the Calder and Saltonstall Mill on Luddenden Brook, possibly the first use of the Holme House Mill site. No medieval records of the mills in Langfield and Todmorden with Walsden have survived.[1]

The mills and their weirs needed periodic repairs. In 1313 the weirs of Soyland and Sowerby Bridge Mills were washed away by floods. As a result of river damage, Sowerby Bridge Mill was replaced in 1379 by a new mill and weir at Luddenden, on the brook of the same name.[2] The mills were normally let to millers – between 1327 and 1335, Stephen Milner paid 36s a year rent for Bridge Mill in Wadsworth[3] – who made their income from the 'multure', the proportion of the tenants' corn which they were allowed to keep. This was one twentieth in Warley and Sowerby. The Wakefield court rolls record fines imposed for going to mills outside the lord's jurisdiction or using hand-grinding stones.

Medieval technology has been described as being based upon the three 'Ws': wind, water and wood. The wind which so often buffets the houses on the high terraces and moor edge in the upper Calder Valley did not have to be harnessed for power because of the abundance of flowing water. Wood, however, was one of the greatest gifts of nature to medieval man. It was used for building houses; making furniture, domestic utensils and farming equipment; as fuel; and even for the moving parts of machinery – not only water wheels, but also the gearing in mills, were constructed from hard wood.

The extensive stretches of timber along the sides of the Calder Valley and its tributaries, especially on slopes too steep to be brought into permanent cultivation, represented a valuable economic asset which was exploited openly by the manorial lords and surreptitiously by their tenants. Substantial sums were recorded for the sale of timber, and a second source of income to the lords of Wakefield was the fines imposed for unauthorised use.

Oak is the wood mentioned most frequently in the court rolls, and carried the heaviest charges and penalties, because of its quality as a hard wood and the length of time taken by the oak tree to achieve maturity. The other trees used by the local woodworkers were alder, birch and 'salghes' (sallow). The wood of the alder, which grew in profusion in the wetter places, is soft. It had no great reputation as timber, although it was used for building timber-framed cottages in upper Calderdale. Other uses of the alder recorded in the early fourteenth century were for making pipes, troughs and dishes, the latter by the appropriately named William Turner. Other woodworking surnames recorded are Cooper, Cartwright and Wainwright.

Alder made the best charcoal, the fuel used in iron smelting. A survey of 1314 mentions an iron smelting forge in the Forest of Sowerbyshire worth £9 12s yearly. The iron was extracted from the ore by the bloomery process, which involved alternately heating till white hot and then hammering to remove impurities. Iron of good quality could be produced in this way, even from low-grade ores, but the yield, as a proportion of the metal in the ore, was low. Most bloomery hearths had a foot-blast, but a water wheel to work the bellows was in operation at Creskeld Park, near Otley, in 1395.[4]

A treadle-operated tilt hammer, known as an oliver, came into use in the fourteenth century. The Wakefield court rolls for 1349-50 record, under the graveship of Warley, the sale of wood for making charcoal to be used at a bloomery equipped with an oliver. This is the earliest known reference to an oliver in England, the next recorded being at Creskeld Park in 1352. It has been suggested that some early olivers, including the one in the Calder Valley, were water-powered, but this is unlikely, as the treadle operation was quite adequate for the task, and was still used in the eighteenth century. Where water wheels are recorded in association with medieval bloomeries, they were probably used for operating the bellows.[5]

Slag heaps associated with bloomeries have been identified at several places in the upper Calder Valley, including Waterstalls in Walsden, Ramsden Clough, Birks Wood, Beaumont Clough in Erringden, and Hardcastle Crags. Some of the sites in the Todmorden area may have smelted ore from Ruddle Scout in Cliviger, where several bands of ironstone occur. Some coal seams outcropped in Midgley and at Dulesgate in Walsden, but there are no medieval records of coal production. Coal mines in Todmorden were leased in 1580 for a term of twenty-one years. The rental for Sowerbyshire in 1607 shows that Henry Farrer of Ewood paid 5s per annum for 'one coollmyn within the graveshippe of Sowerby', but nothing further is known about it.[6]

There are occasional references to local textile workers in the Wakefield court rolls of the late thirteenth and fourteenth centuries. They include websters (weavers), listers (dyers) and walkers (fullers). Fulling was the process of thickening and felting woollen cloth after weaving. Originally this was done by trampling or 'walking' the cloth in a trough of water containing fuller's earth or some other detergent. Fulling was a relatively simple process to mechanise. Two heavy wooden hammers were alternately raised and dropped on the cloth by a trip mechanism operated by a water wheel. Two of the earliest fulling mills recorded in England were in Yorkshire, at Temple Newsham near Leeds in 1185 and at Ripon in 1186.[7] The old name of 'walker' stuck to the trade, however, even to the extent of calling a fulling mill a 'walk mill'.

Brearley Mill and sluice gates; this was originally the manorial corn mill
for Midgley.

In the early Middle Ages the main centres of textile manufacture in Yorkshire were
York and Beverley, both of which produced woollen cloth of a high quality under gild
regulations. During the thirteenth century, the industry spread to other towns, eg
Leeds, Wakefield and Ripon, and over extensive rural areas. One of the features of
this development was the building of fulling mills along the rivers of the West Riding.
Thomas Walker (the fuller) of Warley and Richard Walker of Sowerby are mentioned
in the Wakefield court rolls of 1286 and 1296 respectively. In 1347 Adam le Walker
of 'Hepden brig' was involved in a court case – the earliest reference to the name
Hebden Bridge. In 1382 Richard Nelleson was granted a fifteen year lease of a site in
Heptonstall township to build a fulling mill.[8]

The records available to map the distribution of the rural woollen industry in the
fourteenth century show that cloth production for sale in Halifax and the upper Calder
Valley was modest in scale and had a relatively low ranking within the county of
Yorkshire.[9] Within the locality there was as yet no hint of the future economic
importance of the town of Halifax. The relative economic development of the local
townships is shown by the amounts paid in the taxes known as lay subsidies (the
Church was separately taxed). The tax was paid by the better-off people, whether free

or bond. The earliest surviving return, for 1332-33, lists the taxpayers by name. In 1334 the system was changed to a township quota, which remained the same, apart from remissions granted on account of poverty, until the sixteenth century.[10] The details are:

	1332-3		1334
	Number of payers	*Tax paid*	*Quota*
Halifax and Heptonstall	5	8s 2½d	11s
Sowerby and Soyland	4	9s 8d	16s
Warley	6	10s 4d	16s
Midgley	5	8s	13s
Wadsworth	6	10s 8d	16s
Stansfield	6	10s 10d	16s
Langfield	5	9s 4d	14s

The quotas for the main centres of the West Riding textile industry were much higher, eg Ripon £6 6s 8d and Wakefield £6. There are no separate returns for Todmorden with Walsden, which was part of the multiple township of Hundersfield. It is clear that Halifax itself was no more than a modest village, which had the mother church of a very large parish and a weekly market. There is no market charter, but records of the 'tolls of Halifax' and penalties imposed on the township for concealing forestallers – people who bought privately goods which should have been brought to the market – point to the existence of a local market in the first half of the fourteenth century.

During the second half of the fifteenth century there was a dramatic change in the distribution of the woollen industry in Yorkshire. York and Beverley went into a steep decline. The main reason is thought to be the rigidity of gild regulations and the burden of the charges which were imposed to maintain the gild system. Together these increased costs of production to an extent which made it difficult for weavers to withstand the competition of the unregulated towns and rural areas. It should be noted, however, that cloth manufacture at Ripon, where there is no trace of a clothworkers' gild, had also collapsed by the early sixteenth century.[11]

There was a considerable expansion of fulling capacity in the upper Calder Valley. This was encouraged by the custom of the manor of Wakefield, which allowed people building fulling mills to pay only the normal customary rents, amounting to a few pence a year, for the sites of mill dams and watercourses. In many manors the fulling mill, like the corn mill, was a manorial monopoly, for which the lord could charge a high rent.

Mayroyd Mill, on the Calder near Hebden Bridge, was built in 1429 and Dean Mill on Luddenden Brook in 1440. The Waterhouse family had interests in two mills in 1450, one in Sowerby and the other in Warley. In 1472 one of them became a partner in Sowerby Bridge fulling mill, which had been built about 1465. In 1477 or thereabouts another mill was built on the Ryburn. At least four mills were built between 1495 and 1503, the first on Luddenden Brook in 1495-6. Sir John Sayvile (Savile) granted to John Horsfell, in 1498, land in Stansfield at Keldyz (Callis?) for building a fulling mill, to which the Savile tenants in the township would be obliged to take their cloth. This is the only recorded case of a local manorial monopoly, and

Holme House Bridge Mill, Luddenden Brook, on the site of a medieval fulling mill.

it may have been difficult to maintain in view of the number of mills springing up in the valley. A mill on the Ryburn, probably Asquith Bottom Mill, was built in 1502, and a mill on the Calder between Warley and Sowerby in the following year.[12]

Documentary references to fulling mills come thick and fast after about 1530. They include new mills in the Sowerby Bridge area on both the Calder and the Ryburn, and others on the Calder at Longbottom in Warley and Stubbing (apparently in Erringden); on Luddenden Brook at Luddenden and Luddenden Foot; and on Hebden Water at Midgehole and Lee. At the western end of the area were Hudson Mill, on Colden Water in Stansfield township; two other mills in Stansfield and Langfield; and mills at Gorpley, and Inchfield in Todmorden with Walsden.[13]

The sixteenth century mills were generally small, and powered by undershot wheels, ie wheels driven by paddles dipping into the flow of a short mill race. It was possible to expand on the same site by erecting a second or even a third 'mill', in the sense of additional wheels and fulling stocks, on the same mill race. The references to 'two fulling mills' or 'three fulling mills' in the same location and ownership are probably to such multiple structures. Some sites may have had a relatively short life. Others were continuously occupied over a period of centuries.

The wills of local people in the early and middle sixteenth century contain increasingly frequent references to textile equipment and materials.[14] The item mentioned most often is the shears which were used to crop the cloth after it had been fulled, dried and the nap raised by teazles. They were invariably described as 'walker shears'. Richard Mawde of Warley left to his son John in 1540 two pairs of walker shears, a shearboard and a pair of looms. (A 'pair' of looms had the same meaning as a 'pair' of shears – it meant one loom.) When John died in 1551 he passed on the same equipment, together with a cloth press, to his son Edmond.

The sixteenth century cloth hall, Heptonstall; now used as housing.

Many of these wills also included bequests of land and/or livestock. Testators survived by more than one son normally divided both the textile and the farming resources between the sons, rather than give the looms and shears to one, and the land and livestock to the other. Gilbert Waterhouse, whose family had extensive farming and textile interests in Halifax, Skircoat and Warley, left to each of two sons in 1541 'one half of all my lomes, walker sheres, cloth pressers and sherbordes'. Each son received in addition a substantial bequest of land. By contrast William Grenewood of Shackleton had much less to leave in 1555, but he still chose to divide equally between his three sons and three daughters the following: 7 cows, 2 heifers, a horse, 16 sheep, corn and hay, and a pair of looms.

A clothier with one or more looms, and with other equipment such as shears and presses, represented the apex of a small productive pyramid. A description of the Yorkshire cloth industry in 1588 indicates that for every 4 weavers of kerseys – a coarse cloth which was the staple of the upper Calder Valley – 3 workers were required to sort and prepare the wool, 20 to card and spin it, and 3 more for shearing and allied work, excluding fulling.[15] The weaving and shearing would be carried on wholly or mainly in the clothier's workshop, but most of the carding and spinning was done as outwork by women of the cottager class. The cottagers, who usually combined wage labour with the working of small plots of land, were too poor to bother with the making of wills or inventories.

The main local commercial centre, for the buying of wool and the sale of cloth, was Halifax, where there was a cloth hall in the sixteenth century. There was a secondary cloth market at Heptonstall, where a cloth hall was built in the early sixteenth century. A government commission appointed in 1533 to enquire into allegations that West Riding clothiers were using weft made partly from flocks (hard tufts of wool) listed 182 offenders under Halifax and 60 under Heptonstall (probably meaning the chapelry) out of a total of 542 for the Riding.[16]

Some local clothiers sent their cloth directly to London to be sold at the annual St Bartholomews Cloth Fair or at Blackwell Hall. In 1518 William Harde (Hardy) of Heptonstall bequeathed to his wife and children 'my booth which I have at Sainct Bartholomews juxta London'. Thomas Stancefeld of Higgin Chamber in Sowerby left to his son in 1564 'two bothes in Bartilmew faire at London'.

The reasons why in the period between about 1470 and 1550 the industry of the Halifax/upper Calder Valley area grew more rapidly than that of the West Riding in general are not at first obvious. The material advantages of the area can be summed up in one word: water. The rainfall and topography provided plentiful power, and many suitable sites, for fulling mills. The water draining off the millstone grit moors was soft, ideal for washing wool and for fulling and dyeing. However, these conditions were found in other West Riding localities.

The upper Calder Valley was as badly placed as any part of the Riding for the supply of wool. Sheep farming was relatively small in scale, and remained so until the development in the nineteenth century of new breeds of sheep adapted to the conditions of the ill-drained acid moorlands. The wool was in any case too coarse for the markets which the local clothiers were trying to serve, although it found a use in the cloth industry of East Lancashire. Most of the better quality wool came from outside the West Riding, especially from north Yorkshire and Lincolnshire. Wealthy clothiers bought directly from the graziers, or at wool fairs at Ripon and other market towns. In the early seventeenth century the Priestley family, clothiers of Soyland, had the advantage that one brother lived in London and sent up sacks of wool which he had bought from graziers in Kent.[17] Most clothiers depended, however, on the services of middlemen, who were variously known as woolchapmen, wooldrivers or broggers.

Middlemen were unpopular in the sixteenth century, being accused of monopolistic practices and profiteering. In 1552 an Act of Parliament outlawed their activities in the wool trade. There was an immediate outcry from the small clothiers of the Halifax area who claimed that, being too poor to buy directly from sheep rearers, they were 'nowe like to bee undone and dryven to beggery . . . '. Their agitation was successful, and resulted in the famous Halifax Act of 1555, the preamble to which began:

> Forasmuche as the Paryshe of Halyfaxe and other places theronto adjoyning, beyng planted in the grete waste and moores, where the Fertilite of Grounde ys not apte to bryng forthe any Corne nor good Grasse, but in rare Places, and by exceedinge and great industrye of the inhabitantes, and the same inhabitantes altogether doo lyve by clothe making. . . .

The Act allowed middlemen to sell wool in Halifax 'to such poore folkes of that and other parishes adjoyning as shall work the same in clothe or yarne . . . and not to the riche and welthye clothyers, nor to any one to selle agayne'.[18]

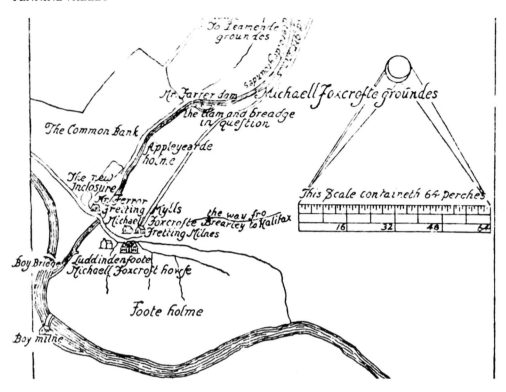

A map of Luddenden Foot from 1599, drawn by Christopher Saxton, in connection
with a lawsuit over water rights for 'fretting' (fulling) mills.

Despite the Halifax Act, the upper Calder Valley was less favourably placed for
access to both wool supplies and markets for cloth than most of the West Riding textile
districts. The root cause of the industrial growth must be sought in the relationship
between the Calderdale people and their physical environment.

Chapter 4 has described the cycles of assarting (clearing land for cultivation),
abandonment of land, reclamation and fresh assarting in Warley and Sowerby before
the Black Death of 1349, and the pressure of population upon resources resulting from
the practice of passing some of the land to younger sons. The mortality of the plagues
reduced the pressure for about a century, but it was renewed in the second half of the
fifteenth century. In 1449-51, Erringden Park was opened for settlement, initially by
eight families. A century later it had fifty households.[19]

Elsewhere there were large tracts of common land above the main terraces, but they
were on the whole too bleak to be developed for the mixed farming of the self-sufficient
peasant household. In these circumstances it is not surprising that in the later fifteenth
century the local people should begin to see the advantages of the loom over the plough,
of developing textiles from a sideline into an activity which balanced the farming side
of the household economy.

Stag Cottage, Heptonstall: a sixteenth century house,
thought to be the oldest in the village.

The starting point of this process was the involvement of some, perhaps most, households in some form of textile production for home use, at least to the extent of carding/combing/heckling, and spinning woollen or hempen yarn. Households without looms sent the yarn to be woven by a 'customer weaver'. Looms could be adapted, by changing the healds and slays, to weave several kinds of cloth, not only different types of woollens but also linen and hempen cloth. The country weavers had the capacity to produce a few pieces of cloth each year, over and above household needs, for sale in the market. The city of York gave them special exemption, in 1551, from the rule that cloth sellers had to be freemen.[20]

The move towards a 'dual economy' involved working the loom for the whole year except the busiest farming periods; providing the necessary support in the preparatory and spinning processes; having a fulling mill within a convenient distance; raising the quality of the cloth from what might have been acceptable for domestic use to market levels; and of course deciding on which kind of cloth to concentrate. Once the finishing and marketing of a particular kind of cloth had become well-established locally, the small producer was drawn to that line as providing the most reliable source of income at the lowest cost and trouble. In the Halifax area the dominant cloth was kersey.

The remarkable economic growth of the Halifax area was the subject of much comment in the middle and late sixteenth century. The antiquary William Camden wrote in 1586 that the inhabitants of the town of Halifax:

> . . . have so flourished by the cloath trade (which within these last seventy years they fell to) that they are both very rich and have gained a great reputation for it above their neighbours.[21]

Camden was mistaken about the timing, as the expansion of the trade can be traced back at least to 1470. More important is his erroneous assumption that the *township* of Halifax, undoubtedly the main market centre for both wool and cloth, was also dominant in manufacture. Sixteenth century records make it possible, for the first time, to make reasonable estimates of the population of the local townships and calculations of their relative wealth, which in turn throw light on the economic effects of the expansion of the textile industry.

A new system of personal taxation was introduced in the reign of Henry VIII. Tax was levied at different rates in the pound on the value of moveable goods possessed or of land occupied. The rate of tax on land was normally twice that on goods. Each taxpayer paid under one heading only, the one which gave the greater yield. Local returns from these assessments have survived for the years 1524, 1545 and 1546. The minimum assessment on land in each of these years was £1, but the minimum for goods varied: £2 in 1524, £1 in 1545, £5 in 1546. The returns are summarised in Table 2.[22]

It will be seen that Heptonstall had been separated for taxation purposes from Halifax, and that Erringden, the former park, now formed another township. Soyland was, however, still included in Sowerby.

The 1545 collection was made in two parts, and one of the returns for Stansfield has been lost. An estimate has been made for this in the percentage figures. The fall in the number of taxpayers between 1545 and 1546 is due almost entirely to the increase in the minimum assessment for goods from £1 to £5. In Langfield, for example, ten people who paid on goods valued at £1-£3 in 1545 escaped tax in 1546, and two more paid on 26s 8d in land instead of £3 in goods.

Between 1524 and 1545 the total assessment of eight of the nine local townships (excluding Stansfield) rose from £725 to £2,311 and the number of taxpayers from 140 to 438. The reduction in the minimum valuation on goods from £2 to £1 accounts for £48 of the latter increase. Other factors were a price inflation of the order of 30-40%, and, probably, some increase in the efficiency of collections. A substantial part of the increase in assessments, however, must be a reflection of economic growth associated with the expansion of the woollen industry. The rate of increase was, however, uneven, with Warley and Sowerby well out in front, Halifax, Heptonstall and Midgley in the middle, and Langfield and Erringden having relatively slow growth. The taxation figures suggest that the western end of the valley had not yet felt the full benefit of the development of the dual economy.

Some rough demographic calculations can be made by bringing together the taxation returns, manorial records and estimates given in the Chantry Surveys of 1548. In 1546-7 Erringden had 23 main tenants and 39 undertenants living in 50 houses and cottages. The taxpayers in 1545 also numbered 23, 46% of the number of households. In 1545 the 5 townships of Heptonstall chapelry had 140-150 taxpayers, including an estimate for Stansfield. Calculating on 5 persons per household instead of the conventional 4½, on the grounds that the 'dual economy' households would be a little larger, gives a figure of 700-750 adults and children. This works out at 44-47% of the

Township	1524				1545				1546			
	Number of taxpayers	Total township assessment £	% of assessment of the 9 townships	Ranking order of assessment	Number of taxpayers	Total township assessment £	% of assessment of the 9 townships	Ranking order of assessment	Number of taxpayers	Total township assessment £	% of assessment of the 9 townships	Ranking order of assessment
Stansfield	13	64	8	5		★	5	7	18	99	5	7
Langfield	4	25	3	9	16	46	2	9	6	27	1	9
Erringden	5	58	7	7	23	94	4	8	12	51	3	8
Heptonstall	11	38	5	8	27	137	6	6	21	103	5	6
Wadsworth	27	175	22	1	52	226	9	4	40	203	11	4
Midgley	15	61	8	6	40	169	7	5	26	146	8	5
Warley	28	88	11	4	78	510	21	2	47	353	19	2
Sowerby and Soyland	22	132	17	3	128	715	29	1	81	581	31	1
Halifax	28	148	19	2	74	414	17	3	43	343	18	3

Table 2: LAY SUBSIDIES FOR 1524, 1545 AND 1546. Percentages are given to the nearest whole number. The symbol ★ indicates a missing return.

Looking north-west from Todmorden towards the headwaters of the River Calder. Left centre: intakes on Todmorden Edge. Right centre: a viaduct on the Todmorden-Burnley railway at Robin Wood, Lydgate.

lower of two estimates of population given in the Chantry Surveys, ie 1,600 (the other estimate was 2,000).[23]

A similar analysis applied to Halifax township gives about 145 households and 725 people in 1545. The township had 32 tenants in a Lewes Priory rental of 1439.[24] This is not the same as a list of households, because of uncertainty about under-tenants, but an estimate of a threefold increase in the population of Halifax between 1439 and 1545 seems reasonable.

The growth of the textile side of the local economy in turn affected the land market. Land which was too infertile or bleak to make a workable mixed-farming holding could present a different picture to a small-scale farmer-weaver. He needed pasture for his cattle and a horse, and land for tentering cloth. The pace of assarting – or intaking as it was now called in the manorial records – quickened in the 1490s, at least in Sowerby and Warley. In these townships, 26½ acres were taken in from 'the waste' in 1489-93, nearly half of it in the Marshaw area of Sowerby. In the next five years, intakes in the same townships totalled over 130 acres. This land was taken on bondhold tenure which, as will be explained in Chapter 6, was in the process of changing into 'customary tenure'.

In the years 1500-1503, contractors took in 258 acres in Warley township, much of it lying between Coldedge and Harewood (now Highroad) Well, and broke it up into small lots for resale or sub-letting. Entry fines for intakes soon rose to £1 an acre, although the rent remained at the customary 4d a year. By this time a considerable gap had opened between the customary rent and the economic rent of the better quality land. Rents of 4s, 5s and more per acre were being paid in the first decade of the century. By about 1560, helped on by the general inflation, the range was mainly between 3s and 10s an acre, with £1 an acre for the smallest lots.[25]

The families of small clothiers were in the market for a few extra acres to keep a balance between their farming and textile activities, or to allow provision to be made for more than one son. The cottager and his family could make a meagre living by carding and spinning for the clothiers, but the occupation of an acre or two, which also brought pasture rights on the common, gave them a greater degree of economic security. Without intaking and sub-letting, the growth of a cottager class would have been inhibited, and the development of the textile industry might have been checked by a shortage of labour. Some intakes were made without licence, but were picked up in periodic surveys by manorial officers.

The lords of the manor of Wakefield did not try to cream off the gain from rising land values, except by increasing the entry fine for intakes. Between 1450 and 1550 there was no noticeable increase in the level of heriot payments on the inheritance of bondhold/customary land, nor in the fines paid on the transfer of tenancies. The profits from higher land values, which accrued to those who inherited substantial holdings, or bought land at the right time, increased the amount of capital available locally for the further growth of the dual economy of textiles and farming.

One Elizabethan commentator, James Ryder, wrote in 1588 that the 'unyealdinge industry' of the people of the Halifax area in 'the use of their trade and groundes . . . enforcinge grounds beyond all hope of fertyllyty' had bred a distinctive spirit of enterprise, including 'a natural ardency of newe inventions . . . after the rude and arrogant manner of their wilde country they surpas the rest in wisdom and wealth'. Herbert Heaton, in his history of the Yorkshire cloth trade, commented drily that the economic growth of the area in the fifteenth and sixteenth centuries, which was 'to contemporaries a matter of awe and wonder', provided the local people with 'a perennial theme for jubilant self-satisfaction'.[26]

6

Land and Society in the Sixteenth and Seventeenth Centuries

Landlords, tenants and enclosure
The development of the manorial structure of the upper Calder Valley until the early sixteenth century has been described in Chapter 3. The pattern in the 1530s, on the eve of the suppression of Lewes Priory, was as follows:

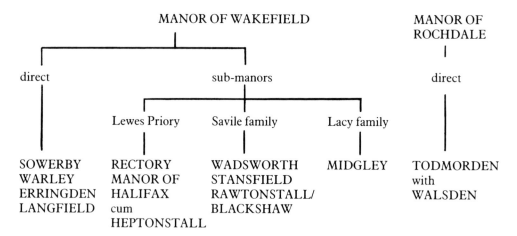

The lords of the manor of Wakefield had only a limited interest in Erringden and Langfield, whereas Sowerby and Warley were integral parts of the manor.

The manors of Wakefield and Rochdale belonged to the Crown until 1625-9, when they were sold to meet the financial problems of Charles I. In 1638 Rochdale was bought by Sir John Byron, whose ancestors had been stewards and lessees of the manor and were landowners in Walsden. The manor descended through the Byron family until it was sold by Lord Byron the poet in 1823. The manor of Wakefield had a succession of owners until 1700, when it was bought by the duke of Leeds.[1]

The Waterhouse family of Shibden Hall, who had been lessees of the rectory manor of Halifax-cum-Heptonstall since the early sixteenth century, acquired the full title in 1545. Sir Arthur Ingram bought the manor in 1609, and sold Heptonstall as a separate manor in 1626 to Charles Greenwood, rector of Thornhill. About 1643 it was bought by Sir William Savile of Thornhill and descended in his family. The sub-manor of Midgley passed by marriage about 1600 to Henry Farrer of Ewood. Both Erringden and Langfield were entirely freehold, and were part of the manor of Wakefield only for civil administration, except for the interest of the lords in Mankinholes Moor. All of the manorial and common rights in Erringden were bought by the freeholders in 1592.[2]

The Saviles, although not resident in upper Calderdale, were the most influential family in the affairs of the valley in the seventeenth century. They were lords of the sub-manors of Wadsworth, Rawtonstall and Stansfield (the latter two now merged into a single unit) and from c1643 of Heptonstall. They often held the stewardship of the manor of Wakefield, and a cadet branch (descended from younger sons) had a substantial interest in Todmorden with Walsden.[3]

The system of land tenure in the upper Calder Valley at the end of the sixteenth century showed considerable variations. In Sowerby and Warley, nearly all the land in the thirteenth and fourteenth centuries had been held in bondage. In the course of time the rules and customs which separated the bondman from the legally free man (as distinct from the tenurial conditions which distinguished bondhold land from freehold land) fell into disuse, and the successors to the bondmen became known as customary tenants. As their title deeds were copies of court roll entries recording their admission as tenants upon inheritance or purchase, they came to be known also as copyholders.

In the sixteenth century, most of the land in what was then the graveship of Sowerby (Warley, Sowerby and Soyland) was copyhold. A rental of c1600 lists 284 copyhold tenures with a total of about 3,240 acres, or an average of 11½ per holding. There were also 92 freehold tenures, averaging about 4 acres per holding, most of them held by the copyholders. These had been created in 1563-4 when Robert Dudley, earl of Leicester, had a grant of part of the common which he sold as freehold intakes, subject to an annual rent of 4d an acre to the Crown as lord of the manor.[4]

The only other townships where copyholders are recorded at this period are Heptonstall, which also had a considerable amount of freehold land, and Todmorden with Walsden, which had 2,531 acres freehold, 1,256 copyhold (including 261 acres of recent intakes in Walsden), plus about 3,500 acres of common. In Wadsworth and Stansfield the tenures were either freehold or leasehold, the latter normally for terms of 20 or 21 years.[5]

The copyholders did not necessarily farm the land themselves. Some had inherited a holding surplus to their needs; others, including local gentry and prosperous yeomen, had bought copyhold tenures as an investment or had taken in land from the common to sub-let in small parcels. A survey of the graveship of Sowerby early in the seventeenth century lists 300 copyholders who had a total of 700 sub-tenants, most of them holding leases of up to twenty-one years.[6]

The manor court operated a very flexible land market for copyholds. They could be sold, mortgaged or sub-let. Copyholders could surrender the reversion of a holding, ie the title to it after the death of a copyholder, in different patterns, usually to share the land between the children. The title to land could be transferred on condition that it could be reclaimed by the parents on demand.

When James I, who came to the throne in 1603, set out to increase his income from the Crown estates, his officials in the duchy of Lancaster could not fail to be struck by the enormous gap between the customary rents for copyhold land in the upper Calder Valley (with a few exceptions, 4d an acre) and the real value of the land as reflected in the rents obtainable by sub-letting, often around 10s an acre. The gap had been greatly widened by inflation and by the growth of the 'dual economy' of farming and textiles which had increased local land values.

It would have been difficult for the Crown to increase the annual rents, as these had been unchanged for centuries. The heriot or inheritance charge (paid for many years in money), and the fines for transfer of title were not uniform, and could have been increased. There was, however, the basis for a reasonable settlement. The king wanted money quickly, and the copyholders realised that complete security of tenure and inheritance, and certainty of heriots and fines, were worth paying for. Negotiations begun in 1607 resulted in a deal which was accepted by nearly all of the copyholders. Rents were unchanged; three years' rent was to be charged for inheritance or sale, with half that for leases and reversions. The charge for the arrangement, made in 1609, was thirty-five times the customary rent, which worked out at 11s 8d an acre, or between one years' and three years' rent at prevailing levels for sub-letting.[7]

In the 1650s the lord of the manor of Heptonstall, Sir George Savile of Thornhill, offered in return for lump sums to fix copyhold fines at the rates set out in the 1609 decree for the manor of Wakefield. In 1657 Thomas Bentley paid £40 for this security in respect of a messuage and land in Hebden Bridge for which the lord's rent was 2s 10d a year.

The average rent for leasehold land in Wadsworth was about 3s an acre, much more than copyholders paid in Sowerby and Warley but well below the cost of sub-let land in the latter townships. In 1600 the Saviles sold four farms in Walshaw Dean, Wadsworth, to the families occupying them, all surnamed Shackleton, for a total of £170 6s 8d. The prudence of this investment, from the point of view of the new freeholders, is shown by the trend in rents, which nearly trebled during the course of the seventeenth century.[8]

Heptonstall had two open fields, North and South, in the middle of the sixteenth century. (These were not necessarily cropping divisions.) South Field was enclosed piecemeal and by agreement in the sixteenth century. A court roll entry of the 25th September 1576 refers to exchanges made for this purpose. North Field, however, remained open until 1783. All of the arable and meadow land in Stansfield and Wadsworth townships was enclosed by 1604, with the exception of sixty acres in Walshaw.[9]

Until the second half of the fifteenth century there was a marked contrast in the landscape of Warley and Sowerby between the old 'oxgang lands', which lay in open fields, and the 'royd land' cleared mainly in the first half of the fourteenth century, which formed small enclosures. The open fields were enclosed piecemeal over a period of about 100 years. When Henry Mawde died in 1472 his holding was described as 'a messuage and 16½ acres of land and meadow lying dispersed between the water of Caldre and the town of Warley'. ('Land' in this context meant arable land.)[10] By the 1490s, however, descriptions such as the following, in Sowerby, were becoming common: 'a close called Harpercroft, two closes called Claylandes, two closes called Overtwarttes, three closes called Snape, 2 acres lying in the Middelfelde, 1¾ acres lying in the Netherfeld' (November 1492). By the 1570s, descriptions of open field holdings were rare, although part of Warley Westfield was still unenclosed.

This early enclosure movement, going on extensively in the Yorkshire Pennines between the fifteenth and the seventeenth centuries, was associated with a change in the management of arable farming, from the regular cultivation of the same permanent open fields with fallows every second or third year, to a system of convertible husbandry in which land was cropped for two or three years and then put down to grass for a rather longer period. The change had a beneficial effect on soil fertility, and upon the yield of both arable crops and pastoral produce. The upper Calderdale farmers could have adopted this system at an early date, if the evidence of Warley and Sowerby applies generally, because of the large amount of 'royd' or 'intake' land which was separately enclosed.

Heptonstall and its former open fields.

The local farmers benefited from an agreement made in 1535 to replace the rectorial tithes (corn, hay, wool and lamb) paid to Lewes Priory with fixed rent charges on the land. The vicar's tithes (calves, milk, pigs, geese, foals and bees) were not affected. The rent charges were quite modest in 1535, and declined rapidly in real terms as prices rose.[11]

The intaking from the common, which had resumed on a significant scale in the late fifteenth century, continued as an important feature of the agrarian scene throughout the sixteenth and seventeenth centuries. Between 1509 and 1565, 239 acres of intakes were recorded in Warley, Sowerby and Soyland, all for entry fines of £1 an acre and annual rents of 4d. During the next decade or so, a large part of the 440 acres of freehold existing at the end of the sixteenth century was taken in under the earl of Leicester's scheme. Not all of the copyhold intakes had been licensed at the time of enclosure. Periodic surveys of the occupied land revealed 'overmeasure', usually described at the same time as having been encroached from the common. In 1560, for

Intakes at Lumbutts, with Langfield Moor behind and Stoodley Pike on the skyline.

example, 25 people were listed as having between them 39 acres of 'overmeasure' in the graveship of Sowerby. They were charged the normal £1 and 4d per acre. There was no additional punitive charge.[12]

A similar practice may account for the apparent concentration of intaking in the Savile sub-manors in certain years. For 1589-91 only 8 acres are recorded in Stansfield and 5 in Wadsworth. In 1597-8, 16 acres were enclosed in Stansfield. In 1599-1600, however, 16 people took in a total of 108 acres in Stansfield, and a further 5½ acres were enclosed in Wadsworth. The records are probably incomplete, but the apparently feverish activity of certain years may conceal a process whereby the lord's steward periodically identified and regularised encroachments.[13]

In the years 1633-7, 30 parcels of intake totalling 83¼ acres were conveyed as freehold in Wadsworth, but most of the 39½ acres enclosed in Stansfield were let as leasehold, for terms of 20 or 21 years, and for 1s an acre annual rent. The acres in Wadsworth and Stansfield were larger than the statute acre (4,840 square yards), which was based upon the perch of 5½ yards. A perch of 7 yards was used in Wadsworth and one of 8 yards in Stansfield, giving local acres equivalent to 1.62 and 2.16 statute acres respectively. The 1626 survey of Todmorden with Walsden also used the 8 yard perch.[14]

The twenty-nine freeholders of Langfield were involved in a struggle to prevent the right of enclosing any part of the township moor being granted to outsiders. In 1605 they sought a judgement in the court of the duchy of Lancaster (of which the manor of Wakefield was a part) against John Priestley esquire, who was claiming title to part of the moor. The land was surveyed in 1606, but the case dragged on until, in May 1614, the duchy appointed a commission led by Sir John Savile of Howley, steward of the manor of Wakefield, to investigate the matter. They reported that the freeholders held about 500 acres of enclosed ground, and shared 400 acres of mainly barren moor. It was agreed in 1615 that the freeholders would jointly pay 4d an acre annual rent for the best 100 acres and ½d for the rest, a total of about £2 5s. The moor could be divided and enclosed by the consent of a majority of the freeholders.[15]

The freeholders of Inchfield, in Todmorden with Walsden, claimed similar exclusive rights over the local commons, which had originally amounted to between 700 and 800 statute acres. Part of this land had been enclosed by 1626, and part was held as 'stinted pasture', ie where each occupier had the right to put on a specific number of cattle or sheep. The copyholders in Walsden had taken the title to some relatively large intakes, although in some cases the land was not physically enclosed. In Todmorden there were both small intakes (2-4 acres) and large-scale enclosures, eg Bearnshaw Tower (65 acres) near Cornholme, said to have been taken in before 1543.[16]

In 1638 the common lands of the manor of Rochdale were surveyed. About 420 acres of Walsden Common (total 2,015 acres in 1626) were divided first into three sections: Salter Rake and Stoney Edge (242 acres); White Slack (121 acres); and Ramsden (54 acres). Each section was then further divided into three roughly equal parts, the middle part in each case being described as the lord's part, and the outer tracts the freeholders' parts. A similar exercise was carried out on 469 acres of Todmorden Common. It is not easy to trace the subsequent history of these tracts, particularly as some of them bounded freehold or copyhold land which was not physically enclosed, but most of the land is still unimproved moorland today.[17]

Manorial and township government

The system of manorial and township government described in Chapter 3 continued with only minor changes for most of the sixteenth and seventeenth centuries. Villein or bondage tenure had been transformed into copyhold, and there was therefore no longer any occasion for disputes about whether a man was bond or free. The three-weekly courts at Wakefield were now concerned almost exclusively with registering changes in the tenure of copyhold land, by inheritance or surrender. Local government matters were dealt with at the twice-yearly tourn (manor court), held for the upper Calder Valley at Halifax. The principal local officials were still the grave and the constables. Since the early fifteenth century, Sowerbyshire had constituted a single graveship. Each year it was the turn of a particular group of farms or landholdings, usually four or five, to provide a grave on a rota system. One of the tenants of the farms was then chosen, perhaps by lot. The grave was concerned, in the sixteenth and seventeenth centuries, almost exclusively with the administration of copyhold land and the collection of rents.[18]

Each township, now including Heptonstall and Erringden, had a constable, serving for one year. He was assisted by 'the four townsmen', otherwise known as 'the four men', also chosen for one year presumably by the township meeting. The constable and the four men jointly presented offenders in the manor court.

Social discipline was imposed as required in two stages: the 'pain', an order or prohibition with a particular penalty attached; and the 'presentment', or accusation made by the township officers. In the case of practices which were permanently forbidden, eg putting diseased animals onto the moors, a general pain was laid, that is to say, any transgression would be committed under pain of a fine of a certain sum. A particular offence or neglect was dealt with by the imposition of a specific pain – the offender being ordered to stop his action or make good his neglect by a certain date under pain of a fine. Anyone who disregarded a pain would be presented at the next tourn, and the jury would impose a fine, usually of the full amount set by the pain, but occasionally of a lesser sum. The jury consisted of twelve men, elected from

An archway made by John Bentley of Heptonstall, one of the lesser gentry, in 1578.

the ranks of the copyholders. In addition, several men were chosen as prosecutors and one or two as defenders.

At each tourn at Halifax, the reports from the townships usually began with a few standard items, describing the state of repair of highways and pinfolds, and the condition of archery butts, militia weapons and punishment devices – stocks, whipping post and ducking stool. The matters regulated through the system of pains and presentments were public order and morality, nuisance, common rights, commerce and highways. Affrays and bloodshed, rather less frequently reported than in the thirteenth or fourteenth centuries, were punished in the same way, by a fine. The court record for October 1620 shows that the system of 'watch and ward' was in operation, whereby men took it in turns on the orders of the constable to mount a nightly guard against thieves and marauders. Three men were fined a total of 10s for assaulting the 'watchmen' at Sowerby Bridge. It was against the law to wander about at night without due cause, but the curfew does not seem to have been strictly imposed except in the town of Halifax. Games involving gambling were also forbidden by law. In 1579-80, William Crabtree of Sowerby was fined 6d for keeping 'one le Bowlinge Ditch'. George Waterhouse of Warley was fined 3s 4d in 1573 for a more serious breach of the moral code – keeping a bawdy house.

The stocks of Midgley township.

The largest single item of township business brought to the tourns was highway maintenance. The Highways Act of 1555 provided that each householder should furnish, according to his station, either two men with a cart or waggon, or one man, to work for four days in the year on repairing the public roads. Later in the century the obligation was increased to six days. An unpaid surveyor of the highways was to be elected to supervise what became known as 'statute labour'. The Act was, however, ignored in the upper Calder Valley, where the townships preferred to continue with the older manorial custom of making the occupiers of land adjoining a particular stretch of road responsible for its maintenance. This system worked more smoothly in an area of dispersed settlement such as the upper Calder Valley than in a landscape of nucleated villages, as many of the occupiers were called upon to repair roads which led to their own farms. Each township appointed 'overseers of the highways', usually two but occasionally four in number, but their duties were confined to inspection.

The roads out of repair were named in a pain laid at the tourn, with an order to carry out the necessary work either by the following tourn, ie six months later, or by a specified earlier date. Pains were often laid by one township against occupiers of land in another. For example, in October 1660, Heptonstall pained the stretch of the Heptonstall-Burnley highway lying between Hartley Clough and Stiperden Bridge in

A rough road on the line of the Long Causeway at Stiperden.

Stansfield, and Langfield pained the road between Marshaw Bridge and Sowerby Bridge in Sowerby. In each case the township was trying to keep open one of its main lines of communication.

In most cases the threat of a fine was sufficient, and the township was able to tell the following tourn that the work had been carried out. For example, Stansfield reported in October 1620 that James and Richard Smith, pained at the previous court in the sum of 10s for 'amending the highway between Todmerden and Hepton brigge . . . in a place called Castlewood', had 'well and truly' repaired the road. A few people, however, proved recalcitrant. In October 1571, John Mitchell of Heptonstall was ordered to repair a way leading between Clarke Mill and High Greenwood. He failed to do so, and was fined the amount pained, 39s, in the following April.

There is no indication of the methods of repair used, except for the cutting back of hedges and the maintenance of drainage holes, which were known as 'sluices' or 'soogh holes'. Presumably holes in the roads would be filled in with stones. There are few references in the court rolls to the repair of causeways, but it may have been taken for granted that where a causeway existed in a highway it must be kept in good order.

Hebden Bridge: the late Victorian bridge, with Bridge Mill on the right.

Apart from 'causeys' the roads had natural surfaces, and if these became muddy in winter, no one was to blame unless the ditches and hedges had been neglected. In law a road was thought of as a right of passage, rather than as something with a particular surface.

The townships did not pay much attention to the legal distinction between a highway, over which all traffic had a right of passage, and a lane, which was open to men, horses and animals, but not to wheeled vehicles. Frequently a road was described simply as a 'way', and occasionally the same road was referred to in the same entry as both a highway and a lane. In October 1660, Stansfield ordered the occupiers of lands on both sides of the *lane* leading between Blackshaw Bridge and Shaw Bridge in Stansfield to repair their several parts of the *highway* before Christmas.

Looking over the North Field of Heptonstall to the former open arable fields of Old Town (left) and the hunting ground of Erringden Park (right).

A pinfold at Langfield.

The view over Todmorden, with restoration in progress on the
Rochdale Canal, 1984.

7

Religious Struggles and the Civil War

Religious Life before the Reformation

In April 1523, Peter Crossley of Horsehold in Erringden made his will, beginning with the devotional preamble commonly used before the Reformation: 'I bewitt [bequeath] my soull to Almyghtie God, our Lady Saynete Mary, and to al the Saynctes in hevyn'. He asked that his body should be buried 'in the south parte of the kirk of Heptonstall' and bequeathed five marks (£3 6s 8d) towards the repair of 'the stepill of the said kirke'. He left his best beast as a 'mortuary', or death duty payable to the church, to the vicar of Halifax, whose parish extended from Stansfield to Shelf and Lindley, and included twenty-two townships.[1]

The word 'vicar' means deputy or substitute. The patronage of Halifax parish, together with the lands in Halifax and Heptonstall which were known as the rectory manor, had been granted by one of the earls Warenne about the year 1100 to Lewes Priory in Sussex. The priory nominated rectors until 1274, when the first vicar was appointed. He received the small tithes (milk, calves, foals, pigs, geese, bees), mortuaries and offerings. The great tithes (corn, hay, wool, lambs) and the rectory manor were appropriated by the priory. In 1291 the priory's income from the rectory manor and tithes was valued for ecclesiastical taxation at £93 6s 8d a year and the vicar's income at £16.[2]

Because of the great size of Halifax parish, two parochial chapels were built, at Elland and Heptonstall. The dates of their foundation are not known, but descriptions of the roof timbers of the old church at Heptonstall, before they were removed in the 1860s, suggest a date not later than the middle of the thirteenth century. The vicar of Halifax paid a stipend of £4 a year to the priest in charge of each chapel. The chapel at Heptonstall, dedicated to St Thomas the Martyr, served the townships of Stansfield, Heptonstall, Wadsworth and Langfield, together with Erringden when the former park was settled after about 1450. Midgley, Warley and Sowerby came directly under Halifax. Todmorden with Walsden lay within the extensive parish of Rochdale.[3]

The increased prosperity resulting from the growth of cloth manufacture from the late fifteenth century led to the building of local chapels. St Mary's Chapel, Todmorden, was in existence by 1476, reputedly founded by the Radcliffe family of Todmorden Hall, which was adjacent to the chapel. Luddenden Chapel was licensed in 1496. Sowerby Chapel was in existence by 1513, and the land for Sowerby Bridge Chapel was bought in 1526.[4] Cross Stone Chapel had been founded by 1537, when Thomas Stansfeld of Sowerby left £5 3s 4d to buy a chalice to replace one lent by Heptonstall Chapel. In the course of time, all of these buildings came to be known as churches, but in the sixteenth century they were described as chapels, to distinguish them from parish churches such as Halifax and Rochdale.

Cross Stone Church, on a terrace overlooking the modern town of Todmorden, was originally the parochial chapel for Stansfield and Langfield.

The chapels at Luddenden, Sowerby, Sowerby Bridge and Cross Stone were all provided, and the chaplains maintained, by the local inhabitants, without any financial help from the mother church at Halifax. This spate of chapel building should not be taken as evidence of an upsurge in religious fervour. What the local communities were buying was convenience. The people were obliged to attend mass on fifty-two Sundays and about thirty holy days in the year, and few questioned the doctrines which made the sacraments, and particularly the mass, essential for salvation.

The final journey, to the grave, still had to be made to Halifax or Heptonstall. St Mary's Chapel, Luddenden, tried to secure full parochial rights in the 1530s, but did not succeed until 1626.[5]

There were important differences, in education, income and way of life, between the vicars of Halifax and the clergy who served the local chapels. The former were normally university-educated, and were known therefore, according to their academic status, as 'Master' or 'Doctor'. They were often pluralists. Dr William Rokeby, vicar from 1502 to 1521, was also archbishop of Dublin and Lord Chancellor of Ireland.[6] All of the other local pre-Reformation clergy of whom we have any record were known by the courtesy title of 'Sir', which was used for non-graduate priests. (They were, of course, far removed in status from the knights who were also known as 'Sir'.) Their surnames suggest that they were local men, who had been 'apprenticed' to a priest of

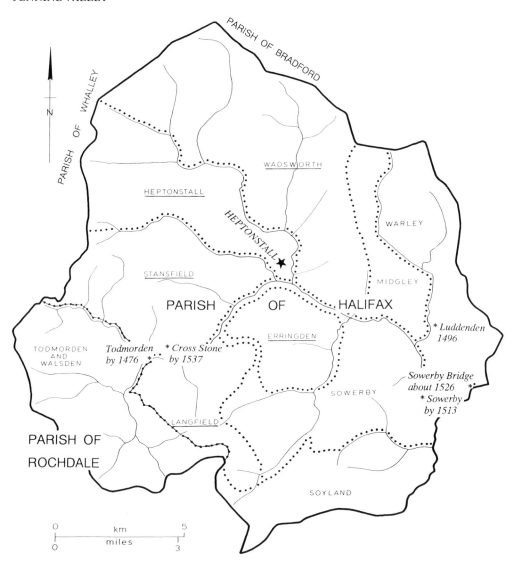

PARISHES AND CHAPELS.
Local chapels with dates of foundations: Luddenden 1496.
Townships in the medieval chapelry of Heptonstall are underlined.

the neighbourhood. The priest in charge of Heptonstall Chapel, normally described as the curate, had an annual stipend of £4 from the vicar of Halifax, plus the fees paid for baptisms, marriages and burials. The chaplains of the non-parochial chapels had to rely upon whatever stipend was agreed with the local parishioners.

The remainder of the clergy lived mainly or entirely from saying masses for the dead. Two of them were incumbents of chantries in Heptonstall Chapel, Our Ladys Chantry, first recorded in 1506 and worth £4 a year in 1535, and the Greenwood Chantry, founded in 1524 and worth £5 a year in 1535.[7]

The duty of the chantry priest was to say mass daily for the souls of the dead, particularly of the family which had founded the chantry. Whethei or not the two Heptonstall priests helped with general parochial duties is uncertain. The incumbents in 1548 claimed to do so, but as the chantries and any other provisions for masses for the dead were about to be suppressed, the plea is a little suspect. The inhabitants of Heptonstall chapelry tried to build up an endowment to support an additional parochial chaplain, but without much success. They started the process in 1528-9, but the annual income was still only £1 3s 4d in 1548. This modest income went to William Aspden, who had been a chaplain at Heptonstall since 1520 if not earlier, and relied otherwise on payments for masses for the dead. There were usually one or two of these 'massing' priests at Heptonstall, relying on bequests, commonly for a 'trental', ie thirty masses, for which the going rate was 6s 8d.

The most comprehensive provision of prayers for the dead is found, not surprisingly, in the will of a Heptonstall chaplain, Robert Browne, dated the 19th March 1517-18. He left several sums as 'conscience money', the largest being 20s to Heptonstall Chapel 'for trespasses and offences that I have done in hitt or in the yerde of the same, in fyndyng or taking away any goodes ayens [against] the pleasur of Almyghty and the health of my soull'. He gave 6s 8d to St Robert's Friary, Knaresborough, to be remembered in the prayers of the friars, and a cope of velvet, worth £6 13s 4d, to Heptonstall Chapel so that his soul and those of his father and mother would be upon the 'bede-roll', ie the list of deceased parishioners for whom prayers were regularly offered, 'to be praid for eyermore'. He left 4d for every priest, and 1d for every clerk, attending his funeral service, and 40s for 'brede, ayll and meytt' for the mourners; 10s was bequeathed for a trental at Heptonstall, to be offered also for the souls of Laurence and Janet Bentley, and £20 for two priests to sing masses for two years, one at Kirkham and the other at Preston (both in Lancashire). In both cases he offered slightly more than the going rate for a massing priest.

The Reformation

The Reformation in England had three main elements: the assertion of the royal supremacy over the Church (1534), which meant not only a denial of papal authority but also increased state control of Church affairs; the confiscation of Church property, especially monastic estates (1536-9) and the chantry endowments (1545-8); and changes in doctrine and worship (from 1549).

The upper Calder Valley was not greatly affected by the developments of the 1530s. It gave little or no support to the rebellion known as the Pilgrimage of Grace (1536), a conservative resistance to unwelcome religious and economic change, in which a large part of Yorkshire was involved. Lewes Priory was suppressed in 1537, but this had little effect on the life of the upper Calder Valley. The priory's local estates had for some time been leased to the Waterhouse family, who finally bought them in 1545.[8]

The doctrinal Reformation began under Edward VI (1547-53). The Latin mass was replaced in 1549 by a communion service said in English. The second Prayer Book of 1552, and a series of directives which culminated in the Forty-Two Articles of 1553, moved the Church of England nearer to the Calvinist position, but not sufficiently to satisfy radical opinion. Images and side altars were removed, and the high altar was replaced by a communion table. The doctrine of purgatory was condemned, adding spiritual justification to the material motives for confiscating chantry endowments. The clergy were allowed to marry.

The gradual spread of Protestant opinions in Halifax parish is shown by the decline, from the late 1530s, of references in wills to the intercession of the Virgin Mary and the saints. They were replaced by declarations such as the following, from the will of Edward Hoppay, a yeoman who lived at Skircoat (1548):

> My beleve is that theire is but one God and one mediator betwixt God and man, which is Jesus Christe . . . A good warke maketh not a good man, but a good man makith goode workes. For a righteouse man lyveth by faithe.

Edward Hoppay, with his affection for the scriptures and belief in justification by faith, had obviously become a thoroughgoing Protestant during the reign of Henry VIII.

Queen Mary, who came to the throne in 1553, brought back the mass and restored the supremacy of the Pope. There was considerable resistance to the restoration of the old order, and nearly 300 Protestants were burned as heretics. Only one martyr went to the stake in Yorkshire.[9]

After the death of Queen Mary in 1558, the government of Elizabeth I tried to produce a religious settlement which would satisfy the consciences of most people and prevent the country being torn apart by doctrinal strife. The 1552 Prayer Book was restored, but with important changes of a conservative nature in, for example, the wording of the central part of the communion service. Images went out again, but most of the traditional vestments stayed in. The office of bishop was retained. The Act of Uniformity of 1559 made it compulsory to attend divine service on Sundays and holy days, on pain of a fine of a shilling for each absence, and required people to receive holy communion at least once a year.

In some parts of Yorkshire, and just across the county boundary in East Lancashire, there was considerable resistance to the new dispensation, at first a stubborn conservatism and then, stimulated by the arrival of Catholic priests trained on the Continent, a sacrificial defence of the old order. Hardly any trace of these movements was found in the upper Calder Valley.

The appeal of Protestantism, and later of what became known as Puritanism, to the upper Calder Valley was undoubtedly linked to the growth of the cloth trade. The Protestant/Puritan religion was the faith of a society dedicated to hard work, thrift and competition, in which the accumulation of wealth – but not extravagance or display – was seen as an outward sign of virtue. The main strongholds of early Protestantism – the clothing districts and the port of Hull – were at a later date equally firm in their support of Puritan ideas. Although the upper Calder Valley was relatively remote, its trading links with Hull and London brought the leading clothiers into contact with 'advanced opinions' in religion.

The natural ideological leanings of the clothiers were reinforced by the 'primitive congregationalism' of the upper Calder Valley. Of the six chapels in the valley above Halifax, five had been established and were maintained by the local people – essentially by the yeomen clothiers. As they themselves hired the chapel clergy, and presumably the schoolmasters also, they would undoubtedly choose ministers to suit their own convictions. Cross Stone Chapel, for example, was the responsibility of six trustees, who chose the minister. In the event of a dispute, the matter was referred to a majority vote of the inhabitants of Stansfield and Langfield. In 1615 Robert Booth was elected curate of Sowerby Bridge by the inhabitants, who paid his stipend (£26 13s 4d a year) by levying a rate.[10]

The government and Church authorities made a determined effort from the 1590s to check the growth of Puritanism, partly because the more extreme Puritans wanted to replace episcopal government of the Church with a presbyterian system. This was seen as a threat to the stability of the State as well as the Church – 'No bishop, no king', as James I put it.

When Puritan clergy were in trouble with the Church authorities it was often for not wearing a surplice (they disliked 'Romish' vestments) or for failing to observe holy days – the Protestant work ethic demanded six days in the week for labour. In 1590 Gilbert Astley, curate of Todmorden, was in trouble for the latter offence. His chapel was in the parish of Rochdale, the vicar of which was Richard Midgley, of Midgley, a man of Puritan sympathies. In 1595 he was succeeded by his son Joseph Midgley, a more extreme Puritan.[11]

The pressure on Puritan clergy increased considerably during the ascendancy of William Laud, bishop of London and from 1633 archbishop of Canterbury, who tried to restore traditional ritual and vestments. Richard Neile, archbishop of York, pursued similar policies. Visitations in 1633 and 1635 identified most of the curates of the parochial chapels in the upper Calder Valley as defaulters. Robert Booth of Sowerby Bridge was said to be unlicensed as a curate and preacher, and to be unorthodox as a preacher. He admitted that his chapel did not have a surplice. Nathaniel Welsh of Luddenden had been licensed in 1629, after about sixteen years in the curacy. His offences, in 1632, included not wearing the required vestments and not observing holy days, and for failure to remedy these deficiencies he was suspended. Nathaniel Rathband of Sowerby suffered a similar fate in 1628. Whether the suspensions were made effective is, of course, another matter.[12]

The Civil War

The accounts of the constable of Sowerby for 1639 record the recruitment, training and equipping (at a cost of £65) of sixteen men, the township's militia quota for an army being raised to fight the Scots, who had risen in rebellion in the previous year against an attempt by Charles I to impose upon them a modified version of the English *Book of Common Prayer*. No doubt similar contingents were recruited from other local townships. The Sowerby men did not have to fight on this occasion. The English army retreated at the sight of the Scottish force north of the Tweed and a truce was made.[13]

The clash with the Scots brought to a head the great crisis which had been developing for some years in English public affairs. It had several interlocking elements. The constitutional issue – whether the king should rule despotically, as Charles had done since 1629, or with the consent of parliament – was related to both economic and religious questions. The first concerned such matters as trading monopolies and the level and kind of taxation. The second involved the forms of worship, the power of the bishops and the use of the material resources of the Church.

The sense of grievance in the upper Calder Valley about arbitrary taxation mounted steadily during the reign of Charles I, who came to the throne in 1625. The king revived an ancient custom by which a man with an annual income from land of £40 or more could be compelled to take a knighthood, or pay a 'composition' to the Crown. The combination of inflation and the economic growth of the upper Calder Valley had brought some of the local yeomen, as well as virtually all the lesser gentry, within the £40 limit. Taking a knighthood was expensive, not only because of the increased taxation which went with the rank, but also through the lifestyle which was expected. The houses which the more prosperous yeomen clothiers were building in the early seventeenth century matched up to the social standing of the lesser gentry. There was, however, a noticeable difference in style of dress between the splendour of the gentleman and the sober garb of the yeoman, who preferred to have 'tin in his buttons and gold in his pockets'.

It is estimated that the majority of the 850 to 900 Yorkshiremen who had to pay compositions for not taking a knighthood were yeomen. Seventy gentlemen and yeomen of the parish of Halifax paid a total of over £1,000. The highest fine, £40, was paid by James Murgatroyd of Hollins in Warley.[14]

In 1627 the county of Yorkshire was ordered to share with the port of Hull the cost of providing three ships needed for the war with France. A petition of protest was signed by 125 men from the parish of Halifax. In 1634, Charles I, denied the normal parliamentary taxes because he would not summon a parliament, began to levy ship money as a regular annual imposition on the whole country. It was assessed on the same basis as the county rate, so that many more people had to pay than would have been caught by the parliamentary subsidies levied on goods and land.[15]

In the 1630s a dispute about the ulnage – the payment for having a seal attached so that cloth could legally be sold – was won by the clothiers.[16] It was not directly the concern of the Crown, but would have seemed to the clothiers to be part and parcel of a system of economic regulation which interfered with their getting on with the business of making cloth and money. There were other causes of economic unrest, however, including normal trade fluctuations and the plague which swept the clothing districts of the West Riding in 1640-1.

In religious matters the upper Calder Valley was strongly Puritan. Religion was not just one of the elements in the struggle which eventually led to civil war. It was both a unifying force for either camp, and a convenient symbol. To the Calderdale men, religion and economics were two sides of the same coin. In the praise of their own virtues which the clothiers trotted out in every lawsuit and petition relating to the trade, two arguments were intertwined: their hard work and enterprise, which found employment for large numbers and made it possible to maintain the 'impotent poor'; and their 'zeal for God's holy religion' which had led them 'freely and voluntarily, at their own Charges', to 'maintain . . . ten preachers, over and above the payment of all tithes and oblations' with the result that there was 'not one Popish recusant' in the entire parish of Halifax. Kersey and the pulpit were the twin symbols of the moral and economic victory over popery, poverty and the 'barren and unfruitfull' hills.[17]

The first phase of the Civil War in Yorkshire (1642-3) was a closely-balanced internal struggle between the parliamentary forces, led by the Fairfax family of Denton near Otley, and the royalists, one of whose commanders was Sir William Savile of Thornhill. Some of the clothing towns changed hands several times. The woollen trade was severely disrupted, causing great economic distress in the upper Calder Valley. With the port of Hull shut off – it was occupied for parliament and besieged by the royalists

– the only market outlet was the hazardous overland journey, by packhorse, to London. Thomas Priestley, a member of a numerous yeoman-clothier family of Goodgreave in Sowerby, risked this journey frequently to take cloth to his brother John, who ran the London end of the family business (and bought wool in Kent as a return load). According to another brother, Jonathan, Thomas bought cloth to add to his own stock, and:

> travelled to London with 8 or 9 horses all the time of the Civil Wars; sometimes he and others that was with him hired convoys [ie armed escorts] and sometimes went without, and were never taken . . . all that dangerous time . . . I have heard my brother Thomas say that he spent £20 every journey and got £20 clear every journey; he got £400 in those times.[18]

On the 30th June 1643, Lord Fairfax's forces were defeated by a greatly superior royalist army at the Battle of Adwalton (or Atherton) Moor, near Bradford. Soon all of Yorkshire except Hull was in the hands of the royalists. John Brearcliffe, a young Halifax apothecary, noted in his diary: '3rd July 1643, being Monday, 1 clok morn, bradford taken and I into Lancashire'. Within a few days Halifax and the upper Calder Valley were abandoned to the royalists and the remnants of the defeated forces took refuge in Lancashire.[19]

Civilians as well as soldiers thought it prudent to leave. The Priestleys of Goodgreave – a committed Puritan family, brought up on a diet of sermons and psalms – went into Lancashire. The father and elder sons went first, and when the father, Joseph Priestley, rode over Blackstone Edge to visit his wife and younger children, he was captured by royalists. He refused to find the £80 ransom demanded, believing that Halifax would soon change hands again, but was taken ill and died within a few days. After the rest of the family had left, 'our house at Goodgreave was ransacked and plundered over and over again'. John Farrar's house at Ewood in Midgley was also plundered, and it is probable that many other houses suffered a similar fate.[20]

For a time in the autumn of 1643 the parliamentarians established a base at Heptonstall, which was protected by cliffs on three sides with a line of retreat over the moors into Lancashire. Three months of skirmishing followed, including an unsuccessful royalist attack on Heptonstall. In January 1644, however, the small parliamentary force withdrew to Burnley because of a threatened royalist move from the direction of Keighley.

The arrival in the north of England of a large Scottish army in alliance with the parliamentarians tilted the balance of the struggle in Yorkshire. On the 28th January the royalists abandoned Halifax, and in April Bradford was retaken from them. At the Battle of Marston Moor on the 2nd July the royalists were heavily defeated. The war was soon over in Yorkshire, except for the reduction of royalist garrisons in several castles, including Pontefract. The lines of communication between the clothing districts and the port of Hull were secure again. The troubles of the upper Calder Valley were not finished, however. In August 1645 there was a new outbreak of plague, which caused 529 deaths in the parish of Halifax.[21]

At Marston Moor the royalists lost Yorkshire. At Naseby (14th June 1645) they effectively lost the war. In the summer of 1646 King Charles surrendered to the Scots, who handed him over to the English parliament in January 1647. Meanwhile the parliamentarians had split into two parties, which became known by their religious labels as the Presbyterians, who had a majority in the House of Commons, and the Independents, who were strong in the army. Differences also arose between the Scots and their English allies. Charles was able to make a secret agreement with the Scots, which brought a Scottish army into England on his side in July 1648. Oliver Cromwell moved against the Scots and their royalist allies in August, drawing provisions from the Calder Valley, and routed them near Preston on the 17th and 18th August.[22]

The Presbyterians were still prepared to try to reach a political settlement with King Charles, but the army leaders felt that he could not be trusted and would not forgive him for re-starting the war. He was put on trial, and executed in January 1649.

After the final parliamentary victory in West Yorkshire, Halifax Church was put on the same footing as the local parochial chapels, with the inhabitants paying, and presumably choosing, their ministers. In 1650 the income of the vicarage – the small tithes and offerings – was divided between the parish church and the parochial chapels.[23]

The ministers in the Calderdale chapels during the Commonwealth period (1649-60) belonged to three groups, Presbyterians, Independents (or Congregationalists) and Antinomians. (There is no record of any Baptist activity until the 1690s.) Henry Root, minister of Sowerby from 1648 after spending two years as a preacher at Halifax, was an Independent. Oliver Heywood, the famous Presbyterian who was minister of Coley Chapel, Northowram, from 1650, preached a sermon every Thursday for several years at the house of Samuel Hopkinson at the Stubbing, Sowerby. Although the difference between the Independents and Presbyterians was essentially a matter of church organisation rather than doctrine, there were rival factions in some places.

Robert Town, minister of Todmorden Chapel from 1643, was accused by the Bury Classis, the committee of ministers and lay elders which under the Presbyterian system had jurisdiction over Todmorden, of Antinomianism, an unorthodox and extreme form of Calvinism. (Antinomians believed that salvation was achieved entirely by divine grace, with no conditions required of the people who were 'saved'.) Town was driven from his post, but ministered later at Elland and Haworth. Heywood described him as 'the famous Antinomian who writ some books . . . the best scholar and soberest man [of the Antinomians] but something unsound in principles'.[24]

The Restoration and the Beginnings of Nonconformity

The revolutionary struggle, in which the upper Calder Valley had been so wholeheartedly engaged, ended in dictatorship. In 1653 Oliver Cromwell made himself Lord Protector. After his death in September 1658 the country began to slide into anarchy, and the restoration of a constitutional monarchy seemed to offer the best hope of political stability.

The return of Charles II in 1660 meant also the restoration of prewar forms of worship and Church government. Deprived Anglican incumbents were restored. In April 1662 a revised *Book of Common Prayer* was issued. The Act of Uniformity, passed in the following month, provided for the expulsion of all clergy who refused to subscribe to the new liturgy.

Timothy Root, who had been curate of Sowerby Bridge for only a year, was ejected on the 3rd September 1662. His father, Henry Root, curate of Sowerby, defied the Act and continued preaching in the chapel for about six months, until he was arrested. He spent several months as a prisoner in York Castle. Oliver Heywood was ejected from Coley Chapel in Northowram.[25]

There are more questions than answers about the affairs of the parochial chapels after 1662. Did the local people choose ministers who were reluctant conformists and who adopted as far as possible a 'low church' style? Did they select them on the basis of their performance as preachers? Was the relatively rapid turnover of ministers a result of disagreements on doctrinal or liturgical questions? Many of the ejected clergymen (who numbered about 1,700 in England and Wales) continued their ministry by preaching in private houses. The government responded with the Conventicle Acts of 1664 and 1670, which made any religious meeting illegal if there were more than five people present in addition to the household. From March 1666 dissenting ministers were forbidden to go within five miles of their former church or any place at which they had illegally preached since ejection. The penalty was a fine of £40.

Oliver Heywood considered that the Five Mile Act, by turning dissenting ministers into itinerant evangelists, served only to promote the spread of Nonconformity. Heywood, Henry Root (until his death, aged nearly eighty, in 1669), Timothy Root and, for a short time, John Ryther (ejected in 1662 from the vicarage of Frodingham, Lincolnshire) served dissenting centres at Sowerby and in the chapelry of Cross Stone (Stansfield and Langfield). Heywood was a Presbyterian and the other three were Independent, but this does not seem to have caused any problems.[26]

Another dissenting sect was established in the upper Calder Valley in the 1650s – the Society of Friends, or Quakers. They were founded by George Fox, who began his mission about 1649 and brought together several existing groups which shared his rejection of all forms of organised religion. Because of the aggressive style of their evangelism (in contrast to the 'quietist' character of later Quakerism), their refusal to take oaths, bear arms or pay tithes, and suspicions that they were politically subversive, they were in trouble with the authorities before the Restoration, and afterwards became the most severely persecuted of the dissenting sects.

An early Quaker convert was Christopher Taylor, the Puritan minister of 'the chapel in the Bryers' – St Anne's Chapel, Southowram. He became a Quaker minister and – with his brother Thomas, a prominent Quaker – established meetings at Halifax, Brighouse and Bradford. Thomas Taylor and another itinerant evangelist, Thomas Goodaire, preached at or near Mankinholes, which became the headquarters of another meeting.[27]

The Quakers did not have an ordained ministry, but recognised those members (including women) who had appropriate gifts, and called them ministers. Thomas Musgrave of Warley, a member of the Halifax meeting, became a minister; in 1686 he went on a mission to Ireland and in the following decade to North America.[28]

The Quakers suffered the normal penalties of dissenting sects. John Sutcliffe, one of the ministers of the Mankinholes Meeting, was fined £50 in 1670-1 for holding religious meetings at his house. Thomas Sutcliffe, another minister, paid £21 10s for a similar offence at his own house. In addition the goods of Quakers were distrained for the tithes which they refused to pay. Sometimes cattle were taken, but more often it was a piece of kersey. As a neat illustration of the importance of the dual economy, John Fielden of Hartley Royd in Stansfield and John Stansfield of Sowerby had pieces of kersey seized in 1678, but livestock in 1683.[29]

In 1672 Charles II, as part of an understanding with his French allies in preparation for the Third Dutch War (1672-3), issued the Declaration of Indulgence suspending the penal laws against both Catholics and dissenters. Licences were taken out for the house of John Butterworth in Warley, and for a meeting house at Quarry Hill, Sowerby, built by Joshua Horton. Oliver Heywood, Eli Bentley, Joseph Dawson and Timothy Root shared the preaching at Quarry Hill, each receiving 10s a week from

Horton. Heywood also preached in Warley once a week. Fifteen Independents, members of the late Henry Root's flock, agreed to join with Heywood's Northowram-based Presbyterians in 'sweet harmony'.[30] The Quakers did not apply for any licences.

Parliament, which had a majority strongly opposed to Catholicism, forced Charles II to cancel his Declaration of Indulgence in 1673, although the licences were not formally revoked until 1674 or 1675. The intermittent persecution of dissenters was resumed, but this could not deter men like Heywood. In May 1683 he preached to a large gathering at the house of John Helliwell in Stansfield. During the sermon the township constable, apparently prompted by Richard Robinson, the curate of Cross Stone, arrived with a warrant for the arrest of the preacher. Heywood dismissed the congregation after a sermon lasting less than two hours – which by Puritan standards was a shortened address – and was able to persuade the constable to let him go. Heywood noted in his diary with satisfaction that, according to his informants, Mr Robinson had announced a sermon in his chapel on the same day (Whit Tuesday and the king's birthday) but no one had turned up.[31]

In 1688 James II (1685-8), who was a Catholic, was overthrown, and William of Orange and his wife Mary, James's sister, became joint sovereigns. One of the fruits of the 'Glorious Revolution' was the Act of Toleration of 1689, which removed most of the penalties against Nonconformists (but not Catholics) and provided for the licensing of their meeting houses.

Houses licensed for Presbyterian/Independent groups (in the upper Calder Valley at this period it is virtually impossible to distinguish between them) included those of John Butterworth in Warley, John Aske in Langfield (1689), Paul Helliwell in Stansfield and John Haworth in Langfield (1690) and Charles Gaukroger in Erringden (1695). Heywood's work in Stansfield was consolidated by Rev Matthew Smith, who settled in Mixenden in 1686. His congregation worshipped for a period in a room in Great House in Stansfield, to which Joshua Cordingley came in 1712 as the first permanent minister. In 1717 the site for a chapel at Benthead, not far from Great House, was purchased. It opened in 1719.

The Quakers took out licences in 1689 for 4 houses in Stansfield (including that of John Fielden at Hartley Royd), 5 or 6 in Langfield (including the house of Thomas Sutcliffe), 2 in Midgley (1 of which was the house of Henry Broadbelt, a minister) and 1 each in Warley, Sowerby (Joshua Smith) and Broad Carr. The proliferation of licensed houses in Stansfield and Langfield shows that the Mankinholes Meeting had no single base, but moved around the houses of its leading members. In 1695 a house at Shoebroad in Langfield was licensed.[32]

The first Baptist congregations in the upper Calder Valley evolved in an unusual manner. Two young men, William Mitchell of Heptonstall and his cousin David Crossley, began to operate in the 1680s as itinerant evangelists, unconnected with any sect. They built up a substantial following on both sides of the Pennines. After the Act of Toleration, their supporters licensed some twenty houses in East Lancashire and the West Riding, including Greenwood Lee and a house at Hebden Bridge. Their main base was Bacup in Rossendale, where a meeting house was built in 1692, and the congregations, still unconnected with any established sect, were known collectively as 'The Church of Christ in Rossendale'.

In 1692-3, Crossley and Mitchell became Particular (ie Calvinist) Baptists, and gradually their network followed suit. In 1703 a meeting house was opened at Rodwell End in Stansfield 'for the use of Protestant Dissenters known by the name of Baptists or Independents', a description which suggests some lingering uncertainty about their affiliation. Another chapel was opened in 1717 in a converted building at Stone Slack in Heptonstall; and the community in the upper Calder Valley worshipped alternately in the two chapels. In the same year the Rodwell End/Stone Slack Baptists formally separated themselves from the Church of Christ in Rossendale.[33]

A questionnaire about the state of the Church of England was sent out in 1705. From the upper Calder Valley, Heptonstall and Luddenden replied. Daniel Towne, curate of Heptonstall, complained that the vicar of Halifax had for several years refused to pay the £4 annual allowance to Heptonstall Church. The 'minister and parish' had been brought to 'a low ebb . . . by reason of so many Conventicles houses set up in nookes and corners within the said parish'. The churchwardens and trustees of Luddenden reported that they had had no minister for six months. The endowment was only £4 a year, and the combination of a depression in woollen manufacture and the competition of 'Dissenters . . . building Chapels verry nigh us' meant that the income was insufficient to pay an adequate stipend: '. . . no clergyman is willing to serve us for so small wages'.[34]

There is not much evidence about the sociology of religion in the upper Calder Valley at the end of the seventeenth century. The Quakers, although they had some poor members, were mainly yeomen clothiers. To survive their early 'sufferings', their activists needed to be independent materially as well as spiritually. The leading members of the Presbyterian/Independent groups seem also to have been men of substance, although the evidence is less detailed than in the case of the Quakers. It must be remembered, however, that dissenters were very much in a minority at this period. Most of the yeomen clothiers, and people of similar rank, must have been either conformist or indifferent.

8

The Age of the Yeoman Clothier

The Dual Economy

One of the most distinctive features of the upper Calder Valley is the survival of large numbers of fine houses built by the yeomen and lesser gentry in the period between the late sixteenth and mid-eighteenth centuries. Some are grouped in villages such as Mankinholes, Heptonstall and Midgley. Most are to be found strung out along the hillsides, mainly on the southward-facing terraces. While showing considerable variety of architectural detail, they give a strong impression of visual unity, deriving from the use of the same building materials – millstone grit walls and low-pitched roofs of thin sandstone slabs – and particularly from the rhythmic patterns of mullioned windows which contribute so much to the harmony of the façades.

That so many of these houses have survived can be explained by the strong influence of topography on the history of the upper Calder Valley. When the valley bottom, previously underdeveloped, was opened up by new transport links from the late eighteenth century, it became the focus of rapid industrial growth, leaving the older hillside settlements intact as evidence of an earlier way of life.

The economic basis of that way of life was the combination of farming and textiles in the same household, the 'dual economy' which, as explained in Chapter 5, developed from the fifteenth century as the response of the local people to the difficulties of making a living primarily by farming. At the base of the economic pyramid was the cottager with a bit of land and access to the common grazing who worked for wages as a weaver or wool comber, and whose wife and children carded and spun. The apex was occupied by a very small number who had attained the status of gentry, but whose living came from the same combination of farming and cloth making. The main human engines of the dual economy were, however, the people who can be conveniently described as 'yeomen clothiers'.

'Yeoman' is a social not an occupational description, denoting the rank immediately below that of gentleman. In the country at large, such men were normally farmers of some substance, including copyholders and leaseholders as well as freeholders. In the dual economy areas of Yorkshire, the same man was often described as a yeoman in one record or a clothier (or some other textile designation) in another. The term 'yeoman clothier' does not seem, on the evidence of contemporary documents, to have been in common use, perhaps because so many yeomen were clothiers, and so many textile producers were yeomen.

Probate inventories, which list and value the moveable goods of a deceased person, provide a major quarry of information for the study of farming, domestic industry and housing, and form the principal source for this chapter. They describe farming stock, crops and gear; industrial equipment and materials in different stages of manufacture;

A cruck-framed house at Inchfield, Todmorden. Crucks were pairs of matching curved timbers, made by splitting a tree trunk and its first main branch. They are rare in the upper Calder Valley.

and furniture and household utensils. Although not directly concerned with real property (land and buildings), they normally list goods by the rooms or building in which they are found, which shows what particular rooms were used for, as well as outlining the structure of the house.

The inventory evidence used in the chapter comes mainly from the period between the 1680s, before which very few Calder Valley inventories have survived (although there is a much longer run of wills), and the middle of the eighteenth century, after which there is a sharp decline in the amount of useful detail recorded.[1] The inventories used here are drawn from a slightly larger area than the normal geographical limits of this book, to give a more accurate picture of the organisation of the local textile industry. Halifax is included as the main marketing and finishing centre, as are the neighbouring townships (particularly Skircoat, Soyland and Norland) which had some substantial textile men whose trading links extended through much of the upper Calder Valley.

The farming side of the dual economy fulfilled several functions. It provided cereals (mainly oats), meat and dairy produce for the households; cash from the sale of surpluses; grass, hay and oat straw to feed transport animals as well as farm stock; and land for tentering cloth. Although farming was subject to its own fluctuations and hazards – wet summers, severe winters, stock diseases – overall it made for a much more stable household, and local, economy than would have been the case if the clothiers had been completely exposed to the vicissitudes of the textile trade. Farming work was also beneficial to physical and mental health, taking people out of the dusty workshop or overcrowded multi-purpose living room into the fresh air and giving them a welcome change of activity.

During this period, local farming was static in technique, although dynamic in other ways. There were no major new developments until the middle of the eighteenth century, when new crops, such as potatoes, came into general use. The emergence of improved breeds of sheep suited to the wet, acid moorland pastures dates from the nineteenth century. This technical conservatism is not surprising. In those parts of western Yorkshire where most of the farmland was held by people engaged also in textiles, new ideas, initiatives and investment went mainly, if not entirely, into the industrial side. In any case, Yorkshire as a whole was slow to adopt the new techniques – the use of clover, turnips and other field fodder crops in new rotations, and improved breeds of animals – which are described as 'the agrarian revolution'. Recent surveys of inventories for the whole of Yorkshire, covering the late seventeenth and the first half of the eighteenth centuries, have shown that the new techniques did not make any significant impact in the county until about 1750, in contrast with farming areas further south, where the agrarian revolution seems to have developed much earlier.[2]

It is clear from both the wills and the Wakefield court rolls that it was the general practice to divide freehold and copyhold land between surviving sons, not necessarily in equal proportions. Unmarried daughters were usually provided for by means of lump sums or annual payments, charged on the properties inherited by the sons, but some parents included daughters in the share-out of the land and buildings. The development of customary tenure, in Warley and Sowerby, into a flexible system which gave the copyholders complete control over the disposition of their estates has been described in Chapter 6.

The subdivision of land on inheritance is one of the reasons for references in the Wakefield court rolls such as:

> the west end of a house called the Cawsey in Warley, the east end of a croft . . . divided from the west . . .

> a messuage in Sowerby now divided into three residences with a croft to each.[3]

There is, however, another explanation for some entries of this kind. The growth of the textile industry led to a brisk demand for farms, cottages and small parcels of land. A substantial proportion of the land in Warley and Sowerby was actually farmed by sub-tenants of the copyholders, who ranged from lessees of substantial farms such as Wood Lane in Sowerby to people who rented a fraction of an acre. A detailed survey of Shore in Stansfield shows that most of the land around 1700 was held in small farms by sub-tenants of freeholders.[4] Sub-letting was common in other parts of the valley, and the desire to secure the maximum income from rent must have contributed to the fragmentation of the smaller holdings.

The need for more land immediately for farming or tentering, the desire to build up real estate in preparation for division on inheritance, and possibly the potential for letting, kept up the pressure to win land from the moor by licensed intakes or unlicensed encroachments. Indeed this process of agricultural colonisation is one of the most distinctive features of local history. It was going on apace, although with periodic checks, in the century before the Black Death (1349). It resumed about 1440, and continued at least intermittently until the maximum extent of improvement was reached about 1860, to be followed before long by a retreat from the moorland margins as the dual economy went into a steep decline. Most of the land taken in from the

Higher Ashes, Cross Stone.

sixteenth century lay around or above the 1,000 feet contour. In a bleak and damp environment, this land was used mainly for pasture or for tentering cloth. It was, however, the practice in parts of the Yorkshire Pennines to take two or three crops of oats off newly-cleared land before laying it down to long-term pasture, and there is evidence of the cultivation of oats at relatively high altitudes in the upper Calder Valley.

In 1670-94, 22 intakes totalling 132 acres were licensed in the manor of Rawtonstall-cum-Stansfield by the lords, the Saviles. The rents for a Stansfield customary acre (2.12 statute acres) varied from 2s down to about 2d an acre for two intakes of 20 and 14 acres respectively, which were probably rather rough ground. In the same period, new clearances were being made in the Saviles' manor of Wadsworth, the locations including Thurish, 1,200 feet above sea level, and Pecket Well Clough.[5]

The earliest detailed picture of the local farming system is provided by a good run of 90 probate inventories from 1688-97. Nearly half of the testators – mainly widows, innkeepers and Halifax traders – were not significantly involved in farming. Of the 47 who were, all had cattle, most had horses, but only 9 kept sheep. The average number of cattle per holding was 6, and three-quarters of the farms fell within the range 3 to 9 heads. Only 8 people had more than 1 horse; 5 had 2 each, and 3 gentlemen had 4, 5 and 6 respectively. There were about 450 sheep and lambs, half of them on 2 farms in Wadsworth and another 54 at Widdop, on the moor edge in Heptonstall township. (The numbers of sheep should not be compared with those of cattle, as cows were worth usually between £3 and £4, and sheep between 4s and 5s.) Only 4 people had pigs – 9 in all – one kept bees, and no poultry is recorded.

The scale of arable cultivation is more difficult to calculate for three reasons. The first is the seasonal factor. Values of corn were much greater in the period from shortly before the harvest, when standing crops were usually valued, until the end of the calendar year than in spring or early summer. Secondly, hay and corn were often valued together. A clear statement such as 'six days' works of oats' which appears in the inventory of Caleb Gudgeon of Warley (1694) is relatively rare. (A 'day's work', otherwise 'a day's ploughwork', was a local measure equivalent to about two-thirds of a statute acre, which was presumably the amount of land that could be ploughed in a normal day's work.) Thirdly some of the 'corn in the chamber' would have been bought in local markets such as Halifax, and taken by the sack to the local corn mill when flour or meal were needed.

Taking together the evidence of ploughs and harrows, valuations of growing corn, references to 'corn in the barn', 'corn and hay', 'for tilth making on the land' and similar entries in inventories, it seems that 35 of the 47 farmers were engaged in arable farming. This figure is not quite as reliable as the details of stock, and there is no way of calculating the scale of production except that, as one would expect, it was lower than in the main farming areas of Yorkshire.

Another sample of 36 inventories for the period 1718-1740 gives a similar picture. All of the 23 people with a significant involvement in farming kept cattle, with an average of just over 6 head each. Robert Sutcliffe of Greenwood Lee had by far the largest number, 22. There were no sheep, and only 11 pigs (including 7 young). On 16 of the farms there was evidence of arable cultivation. Most of the farmers had 1 horse; Robert Sutcliffe had 4; 3 others had 2 each.

Details of the cattle, apart from their stages of growth and sex, are rarely given, but the inventory of Elizabeth Horsfell of Stansfield describes every animal. A white cow was due to calve around May Day, and a red heifer three weeks earlier. A black heifer was due at midsummer and a red cow was 'unbul'd'. A little black cow was destined to be winter fare, ie to be killed in early November. There were two 'twinters' (two winters old), one red and one with a brown back, and two calves. James Riley of Priestley Ing in Sowerby had amongst his cattle a brown-back cow and a 'Holderness white', which was a short-horn breed. These variegated herds show no sign of selective breeding.

From the above inventories, a clear picture of local farming emerges. On the pastoral side, every farm kept cattle but only 9 out of 70 had sheep. The millstone grit moors provided poor feed and unhealthy conditions for sheep. As explained in Chapter 5, the idea that one of the reasons for the growth of the local textile industry was a plentiful supply of good local wool is doubly false: the sheep were few, and their fleeces were poor and coarse. Hardly any pigs were kept. Two large county-wide surveys of inventories of 1688-9 and 1720-2 show an average of less than one pig per farm, even counting a sow and seven young as eight pigs.[6] The ubiquitous pig seems to be as fictional as the well-fleeced mid-Pennine sheep. Daniel Defoe's statement in the 1720s that the local farmers 'scarce sow corn enough for their cocks and hens' is clearly a casual journalistic comment.[7] In fact arable cultivation was widespread, but no poultry are listed in the inventories.

Although no precise calculation can be made, it is clear that the main cereal crop was oats. Inventories normally refer only to corn, but where the crop is specified it is nearly always oats. Many inventories include oatmeal. Wheat and rye were also grown, but oats predominated, as it had in the Middle Ages and would until corn growing virtually died out in the late nineteenth century. The crop could survive cool and damp

On the moorland edge, at Widdop.

conditions better than the other cereals, and as a bonus its straw provided a relatively nutritious feed for cattle and horses. It was eaten both as 'havercake' (oatcake) and as porridge.

One distinctive feature of local farming, revealed by the inventories, is the considerable use of sleds for transporting hay, manure, stone and peat on steeply-sloping fields. We have to look elsewhere for evidence of another important practice, the carrying of lime from Boulsworth Hill, Wycoller and Thursden, just across the Pennine watershed, to the north-east of Widdop and Wadsworth Moors. Some of the tracks used are still marked on Ordnance Survey maps as 'limers' gates'. The Heptonstall constables' accounts record the robbery and murder of a lime-carrier by soldiers in 1779.

To discuss the farming of the upper Calder Valley as though it were a freestanding economic activity is, however, to present *Hamlet* without the prince. Of the 47 farmers in the 1688-97 batch of inventories, 34 were also engaged in textiles to the extent of having one or more looms, finishing tools and/or substantial stocks of textile materials. Some of the others had a second trade, eg as blacksmith, shoemaker or innkeeper. Reversing the ratio, of the 37 people involved in textiles, 34 were also farming, excluding one who had a little arable land but no more. The figures for the 1718-40 group are broadly similar. Of the 23 farmers, 18 were engaged in textiles and 3 more had textile occupations (wood stapler, clothier, white kersey maker) and 1 was an innkeeper. Twenty of the 22 textile operators were also farming. Putting the two groups together, 79% of those who were farming had some association with textiles, and 92% of the textile workers had a farm. In other words, of the people who left probate documents behind, relatively few were living by farming alone, and almost all of these involved in textiles were practising the dual economy.

The cloth most frequently mentioned in the inventories of the late seventeenth and early eighteenth centuries was kersey, woven from short-staple wool after carding and spinning on the 'great wheel'. It was normally made 1 yard wide and 17 to 18 yards long, and a handloom could produce two pieces a week. After weaving the cloth was fulled, to thicken the fabric by shrinking and matting together the surface fibres; dried on tenters; and finished by three dressing processes: the nap was raised with teazles (or a gig mill) and cropped with heavy shears, after which the pieces were interlined with paper and pressed.

For various reasons, not least the expansion of cheap cloth production in some export markets, the Halifax area began to experiment with worsted manufacture in the late seventeenth century. Worsted yarn was made from long-staple wool, which was combed not carded, using pairs of hand combs containing several rows of long metal teeth; and then spun on the treadle-operated Saxony wheel. The yarn was strong and smooth, and worsted cloth did not need to be fulled.

The early history of worsted manufacture in Yorkshire is rather obscure. Coverlets were being made of worsted yarn from the fourteenth century. In the inventories of dual economy households in the Forest of Knaresborough during the second half of the sixteenth century, combs were as numerous as cards and many of the households had both. Bays, a cloth made from a warp of worsted yarn and a weft of carded, woollen yarn, were established in the Rochdale area by about 1600, but do not seem to have become important in western Yorkshire until the last quarter of the seventeenth century. The letter books of Joseph Holroyd, a cloth merchant of Soyland, in 1706-7, show that he was sending large quantities of bays to London and Rotterdam. By the early eighteenth century the manufacture of full worsted cloths – mainly shalloons and serges, with some other types such as 'caddows' (quilts) – had become well-established in the Halifax area, from where it spread to Bradford and Keighley.[8]

In his masterly study of the Yorkshire woollen and worsted industries, Herbert Heaton contrasted the organisation of the woollen and worsted trades at the beginning of the eighteenth century. The mainstay of the woollen industry was the independent clothier, with one, two or three looms, who bought raw wool and processed it, using some outside labour, as far as the weaving stage. Most of the carding and spinning was 'put out' to cottager families. It was estimated that the work of five or six spinners (women and older girls) and several carders (usually children) was needed to keep one weaver supplied. Partly because more capital was required to establish a new branch of textiles, Heaton explains, the worsted master 'was usually a large employer, with a flock of workpeople at his command', including combers and weavers who owned their own equipment but used the employer's materials; '. . . the small independent clothier never existed in the worsted industry'.[9]

Heaton's researches, most of which were carried out before the First World War, have stood the test of time remarkably well, but it would be surprising if a few of his judgments did not need revision in the light of new evidence. There were certainly worsted masters of the kind he describes in upper Calderdale. John Greenwood of Hebden Bridge (1730), who was also an innkeeper (the White Lion), a carrier and a farmer, was engaged in the manufacture of worsteds, mainly shalloons, from the raw wool to the woven cloth stage, doing at least some of his own combing, but putting out the spinning and weaving stages. However, there were 'small independent clothiers' in worsted, eg John Sutcliffe of Sowerby (1724) who had three looms and quantities of uncombed wool, combed wool and worsted yarn. Some households engaged in both branches of the trade, a sensible arrangement as the market for one kind of cloth might be brisk while the other was slack. Robert Halstead of Bankfoot near Hebden Bridge (1725) had wool, several sorts of yarn, 21 shalloons, 10 serges and 14 kerseys. Elizabeth Horsfell of Stansfield (1720) had one loom for 'cloth' (woollens) and another for 'worseth', together with wool, a worsted warp, three spinning wheels and 'cards of all sorts'. John Normanton of Sowerby (1731) had a kersey loom and a shalloon loom, together with warping gear. All three households were apparently putting out the combing stage in worsted.

On the other side of the picture, there were some local men in the kersey trade who by the standards of the time were substantial capitalists, employing large numbers of outworkers. Joseph Gawkroger of Sowerby (1693) had only one loom, but he had finishing equipment – three presses, four pairs of shears, three tenters – about 32 stones of wool and 3 stones of flocks, and the following:

> yarns for 10 pieces £11
> average value per piece £1 2s 0d
>
> 32 new pieces of kersey £37 12s 0d
> average value per piece £1 3s 6d
>
> 86 dressed pieces of kersey £107 10s 0d
> average value per piece £1 5s 0d

The above figures suggest that 88% of the value of the kersey came from the raw wool and the preparatory, carding and spinning processes, with 6% added by the weaving stage and the same amount by fulling and finishing. Broadly similar ratios can be deduced from the price data of other inventories.

Nathan Kirshaw of Soyland (probably of Wood Farm, Hoyle Bank), who died in 1692, had 154 stones of wool, value £17 1s 6d; rape oil and butter, used to treat the wool before carding to make processing easier; a warping frame; yarn to make 12 kerseys and a total of 88 kerseys dressed and undressed; two looms; five tenters; eight pairs of shears; and six cloth presses, one operated by a screw, the other by a 'stang' (pole).

William Thomas of Broadbottom in Mytholmroyd (1714) was a kersey master involved in all the stages of production as far as cloth dressing. His inventory included 33 stones of wool 'at spinning in Lankashir' and yarn for 32 pieces of cloth 'out at making', as well as five looms (the largest number in one household found in the West Riding in an extensive search of probate inventories for the late seventeenth and early eighteenth centuries undertaken by Dr Michael Dickenson).[10] His finishing equipment included four pairs of shears, a screw press, three balk presses and seven tenters, and his stock of cloth consisted of 48 fine kerseys worth £1 16s each, and 71 coarse pieces at £1 10s each. His total textile inventory, excluding trading debts, came to £287. The scale of the putting out of weaving shows that there must have been a substantial number of cottager-weavers, owning their own looms but processing their employer's materials, as well as journeymen weavers who worked some of the looms in the yeomen-clothiers' loomshops.

Gawkroger, Kirshaw and Thomas were engaged in manufacturing as well as finishing, although they may have bought some cloth made by small independent producers. John Wainhouse of Pyenest, Skircoat (1692), and Robert Sutcliffe of Greenwood Lee (1718) were both merchant finishers, buying undressed cloth. Wainhouse had two hot presses, two cold presses, eight pairs of shears and 163 kerseys valued at £1 9s each. Sutcliffe's family owned a gig mill in Stansfield and two fulling mills in Langfield. His workshop contained seven pairs of shears, two presses, forty dozen packs of papers, and 86 white (ie undyed) kerseys at £1 15s 6d each. In the fields were 10 tenters worth £30, bringing the whole textile inventory to £203 10s.

It was unusual for small-scale producers of kerseys to engage in all the stages from carding to cropping, but Jeremy Waddington of Sowerby (1692) had cards, four spinning wheels, a warping wough, two looms, a pair of old shears and two presses, also apparently old. His goods, including £10 17s 4d on the farming side, totalled only £28 6s 7d. Another one-loom man engaged in finishing was William Cockcroft of Mayroyd, near Hebden Bridge (1644), whose inventory survives because it was cited in a lawsuit.[11] In this case, however, the loom was apparently a sideline: Cockcroft had a pair of shears, a press, papers and nineteen kersey pieces in his shop, two presses in his packing house, and five tenters. He was essentially a finisher, rather than a clothier. There is no reference to the dyeing process in any of the local inventories.

A comparison of the inventories for 1688-97 and 1718-40 throws some light on the progress of the worsted industry. Of the 36 weavers or finishers in the first group, 17 were in woollens, 18 are uncertain, and one was a linen weaver. There is no positive evidence of worsted production. In 1718-40, the 22 textile households broke down as follows: woollens 8, worsted 3, woollen and worsted 4, uncertain 7. In both groups, when the type of woollen cloth is specified, it is always kersey.

To return to the balance between the two sides of the dual economy, we have seen that the great majority of those households which were engaged in textiles from the one-loom level upwards were also involved in farming. A key factor in the economic and social history of the area is the relationship between the scale of farming and the scale of textile operations. In some dual economy regions, eg Nidderdale and the Forest of Knaresborough, the relationship between the two sides tended to be complementary, the three-loom weavers having on average a smaller farming operation than the one-loom weavers. This was not the case in the upper Calder Valley. If the farming-textile inventories are arranged in groups, in ascending order of the value of textile equipment and materials, the average farming valuation rises, although by no means proportionately, until the ranks of the wealthy putters-out and merchant-finishers are reached. To illustrate this point in a fairly simple way, twenty-two inventories were selected which fall into four groups of widely-separated textile valuations, with the following result (figures to the nearest £):

Group	Number of Inventories	Range of Textile Valuations	Average Farming Valuation
A	7	under £10	£26
B	6	£18-£38	£28
C	5	£69-£87	£38
D	4	£163-£278	£23

Greenwood Lee.

A more sophisticated statistical analysis could be constructed, but would need considerable qualification. Inventory valuations are not a precise measure of wealth and certainly not of real annual income, as they excluded buildings, land, rents received and the input of labour. Men who were mainly putters-out had capital tied up in materials which loomed large in the valuations. A three-loom clothier who rode weekly to market in Halifax to sell his pieces and top up his supply of wool needed little circulating capital. His three looms might be valued at only £3 altogether, but if worked full time for a year (which would not, of course, happen in practice through the demands of farming) they would produce added value of about £22-£30.

Housing

The extent and strength of the dual economy is undoubtedly one of the reasons for the rich housing heritage of the upper Calder Valley. The Halifax-upper Calderdale area has 24 of the former West Yorkshire Metropolitan County's 35 examples of the aisled house, most of which are thought to have been built in the period 1475-1575. The same district, 17% of the county in area, has 56% of all the houses with datestones from the years 1600-49. This is partly because hillside settlements have suffered less disturbance from later industrialisation than valley-bottom towns and villages, but it is clear that the 'great rebuilding' began at a relatively early date in upper Calderdale.[12]

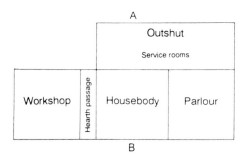

A

Ground Plan

The parlour is the main bedroom

A TWO-CELL HOUSE: Ground Plan

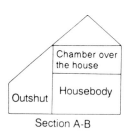

Section A-B

The parlour is the main bedroom

A SIMPLE THREE-CELL HOUSE

OF A YEOMAN CLOTHIER

Some parlours are bedrooms, others drawing room
and dining room

A THREE-CELL GENTRY HOUSE: Ground Plan

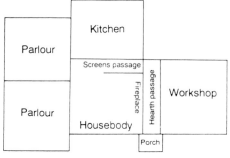

The parlours are used mainly as bedrooms

A LARGER THREE-CELL HOUSE

OF A YEOMAN CLOTHIER:

Ground Plan

Simplified sketch plans of house types.

A major influence on the timing of rebuilding may have been the purchase of freeholds or secure copyholds, described in Chapter 6. The considerations which would influence the decision to remodel or replace a dual-economy house were: the ability to pay for the work; the need for more space for textile activities; the desire for greater comfort; the increased rental potential of a better house; and concern for status. We can imagine many yeomen-clothiers preferring to plough back their profits into an expansion of trade rather than invest in improved housing, but reaching a point at which the first could not be continued without the second.

The vernacular architecture of upper Calderdale is admirably presented in *Rural Houses of West Yorkshire* (1986). The account below concentrates on the relationship between different types of house and the life and work of the yeomen clothiers.

The houses which are clearly described in the inventories can be divided into three main groups:

Type A: smaller than two-up and two-down

Type B: two-up and two-down, otherwise known as a two-cell house, with or without an outshut at the back

Type C: a three-cell house, one room or two rooms deep, with or without an outshut

Most of the surviving houses with dates earlier than 1700 are type C, a picture reinforced by the inventory evidence. Of the 34 houses clearly described in inventories for the years 1688-97, 25 are type C, 8 type B and only one type A. The hearth tax returns for 1672, summarised in Table 3, suggest that, in the community as a whole, type A houses would have been the most numerous, even in the townships most heavily involved in the textile trade.[13] However, most of the people who left probate records behind could afford to live in something better.

The type B houses consisted, on the ground floor, of a housebody, often described simply as 'the house', less frequently as the hall or hall-house, and a parlour; with two chambers above. In the seventeenth century the housebody was the main living and dining room, used also for cooking (for the type B houses had no separate cooking kitchen, although they might have a 'dairy' at the back), and accommodating light industrial work such as spinning. The parlour was the principal bedroom, although it might also be furnished for other uses. Where there were two chambers, the usual pattern was for one to contain beds and the other to be used for storage.

In the three-cell (type C) houses, the housebody occupied the middle of the façade, with a parlour on one side and a workshop (or in a few cases another parlour) on the other. About half of the above inventory sample had a second parlour behind the front one, and 15 of the 25 houses had a kitchen, although in some cases there were cooking implements in the housebody as well.

Nearly all of the houses were stone-built. In a few cases, eg Westfield in Warley, an older timber-framed house was encased in stone in the seventeenth century. One feature carried forward from the timber-framed style was the cross passage, which ran behind the main fireplace from the front of the house to the back, a door in the passage beyond the fireplace giving access to the housebody. The front entrance was in some cases protected by a two-storey porch, as at Greenwood Lee.

The parlour, or if there was more than one at least one of the parlours, had a fireplace in the wall opposite the housebody. The principal bedroom was almost invariably a parlour. A majority of homes with two or more parlours had one of them furnished as a dining/sitting room. Of the three gentry houses amongst the 25 type C buildings, Wood Lane Hall in Sowerby had five parlours, three of them bedrooms; Murgatroyd

	Number of dwellings	Exempt because of poverty	Number of hearths taxed			% 3 hearths or more	%1 hearth or exempt
			1	2	3+		
Stansfield	180	16	122	30	12	7	77
Langfield	59	9	32	12	6	10	69
Erringden	73	15	31	16	11	15	63
Heptonstall	102	—	61	28	13	13	60
Wadsworth	178	42	91	22	23	13	75
Midgley	90	20	35	13	22	24	61
Warley	188	—	105	43	40	21	56
Sowerby & Soyland	350	12	180	71	87	25	55
Halifax	463	150	61	81	171	37	46

Table 3: A SUMMARY OF THE 1672 HEARTH TAX RETURNS.

in Warley had a parlour-bedroom, a dining room and a 'withdrawing room'; and the house of Richard Thomas of Heptonstall had three parlours, two of which had three four-poster beds between them.

On the opposite side of the cross passage was the 'low end', nearly always consisting of the shop containing looms, or shears and presses, or other working gear. It might or might not have had a fireplace; some industrial processes such as combing generated their own heat. The low end was sometimes architecturally inferior to the upper end, with less attention devoted to the details of windows and masonry work. In two of the gentry houses mentioned above, the lower end had parlours in place of the shop, but the house of Richard Thomas had a shop with two looms.

The lower end was often only one room deep. The remainder of the house might be fully two rooms deep, and/or have a projecting two-storey wing, accommodating the kitchen and kitchen chamber, behind the housebody. The main features of the houses which catch the eye are the mullioned windows, sometimes single, sometimes double, and varying in recessing and other details; and the gabled wings. The latter are found commonly at the parlour end only, as at Greenwood Lee, but occasionally at both ends, as at Colden, a late sixteenth century house in Heptonstall township. The roofs are of 'slatestone', thin sandstone slabs.

In some houses there was no communication at first floor level between the shop chamber (normally used for industrial processes or storage, but sometimes having a bed as well) and the chambers over the main part of the house. The outside stone staircase leading to the shop chamber is generally a later feature, built for convenience when the business had become concerned mainly with 'putting out'. The separate character of the shop wing shows up very clearly in the illustration of Great House Clough Farm in Stansfield. Although chambers over the remainder of the house were sometimes used for textile storage or even processing, the three-cell house of the yeoman clothier was basically two-thirds residential and one-third industrial. Someone of a comparable social standing without a significant involvement in textiles would not need the shop wing. Delete the latter at Great House Clough and we have a two-cell

Swallowshaw, Stansfield.

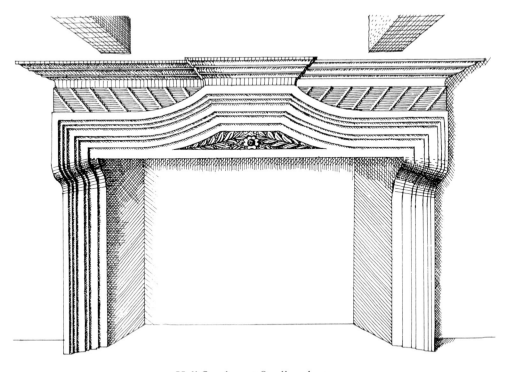

Hall fireplace at Swallowshaw.

Great House, Colden.

house similar to Flailcroft, in Todmorden with Walsden. Built apparently in the second half of the seventeenth century, it had no need for a cross passage, and entry into the housebody was through a door in the gable end. An outshut was added in the eighteenth century.

The fact that nearly all of the three-cell houses occupied by families of the yeoman class had shop wings has already been noted. In the inventories for both 1688-97 and 1718-40 we find that whereas many of the one-loom farmer-weavers had a two-cell or smaller house, every family with two or more looms, or with a comparable amount of other textile equipment and/or materials, had a three-cell house. The preponderance of three-cell houses in the upper Calder Valley is therefore a product of the dual economy, not merely in the general sense that the yeomen clothiers could afford to build them, but because they were a functional requirement. As already explained, the larger-scale textile men also tended to be the larger-scale farmers (below the level of the wealthy merchant finishers) and the three-cell house normally had a large barn.

In his journey through the area in the 1720s, Daniel Defoe noted that 'among the manufacturers' houses are likewise scattered an infinite number of cottages or small dwellings, in which dwell the workmen which are employed'.[14] One architectural consequence of the growth in the number of outworkers was the building of short terraces of cottages with 'weavers' windows', ie stone-mullioned windows extending the full length of the first floor to give the maximum natural light.

Great House Clough Farm.

Wood Lane Hall, Sowerby.

Weavers' cottages at Luddenden.

The probate documents for the valley above Halifax for the two year period 1770-2 were examined to find out whether the dual economy was still dominant and the sub-division of landholdings was still practised (answer, yes to both questions), and whether informative inventories were still to be found (answer, no). Of the 19 people leaving wills, 4 were described as yeomen, 2 of whom were engaged in textiles; 1 was an elderly husbandman whose only son was a weaver; 9 were weavers, 7 of them in worsted; 1 was a comb maker; 1 an innkeeper-weaver; a man with no description had an old linsey loom (for weaving a mixed linen-worsted cloth); and the remaining 2 were a cordwainer and a widow.

The society of the upper Calder Valley on the eve of the Industrial Revolution was far from egalitarian. The fundamental division was between the families which could be described as economically independent – combining farming with textile operations in which they owned their own equipment and materials, or in a minority of cases living by farming alone – and those who gained a livelihood mainly by selling their labour. The lower and much larger group was itself a gradation from skilled workers who had a little land, down to those who lived intermittently or permanently in poverty. The upper group ranged from modest farmer-weavers to the prosperous putters-out and merchant-finishers.

Flailcroft, Todmorden.

This yeoman class had a dominant influence on local society, filling the important township offices (as described in Chapter 9) and giving the valley its distinctive religious and political outlook. They had one great social advantage compared to people of a comparable rank in areas dominated by resident squires and well-beneficed parsons: they did not have to look up to anyone. The few resident lesser gentry lived in rather more comfort than families such as the Sutcliffes of Greenwood Lee, but did not have a dominant role in local society. The wealthy yeomen-clothiers were themselves considerable employers of labour and had a respected place as the driving forces of economic life and social organisation. The spirit of their age is captured by the grace and dignity of the surviving yeomen's houses.

9

Community Life in the Eighteenth and Early Nineteenth Centuries

The Social Framework

The organisations out of which the framework of local community life was constructed were the county, the parish, the manor, the township and the settlement, ie town, village or hamlet. The counties, locally the West Riding and Lancashire, were concerned with the administration of justice, through the Quarter Sessions presided over by a group of justices of the peace. They maintained Houses of Correction at Wakefield and Preston, originally intended for the reform of 'idle vagabonds' by a combination of whipping and industrial training. The old-established county jails at York (serving all three Ridings) and Lancaster continued in use, especially for prisoners awaiting trial. The counties were also responsible for major bridges. A county rate was levied for 'bridge money' and judicial costs.

As a social unit, the county mattered only to the gentry. Only a handful of lesser gentry lived in upper Calderdale, and it was often difficult to recruit enough JPs.[1]

The parishes – Halifax with its twenty-two townships, and Rochdale which included Todmorden with Walsden – were too large to be significant in terms of either local loyalties or social administration. Even the ancient chapelry of Heptonstall contained five townships, each with its own churchwarden keeping separate township accounts. The manor of Wakefield, with its twice-yearly tourns regulating community affairs, was a much more relevant institution, even in the eighteenth century.

The remaining units were the township and the settlement. Over most of the area settlement was dispersed, although there were a few nucleated villages such as Heptonstall, and therefore the township had the key role in social regulation. In the eighteenth century some of their officers (constables and surveyors) operated within a dual system, being responsible both to the manor court and to the JPs.

The Constables

The constable was both the principal officer of the township and the one with the heaviest and most varied duties.[2] His responsibilities included law and order, weights and measures, the pinfold, turbary, the militia and tax collection. At regular intervals the constables carried out a 'privy search' for vagrants. Dealing with them could be expensive. In 1762 the Wadsworth constable spent 22s on guarding a vagrant, taking him to the nearest available JP at Bradford, and delivering the miscreant to the house of correction at Wakefield. The 'hue and cry' system, of calling out a posse of local men to pursue criminals, was still occasionally used until its abolition in 1828. Several townships had their own 'dungeon' or lock-up.

The White Lion Inn, Hebden Bridge.

The traditional punitive instruments – stocks, whipping post and ducking stool – were still maintained, although there is no reference to whipping in the eighteenth century records. Most local townships still possess at least the remains of their stocks, the best preserved being at Cross Stone. A spell in the stocks, usually for a few hours, was used to punish drunkenness and other minor offences. The Heptonstall stocks were used as late as 1841, when two men were locked in for six hours, for being drunk and disorderly at Christmas.

The constables sometimes dealt with serious crimes, including murder. In 1779 John Greenwood of 'Hirstin' (?Thursden), a lime carrier, was murdered by soldiers. The calendars of the Wakefield house of correction show that a disproportionate number of inmates came from upper Calderdale, Midgley having a particularly bad reputation. Some offenders received a much more severe punishment than a few weeks on the Wakefield treadmill. In 1832 a man who stole a ham from the White Lion Inn, Hebden Bridge, was transported for seven years; two years later, four men involved in the theft of twenty pounds of wheat from Champion Murgatroyd (who often served as churchwarden for Midgley) received the same sentence.[3]

In the history of law and order in the upper Calder Valley, the most famous episode is that of the Cragg Coiners. The counterfeiters clipped shavings from the edge of gold guinea coins, filed on a new edge and returned the coins (now about fifteen per cent lighter) into circulation. The clippings were melted down and struck into imitations of Portuguese gold coins then widely circulated in England. (Some of the dies used are preserved in Heptonstall museum.)

This activity was widespread in upper Calderdale in the 1760s. The Cragg Vale coiners were the most active, as well as being the most difficult to catch red-handed. Most of them were farmers or weavers or both, who lived in isolated farmhouses approached by hillside tracks which could easily be watched. The 'considerable halo of romance' attached to the coiners (to quote Ling Roth) is hardly deserved. To protect themselves they committed two murders, including that of William Dighton, supervisor of customs and excise in Halifax. When they were cornered, they readily betrayed each other in an attempt to save their own skins.

In 1769-74 many of the leading coiners were put on trial for counterfeiting (a capital offence) and other crimes. Most were acquitted because of conflicts of evidence, but several were hanged, including the murderers of Dighton, and the self-styled 'king' of the Cragg Coiners, David Hartley of Bell House in Erringden. A fuller account of the coiners is given in a separate book by one of the present authors.[4]

Stray animals were impounded by the township pinder, but the maintenance of the pinfold was the responsibility of the constable. There are several pinfolds still in a fair state of preservation, eg at Pinfold Lane, Heptonstall, and at Midgley on the lane leading to the old workhouse at New Earth Head.

In the seventeenth century, particularly during the ascendancy of the Puritans, the constables were kept busy on Sundays pursuing those who profaned the Sabbath by drinking or gambling. Perhaps surprisingly, the Sunday observance laws were still being enforced in the late eighteenth and early nineteenth centuries. In 1805 the Stansfield constable fined one man for not going to divine worship (under an Act of 1559), another for swearing on Sunday, and three others for Sabbath-breaking. As late as 1830 three Sowerby men, convicted of gambling on Sunday, were fined and put in the stocks.

The constable had to collect, in addition to his own and the county rate, land tax and window tax (in operation from 1695 to 1851), and acted as inspector of weights and measures. He took care of militia weapons, and organised the ballot by which a quota of militia men was raised from each township. The 1757 Militia Act allowed those chosen to hire substitutes. During the Napoleonic Wars, Erringden and Warley had militia clubs, the subscriptions being used to pay substitutes. A Warley town meeting in 1810 authorised the overseers of the poor to augment the funds of the militia club with 140 guineas out of the poor rate. In this period about a quarter of the Heptonstall poor rate was spent on the wives or widows of militia men.

One wonders what happened to Jeremiah Riley, constable of Sowerby in 1711-12. The only entry, in his otherwise completely blank pages, is a rhyming couplet:

Remember man that die thou must,
And, after death, return to dust.

Was he trying to suggest that a constable's lot was not a happy one, or is there a more prosaic explanation, eg that he kept his accounts on separate sheets and forgot to copy them into the book?

The Churchwardens

The office of churchwarden rivals in antiquity that of the constable, and it is the only one of the four township offices to survive to the present day. The principal duties

Heptonstall Old Church.

were the maintenance of the church building and its furnishings, the upkeep of the churchyard, and the provision of vestments, a Bible, a *Book of Common Prayer* and a *Book of Homilies*. The churchwardens also had certain responsibilities under the Tudor poor laws, and made payments for the destruction of vermin. The church at Heptonstall served five townships: Heptonstall, Stansfield, Langfield, Erringden and Wadsworth. Each township had its own churchwarden – Heptonstall always had two – and kept separate accounts. The churchwardens were unpaid, but minor function-aries, including the clerk, sexton and bell-ringers, received small payments.[5]

The fabric of Heptonstall Church, most of which was by now over 300 years old, was in constant need of repair. The churchwardens made regular payments for wood, laths, nails, hair for 'plaistering', ironwork and other materials. Each autumn, several days were spent by labourers packing the roof slates with moss to make them watertight, not always effectively as entries such as the following show: 'February and March 1792, paid sexton for getting snow out of church three times, 1s'. The inside of the church was regularly whitewashed.

Although a 'singing loft' had been made in the north chancel in 1720, there is no mention of a choir until 1786, when 7s 2d was spent on 'Book Frame for Singers and other Iron work' and a further 5s on 'Singers, for books'. This latter item was repeated annually. The singers were accompanied by string and wind instruments.

The expenses of the chapelry were shared by the five townships in a ratio probably determined by some earlier rateable valuation: Wadsworth 33%, Stansfield 25%, Heptonstall 22%, Erringden 11%, Langfield 8%. Having calculated the amount to be met by their own township, the churchwardens then added their personal expenses, and levied a church rate to raise the amount needed. The average annual expenses of the chapelry were about £25 in 1750-1800, and the townships could meet this by levying a rate of two pence in the pound.

A small income also came from payments made for burials in the church. The fees for the usual burials in the churchyard went to the minister, but the income for burials in the church itself went to the churchwardens: 6s 8d for the chancel, and 3s 4d for elsewhere in the church. In 1494 William Grenewod of Heptonstall left 3s 4d so that he could be buried 'in the chapel of St. Thomas of Heptonstall' – the charge had not changed in 300 years.[6]

A milestone at Blackshaw Head, on the line of the Long Causeway.

A causeway on Langfield Moor.

Roads and Bridges: The Surveyors of the Highway

The system of highway maintenance used in the seventeenth century has been described in Chapter 6. The Highways Act of 1555, which provided for the township roads to be repaired by compulsory labour, was ignored. The older custom of making the occupiers of land adjoining a stretch of road responsible for keeping it in good order was maintained. The 'overseers of the highways' inspected the roads, and the court of the manor of Wakefield enforced, in a rather leisurely way, the orders for necessary repairs.[7]

Erringden never appointed surveyors, being content with the system of maintenance 'by reason of tenure'. Partly because the township was a park until the middle of the fifteenth century, no major routeways passed through it. The land was either physically enclosed or allocated in parcels to the freeholders, so that every piece of road had an occupier or occupiers who accepted responsibility for it.

The records of Wakefield Manor and of the quarter sessions, which could order the repair of highways, show that tenured maintenance continued for minor roads in other townships. In 1738, for example, the quarter sessions indicted the occupiers of land along what is now the Hebden Bridge-Todmorden road, then a 'horseway', for neglect of maintenance. In 1765 the quarter sessions ordered that the road from White Lee Clough (Mytholmroyd) to Hebden Bridge Mills should be maintained at the charge of the owners of lands and tenements in Wadsworth 'as the other highways there are maintained'.

The surveyors concentrated on the upkeep and improvement of the main routeways. Before the turnpike road was made, these ran along the hillside terraces, descending at intervals to cross the steep-sided tributary valleys. The line of the principal routeway, from Halifax to Burnley, is picked out in the packhorse driver's jingle:

> Burnley for ready money
> Mearclough don't trust
> You'll be taking a peep at Stiperden
> And call at Kebs you must
> Blackshawhead for travellers
> and Heptonstall for trust
> Hepton Brig for landladies
> Midgley by the moor
> Luddenden's a warm spot
> Roils Head's very cold
> But if you get to Halifax
> You must be very bold.

The steep climbs on these routes made them unsuitable for wheeled vehicles, and goods were carried by trains of packhorses. For the latter a permanent and hard-wearing surface was provided by paved causeways, the maintenance of which was the main business of the surveyors in the pre-turnpike period. Causey stones, usually about four feet by eighteen inches, were the usual covering, with smaller stones packed in at the side to give a total width of about eight feet. Examples from the surveyor's accounts are:

Heptonstall 1732   20 Rood of Stones for a new Causey in the Slack, £1 10s 0d
[A rood was locally 7 yards]

Wadsworth 1760   32 Rood of Causey near Widdop £3 4s 0d

Each township had its own tools: spades, mattocks, picks, mauls, wedges, crowbars, and sledges for hauling stones.

When it was necessary to employ labour, and buy tools and materials, the money could be raised either by means of a 'levy' or rate, or by collecting 'composition money' in lieu of statute duty. In 1768 the Heptonstall scale for composition money ranged from 4d a day for a labourer to as much as 3s a day for a farmer and his son.

The major bridges, as already explained, were maintained by the county. Originally made of wood, Hebden (Old) Bridge, Sowerby Bridge and Luddenden Bridge were rebuilt in stone in the early sixteenth century.[8] Mytholmroyd Bridge, not a county bridge, was rebuilt in stone in 1684. It was repaired in 1722 with Sowerby paying one

Hebden Bridge, looking up Hebden Water. In the right foreground is the aqueduct carrying the canal over the River Calder. Of the three bridges over Hebden Water, the middle one is the stone bridge built about 1510 to replace the wooden bridge first recorded in 1347. The lower bridge was built for the turnpike road in 1771-2.

The old roads climbing out of Hebden Bridge: (above) the Buttress, leading to Heptonstall; and (below) Stubbing, on the Wadsworth side. The steepness of the roads is indicated by the handrails.

half of the cost, and Wadsworth and Erringden the other half. Heptonstall and Stansfield shared the maintenance of Jack Bridge on Colden Water, rebuilt in 1778, and Midgley and Wadsworth were jointly responsible for Foster Clough Bridge, rebuilt in 1761.

The industrial growth of the West Riding and East Lancashire during the first half of the eighteenth century meant extra traffic on the roads, an increasing proportion of which was, as far as the townships were concerned, through traffic rather than local. To deal with this problem, turnpike trusts, which improved and maintained main roads out of the income from tolls, were set up by Act of Parliament. The earliest trust in the West Riding was established in 1734 for the road from Rochdale over Blackstone Edge to Elland and Halifax. Six more Acts for Yorkshire roads were passed in 1741, and by the end of that decade the industrial West Riding had a substantial network of turnpike roads, including Elland-Cleckheaton-Leeds, and Halifax-Leeds-Selby. By 1752 the Halifax-Rochdale road had been improved and widened.[9]

It was not until 1760 that an Act of Parliament was secured for the construction of a turnpike road along the Calder Valley from Halifax and Sowerby Bridge to Todmorden, with branches from there to Burnley and Littleborough (on the way to Rochdale) respectively. This route offers the easiest crossing of the Pennines south of the Aire Gap. However, most of the early turnpike trusts were able to take over existing highways; in upper Calderdale, most of the line consisted of bridleways and rough 'occupation' roads (used by local occupiers, not as through roads).

In 1761 work began on the Todmorden-Hebden Bridge stretch, hitherto a bridleway. The first toll house was built at Charlestown in 1763. For the eastern section the line King Cross-Cotehill-Causeway Head-Lower Longbottom-Luddenden Foot (with a toll house at Longbottom) was chosen in preference to the higher route through Highroad Well and Warley Town. The contract for the Mytholmroyd-Hebden Bridge section was not let until 1767. Existing bridges were widened and new ones built. The old, narrow bridge at Hebden Bridge was replaced by a new bridge further downstream, built in 1771 by the county at a cost of £210.

It was not until 1781 that the whole line was completed. The turnpike could then begin to attract through traffic to and from the Rochdale area away from the hillier Blackstone Edge road.

There was a long-running dispute between the turnpike trustees and the townships through which the road passed, about the amount of statute labour, or money in lieu, which should be allocated to the turnpike. In the end the trust had to settle for modest contributions. The townships, however, came to appreciate the advantages of the turnpike road, as for the first time heavy wheeled vehicles, carrying coal, cotton, wool and cloth, were able to move freely along the valley bottom. They began to widen their own narrow tracks and to make new roads so that wheeled vehicles could reach the hillside settlements. In 1782-3 a new road was built from the turnpike to Heptonstall at a cost of £300, to replace the steep Buttress which climbed from Hebden Old Bridge. Its completion was greeted by celebrations and bell-ringing. However, the next major venture of the Heptonstall surveyors, a road through Lee Wood to Slack, by-passing Heptonstall village, was dubbed by the locals 'the Needless Road'.

Road building and widening continued to be an important activity for a generation, including New Road in Hebden Bridge; Midgley Road down into Mytholmroyd; Birchcliffe Road down the Wadsworth hillside as an alternative to the even steeper Heights Road; and New Road on the Midgley side of Luddenden village, which cut out one of the steepest of the old packhorse tracks. Many of the new lines of road had gradients which would be regarded as crippling away from the Pennines, but they were at least passable with horses and carts.

In the township records, 'causeys' are no more. The new vocabulary is 'setting' – fitting small rectangular stone setts; and 'boldering' – the construction of roads made entirely of small stones, to a depth of a foot or even more.

The Overseers of the Poor

The account books of the local overseers of the poor are unrivalled sources of information about the life and condition of the poor during the eighteenth and early nineteenth centuries.[10] No local overseers records earlier than 1716 have survived, and it is possible that the local townships (as distinct from the parish of Halifax and the ancient chapelry of Heptonstall) did not assume responsibility for the poor until after the 1662 Act which provided for the division of large parishes in the North of England. In effect, this Act made the township the unit for poor law administration, as it already was for law and order and, under the manor of Wakefield, for highways.

The overseers levied a poor rate on the annual value of land and buildings, which was used to relieve the 'impotent poor' (the old, the sick and small children), apprentice poor children, set the unemployed to work and finance a variety of other tasks. In the first half of the eighteenth century the poor rate was comparatively low, but during the second half, with its growth of industry and population and its frequent wars, together with the setting up of workhouses, there was a sharp increase. The rate in the pound for Heptonstall rose from 1s 10d in 1716 to 4s in 1766 and 7s in 1800. In Midgley the figure increased from 2s 4d in 1754 to 13s in 1812.

Pauper children were apprenticed, usually at the age of seven, to a master who would undertake to teach the child a trade and provide maintenance until the age of twenty-one for a boy and (normally) eighteen for a girl. The average premium paid by Wadsworth in the eighteenth century was about 30s and the apprentice was also supplied with a new set of clothes. In 1730 Heptonstall township spent 11s 8½d on new clothes for Jonathan Crabtree, including a harden 'sark' (shirt), breeches, waistcoat and coat, and 'a new hat 1s; stokings 1s, clogs 6d; an Apperon 6d'.

The overseers tried to avoid the burden of illegitimate children by arranging marriages, sometimes at considerable expense. In 1780 the Midgley overseers gave Sarah Hargreaves £2 9s 4d to 'adorn or beautify herself ready for Marriage'. On such occasions, overseers' accounts included the cost of arresting and detaining the husband-to-be, as well as paying for the wedding reception.

Allowances made to paupers in money were of two kinds: regular monthly payments or 'constants' made to the old and infirm; and irregular payments, known as 'accidentals' or 'inconstants'. Under an Act of 1696 the regular paupers had to wear on their shoulders a cloth badge showing the letter 'P' and the initial letter of the township name. There are many references to badging, eg in Stansfield (1752): 'Cloth to badge the poor and to Wm. Dearden for badging them, 10d'. The regular allowances varied, but were generally in the range of 1s 6d to 4s a month in the early eighteenth century, and 3s to 5s 6d by the end of the century – with a few as high as 10s.

The irregular payments take up the greater part of the accounts. In 1774-5 there were over 500 'accidentals' in Wadsworth. The Heptonstall accounts contain both conventional entries – 'Pd. John Burne out of health 1s' – and more expressive comments – 'Math. Sutcliffe lad sik, sik, sik 1s'. Payments in kind were numerous, mainly such items as coal, clothing, bedding and furniture, the last often provided on permanent loan. The records have a sprinkling of ambiguous entries including (Heptonstall 1769) 'Stays and a skin to cover Wm Dewhirst daughter 2s 2d'.

Rents, rates and land taxes were often paid by the township on behalf of paupers. In 1722, £14 was paid in rent for twenty-four poor persons in Todmorden and Walsden.[11] The homeless poor occasionally had cottages allotted to them, but were usually lodged with other people, many of whom were paupers themselves. For example, in 1718 Heptonstall paid 'Widdow Ryley' 2s for 'Margrit Tattersall hous room'.

One of the duties of the overseers was to find work for the able-bodied unemployed, and there are many references in the accounts to the supply of textile equipment, including cards, spinning wheels and looms. An Act of 1723 authorised, but did not require, townships to establish workhouses and to refuse poor relief to paupers declining to enter the house. All of the local townships had workhouses at one time or another during the second half of the eighteenth century, but they do not seem to have been used as a means of deterring applications for outdoor relief. Some of them were literally work-houses, but others were essentially shelters for the homeless poor.

Most of the workhouses consisted of converted farm buildings taken on lease. Midgley rented New Earth Head, a farmhouse above the pinfold and on the edge of the moor, for £20 a year from about 1770. Wadsworth had a succession of premises, including Spinks Hill Farm near Pecket Well, which was in use for several decades. In 1770 the activities of the Wadsworth workhouse were farming, clog making, spinning and weaving. In general the operation of a workhouse, including the salary of a 'master' and/or 'dame', was found to be uneconomic.

Judging by the variety and quantity of the food supplied to the local workhouses (we know nothing, of course, about the quality or the cooking), the inmates were fed much better than they would have been on outdoor relief, and infinitely better than the paupers in the post-1834 union workhouses. The inmates of the Heptonstall workhouse regularly received ample supplies of oatmeal, sugar, treacle, butter, beef, mutton, veal, liver, cheese, suet, bacon, beans, turnips, potatoes, cabbages, onions, malt, hops and tobacco, as well as essentials such as bread, flour, lard and salt, etc. At Christmas they enjoyed extras such as apples and currants, and increased rations of tobacco.

The main principle of the 1601 Poor Law Act was that each parish or township was responsible for its own poor. The Act of Settlement of 1662 provided that any stranger could be removed from a parish or township unless he rented a holding of £10 a year or found security to relieve the township of any expense incurred on his behalf. A further Act of 1691 provided that serving a township office, being bound apprentice there, or (if unmarried) being a year in service there, or paying the township rates, gave the right of settlement. The 1696 Act allowed a poor person to enter another parish or township if he or she brought a 'settlement certificate' from the home township, guaranteeing to take responsibility if the migrant became chargeable to the poor rate.

Sowerby has about 100 settlement certificates, and Heptonstall about 60. They were very carefully preserved, because they could prove to be of value after a considerable lapse of time. An extreme example is the case of a man, aged eighty, removed from Sutton to Heptonstall in 1791 because of a settlement certificate granted to his father in 1737, fifty-four years earlier. Legal action to determine the place of settlement could be protracted and expensive. Sometimes the townships found a judgement of Solomon more convenient. In 1784 Wadsworth and Heptonstall agreed to share the costs of maintaining Henry Horsfall, an inmate of Wadsworth workhouse.

Paupers labelled as 'rogues and vagabonds', which usually meant that they had been begging, were treated more harshly. Ann Holland and her son John, aged about seven, were apprehended in Bristol in 1741 and adjudged to be vagabonds. They were ordered to be sent from one house of correction to another as far as Wakefield, and thence to Heptonstall. It turned out that their settlement was actually in Erringden, and a further five shillings was spent by the constable of Heptonstall in removing them there.

The overseers' accounts are very revealing in respect of the prevalent diseases and ailments of the period, and the remedies used. Most of the 'inconstant' items, in money or kind, related to illness. To quote from the Midgley accounts:

> November 1768. To Richard Walton [probably an apothecary] for Sena prunes Syrop Buckhorne for Amos Eastwood, 6d.

> September 1772. Gooing to Blud Grace Sutcliffe, 2d.

> 1785. To a Daffy Bottle for Timothy Fawthrop, 1s 3d. [Daffy's Elixir was a favourite eighteenth century panacea]

The great scourge of the eighteenth century was smallpox. Until vaccination was introduced, it took a heavy toll in epidemic years:

> Midgley. April 1768. Thomas Briggs, his children in the small poxlies, 2d.

> Heptonstall. January 1749. Pd. Henery Sutclif, all his fallimey deed o' the pocks, 2s.

There does not appear to have been a resident doctor in the area during the greater part of the eighteenth century, and in consequence we find physicians being called in from either Burnley or Halifax, or, occasionally from Elland. By 1791, however, a Dr Heyworth was serving as medical officer for the township of Langfield. From September 1791 to January 1792 he would appear to have had a fairly easy passage; during these four months he had administered 'three Blister Plasters, three Stimulating Mixtures, two Pots of Digestive Liniment, a Rubbing Bottle, and some Healing Salve', his total bill amounting to only 12s 10½d.[12]

In addition to paying for midwives and christenings, the overseers paid for pauper funerals, and even for a simple meal at such times, the average total cost to the township being about 10s. In 1745 the Heptonstall overseer complained that the 'extravigant Burial' of Jennet Broxup had cost 15s.

A study of the overseers' accounts leaves the distinct impression that their work, often difficult and tedious, was on the whole carried on very conscientiously, and with no small degree of compassion. All of this work was unremunerated, at least until 1814, when Heptonstall began to employ a paid overseer at an annual stipend of £20-£30 a year.

The operation of this system strengthened the identification of the local people with their township. The settlement laws did this for the 'labouring poor', that is to say, not only the regular paupers but also the many people who might have to turn to the overseers for temporary help in bad times or for a bottle of patent medicine in sickness. The responsibilities of office did the same for the substantial men of the township. This factor was at the root of the local opposition to the new poor law of 1834, which is described in Chapter 12. The autonomy of the township was part of the fabric of community life and was not going to be surrendered without a struggle.

10

The Industrial Revolution

Spinning Frames and Water Wheels: The Early History of the Textile Mills
In 1779 the magnificent Piece Hall was opened in Halifax to replace the old cloth hall which dated back to the sixteenth century. It cost £28 4s to purchase one of the 315 rooms, and worsted and woollen manufacturers from the upper Calder Valley were well represented there. Their cloth was still made, as far as records indicate, entirely by hand, except for the use of water-powered fulling and gig mills. As the trade expanded, the disadvantages of the 'putting-out' system increased. Worsted manufacturers had to send wool for spinning as far as upper Ribblesdale and the North Riding dales. The transport of wool and yarn was time-consuming and tied up capital, and it was difficult to maintain quality. From the same 'tops' (combed wool) the rural spinners produced yarn as heavy as 16s (16 hanks to the pound weight) and as light as 24s.[1]

The invention in 1733 of Kay's flying shuttle speeded up the weaving process and thereby increased the number of spinners needed to supply each loom. Its use spread slowly, however. It was widely used in Lancashire by about 1760, was gradually adopted in the Yorkshire woollen trade between the 1760s and the 1780s, but was apparently not introduced into some branches of the worsted trade until about the end of the century. It is therefore very difficult to assess its importance in a mixed woollen-worsted area such as the upper Calder Valley.[2]

The twin problems of yarn supply and quality control were eventually solved by the development of effective spinning machines, based on the inventions of Hargreaves, Arkwright and Crompton in the 1760s and 1770s. James Hargreaves, in designing his spinning jenny (c1764), imitated the action of the hand-operated spinning wheel. A moveable carriage drew out and twisted the yarn, and was then reversed to wind the yarn on to bobbins. The alternative approach, brought to a workable state by Richard Arkwright in 1769, married the flyer-and-bobbin of the Saxony, ie treadle-operated, wheel, which spun and wound simultaneously, to rollers revolving at different surface speeds which provided the draft.

In cotton the jenny and the roller frame were complementary. The jenny produced yarn with a soft twist, suitable for weft; the roller frame spun yarns with a harder twist, for warps. The jenny was essentially a hand-operated machine, but water power was soon used for the roller frame, often referred to in consequence as the water frame. By 1775 Arkwright had developed a family of water-powered machines for the carding and spinning processes which could be tended by the cheap labour of women and children, and provided the foundations of the factory system.

Samuel Crompton's mule (c1779) was so called because it was a cross between the jenny and the roller frame, having both a moveable carriage and rollers. The mule was

The Piece Hall, Halifax.

at first hand-operated, but it required more physical effort than the jenny and water power was applied during the 1790s. It produced even yarns, to very fine 'counts' (length of yarn per unit of weight), and was later adapted to spin warp yarns as well. The mule was very flexible in operation, but required highly-skilled male operators.[3]

In every branch of textiles there was a considerable time-lag between the general adoption of machine spinning and the victory of the power loom over the hand loom. The mechanisation of weaving was not only more difficult technically, but offered only modest benefits compared with the enormous productivity gains achieved in spinning. Even a hand-operated jenny could have as many as 120 spindles. Cotton led the field in every aspect of textile technology. The cotton fibres, being short, even and elastic, presented fewer technical problems in machine spinning than did wool, worsted or flax. In consequence, mills for carding and spinning cotton were established in traditional woollen and worsted areas, particularly those close to Lancashire.

The first cotton mill in upper Calderdale of which there is any record was built on the Willow Hall estate, in Warley Clough near Sowerby Bridge, and was apparently in use by 1780. In the 1780s the foundations of the cotton industry which created the town of Todmorden were laid by two members of the Fielden family, both of whom came from the ranks of the yeomen clothiers and had been in business as worsted manufacturers. In 1782 Joshua Fielden, of Edge End Farm, began spinning with hand-operated jennies in some converted cottages at Laneside. In 1784 he acquired some leasehold property at Laneside, together with a spring of water in Swineshead Clough. He mortgaged his properties in the same year for a total of £649 at five per cent interest, probably to develop the small water-powered mill from which the Waterside complex later grew. In 1786 John Fielden, son of Samuel Fielden of Swineshead Farm in Langfield, built Clough Mill in Walsden. It was a small three-storey building, containing carding and spinning machinery driven by a water wheel.[4]

Mytholm Mill, Hebden Bridge – on Colden Water near its confluence with the River Calder – was built about 1789 by James King of Mytholm. He had previously been in business as a worsted manufacturer, with a room in the Piece Hall at Halifax. By 1791 King and his partners had a second mill at Mytholm, with a dyehouse. The firm machine-spun cotton and wove (by hand) fustians and velveteens, the earliest reference to the trade which grew to dominate Hebden Bridge.[5]

By 1801 there were about 32 cotton-spinning mills in upper Calderdale. Ten years later Samuel Crompton visited 56 mills in the area, at least 45 of which can be identified from other sources as spinning cotton. He counted 106,735 mule spindles, 15,944 throstle spindles (the throstle was an improved version of the roller frame), and 1,590 jenny spindles. He would not, of course, have been able to record the jenny spindles in domestic workshops. Seventeen of the mills had both mules and throstles.[6]

In 1801 the valley had only five worsted mills, including Rodmer Clough Mill on Colden Water, built in 1793, which also spun cotton. One cause of the relatively slow progress was technical. Early mill-spun yarn was said to be 'rough and hairy'. Roller frames were used at first, but later the mule was adopted for spinning the finer yarns.

The first worsted spinning mill in England was set up at Dolphin Holme near Lancaster in 1784 by the Edmondson family. The pioneer worsted mill in the upper Calder Valley was Lobb Mill in Langfield, a fulling mill bought in 1785 by Christopher Rawdon, which had been adapted for worsted spinning and enlarged by 1790. Two worsted mills opened in 1792, Hand Car or Clough Mill at Stubbing Holme in Sowerby, and Mytholmroyd Mill, built by Thomas Edmondson of Dolphin Holme. The latter had a long mill race running from Hawksclough to drive the wheel. The mill and contents were insured in 1795 for £3,500 and in 1797 for £6,000, which gives some indication of the rate of expansion. Scarbottom Mill, Mytholmroyd, which was on or near the site of a fulling mill recorded in 1607, was occupied as a worsted mill in 1794.[7]

Technical developments in the woollen trade followed quite different lines from those in cotton or worsted. Roller drafting was unsuitable for woollen fibres, and therefore the jenny held its place until the development of the woollen mule, a modified version which did not use rollers for drawing out. As we have seen, the jenny could be worked by hand and the advantages of making it power-driven were not great. On the other hand, carding machines could be applied to wool, and the trade had for centuries used water power for fulling. It was a relatively simple matter to install a scribbling machine (scribbling was the first stage of carding in wool) in a fulling mill, driven by the same water wheel. At first the scribbling facility was offered to customers for payment, as fulling had always been. Soon, however, entrepreneurs began to buy, or build, fulling-scribbling mills, and adapt them for their own manufacturing processes. Power-driven carding machines, to complete the carding process, were added. The next stage was the introduction of the 'slubbing billy', a machine derived from the jenny, which was used for the first stage of spinning. The billy could be water-powered, but was more commonly hand-operated. So too, as we have seen, was the jenny, which completed the spinning process.

These developments are well documented in the upper Calder Valley. The earliest record of scribbling engines is dated 1785, when Samuel and John Waterhouse insured Hollings Mill, Sowerby Bridge, as a fulling and scribbling mill for £1,000. Hollings was an old fulling mill, which would have needed extension, and an increase in power, to cope with its new role. By the mid-1790s, several of the larger woollen mills had developed into 'hybrids', with a mixture of mechanical and hand processes brought together in the same premises. Sowerby Bridge Mill had a handloom weaving shop in 1792, and its insurance valuation increased from £8,500 in that year to £9,900 in 1795, and £12,500 in 1797. Hollings Mill had a handloom shop in the latter year. William Currer of Luddenden Foot Mill had scribbling, carding, slubbing and spinning engines, a fulling mill with a handloom shop over it, and a large carpet-weaving shop.[8]

The numbers of mills which date back to 1801 or earlier, and those first recorded in 1802-22, are as follows (counting twice the mills processing two fibres, eg cotton and worsted):[9]

	To 1801	1802-22
Cotton	32	38
Worsted	5	5
Wool	12	4
Fibre unknown	3	12

These figures exaggerate the dominance of cotton in the early factory system because the cotton mills were on average smaller than the woollen or worsted mills. Most of the recorded insurance valuations of cotton mills were under £1,000. All but two of the woollen and worsted mills exceeded this figure and Hollins Mill had £15,000 cover by 1801.[10] Over half of the cotton firms established before 1800 had a life of less than twenty years, although about three-quarters of the mills continued the processing of cotton under a different management. Most of the woollen and worsted mills continued in operation for many years, often under successive generations of the same family.

In the mid-1820s there was little geographical specialisation within the valley apart from the dominant position of cotton in Todmorden. There were cotton mills all the way down to Sowerby Bridge, woollen mills from the latter up to Underbank between Hebden Bridge and Todmorden, and worsted mills in a slightly smaller area between Luddenden Dean and Langfield. Many firms were processing more than one fibre, although not necessarily in the same mill. For example, Christopher Rawdon was involved with worsted at Lobb Mill, and woollens at Callis and other mills. His partners in Lobb Mill, Ingham and Knowles, were also spinning cotton at Oldroyd Mill.[11]

Most of the water mills were situated on the tributary streams which fed the River Calder. The main river offered the advantage of a substantial volume of water, but the fall of only about fifteen feet per mile between Todmorden and Sowerby Bridge placed limits upon the number and height of the mill weirs which could be constructed. The main tributary streams fall by an average of 180 feet per mile, which made it easy to locate mills close together; on the other hand the flow is much smaller and less reliable. These contrasting conditions required different types of wheel.

Before the eighteenth century, the wheels of corn and fulling mills on the Calder were almost certainly undershot, generating one or two horsepower each. Small

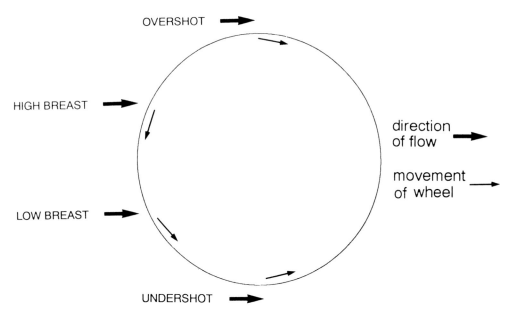

OVERSHOT

HIGH BREAST

direction
of flow

movement
of wheel

LOW BREAST

UNDERSHOT

Types of water wheel.

overshot wheels may have been used on the tributary streams. At several seventeenth century fulling mills, power was increased by arranging two or three undershot wheels in a row. Lobb Mill apparently had three wheels when taken over in the 1780s for redevelopment as a worsted mill.[12]

The wheels installed in textile mills on the River Calder were in general smaller in diameter but much wider than those used high up the tributary streams. The low breast wheel at Mayroyd Mill, 16 feet in diameter and 15 feet wide, generated about 40 horsepower. There was insufficient head of water for a high breast wheel of the same dimensions, which would have been much more efficient. The high breast wheel at Lumb Mill on Luddenden Brook, 36 feet in diameter and 5 feet wide, generated about 20 horsepower. The wheels of the greatest diameter were located in the steep-sided Colden Valley, where the fall is 225 feet per mile and it is easy to bring a mill race along the hillside. According to the sale catalogue of the Mytholm estate, when it was put up for auction in 1868, the wheels at Lower Lumb and Mytholm Mill were respectively 53 feet and 52 feet 6 inches in diameter. The latter wheel was 9 feet 6 inches wide; most of the others on Colden Water were between 6 and 7 feet.[13]

The main problem for water mills on the tributary streams was low water in dry weather. To ease this problem, storage reservoirs were constructed, some for an individual mill, others for a group of mills with a common interest. Some millowners in the upper Luddenden Valley began building reservoirs from 1806. Later ten millowners in the area formed the Cold Edge Dam Company, and by 1836 three reservoirs, with a total capacity of 23 million gallons, had been completed.

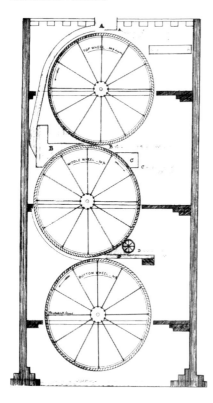

Lumbutts Mill water wheels.

The water wheel at Spring Mill, Wainstalls.

Gibson Mill, on Hebden Water at Hardcastle Crags, was originally a water-powered
cotton spinning mill.

The most spectacular arrangement of water wheels was found at Lumbutts Mill,
near Todmorden. Water was piped from three reservoirs on the hillside above the mill
and fed to four points on the wheels. In addition, water from the higher wheels fell
on to the lower ones. Each wheel was 30 feet in diameter and 6 feet wide.[14]

The Rochdale Canal
The first step in the transport revolution which turned the Calder gorge from an
obstacle to movement into a main communications artery was the building of the
turnpike road, begun in 1761. A few years later the idea of using the same route, the
easiest crossing of the Pennines south of the Aire Gap, for a canal was first seriously
considered. On the Yorkshire side the Aire and Calder Navigation, begun in 1699 with
major improvements in the 1770s, had extended the navigable water of the Humber-
Ouse system to Leeds on the River Aire and Wakefield on the Calder. Between 1758

Lumbutts Mill, with the dam in the foreground.

and 1774 the Calder and Hebble Navigation brought this network as far as Sowerby Bridge. (The branch canal to Halifax was not opened until 1828.) The navigation works involved the selective deepening of the river, and by-passing weirs and other obstacles by means of short cuts. On the other side of the Pennines an early true canal, the Bridgewater between Worsley colliery and Manchester (1759-61), became part of an extensive network of navigable waterways in South Lancashire.[15]

In 1794 an Act of Parliament was secured for the construction of the Rochdale Canal, linking the Calder-Hebble Navigation at Sowerby Bridge with the Bridgewater Canal in Manchester. The promoters originally wanted the right to use the water from all streams within 1,000 yards of the canal, a proposal strongly opposed by the owners of corn, fulling and spinning mills, which were all water-powered at this time. It was agreed that the canal company would have only limited access to certain streams, and would draw most of its water from specially-constructed reservoirs. A great quantity of water was needed because the canal had a total of 92 locks, 36 on the Yorkshire side (a climb of 316 feet) and 56 on the Lancashire side (514 feet).

The supervising engineer was William Jessop, who took over the original scheme devised by John Rennie and modified it by eliminating a proposed summit tunnel. The canal ranks as one of the great engineering achievements of the Industrial Revolution. Between Sowerby Bridge and the Summit, in addition to the locks, there were several deep cuttings, four aqueducts (at Luddenden Foot, Hebden Bridge, Todmorden and Gauxholme) and forty-four bridges over the canal.

By August 1798 the 10½ miles from Sowerby Bridge to Gauxholme had been

The canal basin and Calder and Hebble Canal at Sowerby Bridge.

completed and brought into use, but the whole length was not opened until December 1804. The original estimate had been £360,000, but the final cost, including reservoirs, wharves and buildings, was nearly £700,000. The canal company did not, until later in the nineteenth century, act as a carrier. Its revenue was derived from tolls, initially at the rate of 1½d or 2d per ton mile, on the cargo of the canal boats. The canal was a commercial success, competing effectively with its two cross-Pennine rivals, the Leeds-Liverpool (Act of 1770, completed in 1816) which took a circuitous route via the Aire Gap, and the less efficient Huddersfield Narrow Canal (opened in 1811) which had 74 locks in only 20 miles.

The income from tolls rose from £13,000 in 1807 to £41,000 in 1825, by which time the annual tonnage carried was 500,000. The latter figure reached 875,000 in 1838 and 980,000 in the boom of 1845. However, the competition of the Manchester-Todmorden-Leeds railway, opened in 1841, forced a cut in rates which brought the income down from £62,000 in 1838 to £28,000 in 1845. A dividend of about seven per cent on the nominal value of the shares capital of nearly £500,000 was paid in 1839, but the shares had lost much of their value by 1845.

In 1819 nearly a third of the tonnage of just over 300,000 was made up of coal. Other main items were: stone 45,000 tons, corn 40,000, lime 13,000, timber 6,000 and wool 4,000. Finished textile goods are lost in the figure of 21,000 tons of 'merchandise'. It is not possible to separate through traffic from shipments to and from the Sowerby Bridge-Gauxholme stretch, but the greatest benefit to the area was the supply of cheap coal.[16]

Reflections in the canal: Edwards Mill, Sowerby Bridge.

The canal basin at Sowerby Bridge.

Canal locks near Gauxholme.

Steam Engines and Power Looms

The age of steam came late and slowly to the upper Calder Valley. Water-driven spinning mills had been in operation for two decades when the first steam engines were installed in 1802. Steam did not become the major source of power for new mills until the mid-1820s, and did not establish an overall lead over water power until about 1850. The climate, geology and topography of the valley combined to make the supply of water abundant and its use for power relatively cheap.

Steam engines with a simple up-and-down motion of the beam had been in use for draining mines since the early eighteenth century. By 1776 James Watt's new design of beam engine, which used much less fuel, was available; in 1782-4 he improved it still further and adapted it for rotary motion. The enterprising Lodge family of Willow Hall, who operated the first recorded spinning mill in the upper Calder Valley, were also responsible for the installation of the first steam engines. Thomas Lodge was chairman of the company which built Regulator Mill, a subscription corn mill, on the canal side in Sowerby Bridge, in 1801-2. Timothy Bates of Sowerby Bridge installed a beam-and-crank engine designed by Boulton and Watt. In 1802 the Lodges installed two Boulton and Watt sun-and-planet engines in their Willow Hall cotton mills, a new one rated at 30 horsepower, and a secondhand 10 horsepower engine.[17]

As far as the records go, there was no great rush to follow the example of the Lodge family, even though the completion of the Rochdale Canal in 1804 extended the benefits of cheap coal along the length of the main valley. Of the 28 mills supplying information to the Factories Inquiry Commission in 1833, 18 ran on water only, 7 on steam only, and 3 used both forms of power. Most of the steam-powered mills were in the valley bottom, near the canal. At least five steam engines were installed in the industrial village of Todmorden in 1822-5, and Fielden Brothers used a sixty horsepower engine to power their large weaving shed opened in 1829.[18]

Steam power had overtaken water in the Todmorden area by about 1840, but this did not happen at the lower end of the valley until the 1860s. As late as 1862 a new mill in Cragg Vale (Victoria Mill) was planned to run on water power alone for half the year, but the project was interrupted by the cotton famine.[19] In the 1860s the dual use of power was still widespread, eg in 1868, Dean Mill in Luddenden 58 horsepower steam and 40 horsepower water; and Hollings Mill, Sowerby Bridge, 20 and 45 horsepower respectively.

There was a close connection between the expansion of steam power and the development of weaving by the power loom, illustrated by the habit of referring to the latter as 'the steam loom'. By the time the power loom came to be generally adopted, nearly all of the convenient water-power sites in the upper Calder Valley had been occupied. The weaving shed and the mill chimney soon became familiar twin features of the local industrial landscape, particularly in the Todmorden area.

There were three reasons why the power loom made much slower progress than mechanical spinning: the technical problems were greater; the productivity gains were much less; and the competitive advantage of the power loom was reduced by the fall in the wages of handloom weavers after 1815. One of the benefits of the power-loom system, the better supervision of workers to maintain quality and prevent waste and embezzlement, could be achieved by setting up a handloom workshop.

Rev Edmund Cartwright produced a crude prototype of a power loom in 1786, but the first successful machine was devised by William Horrocks in 1803. A much improved version patented by Sharpe and Roberts in 1822 was widely adopted for cotton during the investment boom of 1823-5, but it was not until 1829 that Fieldens installed at Waterside the first power looms recorded in upper Calderdale. During the next boom period, 1832-6, the power loom began to make a serious impact on worsted, helped by improvements in the spinning process which produced a stronger yarn. In woollens, where both warp and weft were relatively soft and loose, the power looms, especially in broadcloth, could for a considerable time run hardly any faster than the hand loom, and it was not until about 1860 that the victory of the power loom was assured.[20]

An incomplete return of power looms in upper Calderdale in 1835 gives 1,902 in cotton, 307 in cotton and worsted, 59 in one woollen mill, 36 in a mill producing both woollens and worsted, and none indisputably in worsted alone. The cotton/worsted mixtures included union cloths (cotton warp and worsted weft), popular as dress and furnishing fabrics, and 'gambroons' made by Buckleys of Todmorden from a mixed cotton/worsted yarn and used for men's coats. In 1835, Waterside Mill reported 405 operatives and 810 looms (a visitor in 1841 counted 1,058 looms and a total labour force of 571), but some mills had apparently only one loom per weaver.[21]

Other technical developments contributed to the great advance of the textile industry in the years 1832-6. Richard Roberts's self-acting mule, devised in 1825 with improvements patented in 1830, not only achieved a higher degree of automation but incorporated a number of other refinements. Because of the complexities of mule spinning, it was not possible to dispense with the skilled male operator, as some employers had hoped, but there were considerable reductions in production costs. John Jellicorse, spinning cotton at Stansfield Mill, Sowerby, from 1830, thought that in 1833 he had the only mill in the country where all the mules were self-acting. At Fieldens' Waterside works it was estimated in 1841 that a mule spinner produced six times as much output as in 1810. The mechanism of the self-actor was also adopted in woollen spinning to produce the 'woollen mule' – strictly speaking a self-acting jenny as roller drafting was not used – which displaced the hand-driven jenny except in domestic workshops.[22]

The improvements in the speed, efficiency and sophistication of textile machinery had required parallel advances in the performance of the engineering industry. By 1835 there were at least fifteen firms in the upper Calder Valley engaged in millwrighting, iron and brass founding, and machine making. Some of the concerns had a relatively short life, but three – Bates, Jackson and Lord – had a long record of success.

Timothy Bates of Sowerby Bridge started business in 1778 as an iron-founder and millwright, making water wheels and corn-grinding machinery. He moved into steam engines in 1801, but the firm also maintained its original lines.

Jeremiah Jackson of Walsden, in business from 1813 or earlier, made a wide range of textile machinery, including carding engines, roving frames and mules, as well as supplying spare parts and undertaking repairs.

One of the familiar routes to success in textile engineering was taken by John Lord and some of his sons. They had worked as mechanics at Waterside Mill and moved out in the mid-1830s to set up their own machine-making business. At first they took a spare room with power at Clough Mill, but after a few years were able to build the Canal Street Works, where they prospered as one of the leading engineering firms of the area. Later they went into cotton spinning as well. Some of the local firms, including Lords, patented improvements to textile machinery.[23]

In addition to the 15 engineering firms, other enterprises ancillary to textiles in 1835 included 10 dyeworks, a chemical manufactory, a size works, 3 bobbin manufactories and a reed maker. There is a case for putting the three paper mills in the same category,

Railway, river, canal and road at Luddenden Foot, seen from above Brearley.

as this local industry probably developed to meet the heavy demand from the woollen trade for papers and boards for use in pressing, finishing and packing. In 1726 John Midgley was making paper at Dean Mill on Luddenden Brook, where fulling had been carried on since 1440. An inventory of Dean Mills in 1784 mentions two water wheels, one used for the glazing mill. These mills were operated from 1792 to 1921 by the firm of Jonathan Bracken and Sons, who employed eighteen men and eighteen boys in 1851. They included rag sorters and a rag engine feeder, a reminder that the textile industry was a source of supply as well as demand for paper making.[24]

It is perhaps surprising to find that there were about twenty-five corn mills in the area in 1835. Most of them were small, and a few shared their buildings and power with textile processes. With only a few exceptions they were water-powered.

By the mid-1830s the local textile industry had settled into the distribution pattern which was to remain for the rest of the century. A nearly complete record of mills shows that Warley and Sowerby townships had 15 worsted mills, 10 woollen and 6 cotton. In the rest of the valley, 49 out of 59 mills were cotton, with 3 worsted, 1 woollen and 6 mixed. The contrast is lessened a little if hand workers are brought into the picture, but cotton was clearly dominant in the upper part of the valley, with fustians emerging as an important fabric in and around Hebden Bridge.

There was another distinction, between the valley bottom where the mills and chimneys and terraces of workers' houses were spreading rapidly, and the hillside settlements, still clinging to hand processes, often combined with farming. A rough overall calculation for 1835, from a variety of sources, gives 25-30% of the working population in mills and attached workshops; 35-40% handloom weavers, combers and other outworkers; and 35% others, including ancillary trades, craftsmen, shopkeepers and farmers not engaged in textiles.

Fifty-five years after the opening of the first recorded spinning mill in the upper Calder Valley, there were more textile workers outside the mills than inside them. The machines were, however, advancing rapidly at the expense of the hand workers, except where there were still major technical problems to solve, as in wool combing and woollen weaving. Some finishing trades, eg fustian cutting, were to remain hand operations for several decades.

11

Church, Chapel and School

The Evangelical Revival

Chapter 7 described the emergence in the late seventeenth century of three main groups of dissenters: Quakers, Baptists, and Presbyterians or Independents. In the 1740s the Presbyterians had chapels at Sowerby Town, Warley Town and Benthead (Eastwood) in Stansfield, with a total of 500 adherents. About 80 people attended the Particular (Calvinist) Baptist chapels at Stone Slack and Rodhill End, and 100 Quakers worshipped at their meeting house at Shoebroad in Langfield. According to the local Church of England clergy, only eleven per cent of families in the Yorkshire section of the valley were dissenters, but there is no reason to believe that the remainder were all ardent Anglicans. Only fifteen per cent of those described as 'communicants' actually received the sacrament at Easter. The geography of the valley did not help, as for many people the nearest parochial chapel was several miles and a steep climb away.[1]

The upper Calder Valley was already experiencing the first stirrings of the Evangelical Revival. From 1747 John Wesley and his brother Charles paid many visits to the area, to consolidate and extend the work of local evangelists. The main pioneers of what became known as Methodism were two men strikingly different in background and style, William Grimshaw and William Darney – the parson and the pedlar. Grimshaw (1708-63) was curate of Todmorden from 1731 to 1742, and then became perpetual curate of Haworth. His preaching there attracted crowds of 'weeping and roaring sinners', trembling at 'the wrath of God'. Darney was a pedlar selling drapery, who from 1741 combined his trade with that of a preacher, setting up societies in several places in upper Calderdale. 'Scotch Will' was 'a man of prodigious size . . . and when dwelling on the terrors of the Lord, terrible to behold'.[2]

Darney annoyed Charles Wesley, the greatest of Methodist hymn writers, by combining Calvinist leanings with a penchant for writing doggerel hymns. He published a collection of 200 of these compositions, of which the following example is by no means the worst:

> Sometimes there's Mist and Foggs that rise
> Before me in this Wilderness;
> Till these blow off I cannot see
> O Lord, my God, to follow thee.

Darney would have been purged by the Wesleys in 1751 but for the protection of Grimshaw, who argued that his homespun style suited the local people. Grimshaw combined his duties at Haworth with the superintendence of the Haworth Round, a

Dan Taylor's first chapel.

prototype Methodist circuit which stretched from Todmorden to Whitehaven in Cumberland.[3]

John Wesley's diaries are full of references, on his visits to upper Calderdale, to 'large and earnest congregations' hearing him in the open air. On one occasion a drystone wall at Stoneshey Gate in Heptonstall collapsed under the weight of his hearers, but '. . . not one was hurt at all . . . nor was there any interruption either of my speaking or of the attention of the hearers'.[4] Methodist converts were encouraged to attend their parish church – the Wesleys were both Anglican priests. Buildings were adapted or erected for Methodist worship, but there was to be no clash with the times of church services. There is little doubt, however, that for most committed Methodists their religious life was centred on their local Methodist chapel and society.

The Evangelical Revival had a powerful impact on the older dissenting sects. Some of Grimshaw's converts became Particular Baptists and built a chapel at Wainsgate, near Old Town, in 1750. In 1764 a young disciple of Grimshaw, John Fawcett, became the pastor. He was a liberal Calvinist: 'Christ . . . gives everlasting life to all . . . who believe in him'. This was not far from Wesley's creed of 'He died to save us all'.[5]

In the early 1760s the balance between dissent and Methodism was shifted by defections from the latter. Titus Knight and James Crossley, leading Methodist lay preachers in the Halifax area, joined the Independents and became ordained ministers with churches at Halifax and Booth respectively. Their secession may have been influenced by the fact that an Independent minister had both more autonomy, provided that he was in harmony with his congregation, and a much higher status than a Methodist preacher.[6]

The second Birchcliffe Chapel (1825), left, and Sunday school (1827), right.

A third rebel was Dan Taylor, a young coalminer from Northowram, who became a Methodist local preacher in 1761, but soon rebelled against John Wesley's 'dictatorship'. He formed a little flock in Wadsworth, but faced a doctrinal problem. He accepted 'believers' baptism' but rejected Calvinism, and therefore could not join the Particular Baptists. Instead he joined the General Baptists, who were not Calvinists, and was ordained by them in 1763. By December 1764 a small General Baptist chapel had been built at Birchcliffe, near Hebden Bridge. Taylor soon found, however, that he had attached himself to a declining cause. The General Baptists were paralysed by doctrinal controversies, with many of them drifting towards the Unitarian position. In 1770 Dan Taylor and a few allies formed the General Baptist New Connexion, which borrowed some features of Methodist style and organisation.[7]

The year 1764 also saw the opening of the great temple of Calderdale Methodism, the octagonal chapel at Heptonstall. Although by no means the earliest Methodist chapel to be built, it is believed to be the oldest one in continuous use to the present day.[8]

Dan Taylor and John Fawcett became close friends, and combined to form the Heptonstall Book Society, a library-cum-lecture society, in 1769. Both wrote major theological treatises. Taylor had enormous energy, combining his pastoral work and the national leadership of the New Connexion as chairman of its annual meeting with running a farm and school so that his congregation would not have to help him. He founded five new chapels, including Shore and Haley Hill, Halifax, both of which opened in 1777. He wrote to a friend: 'We ding, ding, ding on, in a corner of the world unenvied, unvisited and almost unknown'. Calderdale was a rather remote base

The octagonal Methodist chapel at Heptonstall, built in 1764.

Sowerby Independent (Congregational) Chapel, now demolished.

for the national leader of the Connexion and at the request of the latter he moved to London in 1785.[9]

John Fawcett developed his mission in two ways. As his congregation had outgrown the small Wainsgate Chapel, he promoted the building of Ebenezer Chapel in the growing industrial village of Hebden Bridge. It held 500 people, and opened in 1777. Fawcett ministered at Ebenezer, where he started a Sunday school in 1786, for forty years. His second major activity was running an academy for the training of Particular Baptist ministers, first at his farmhouse near Wainsgate, from 1776 to 1786 at Brearley Hall and finally at Ewood Hall until 1804, when he merged his institution with the new Horton Academy.[10]

Meanwhile the dissenting groups which had not been re-invigorated by the Evangelical Revival were in decline. The old Particular Baptist chapel at Stone Slack had no regular minister after 1772 and Rodhill End closed in 1783. The Presbyterian ministers increasingly questioned the doctrines of the Holy Trinity and the divinity of Christ, and adopted a position of 'rational dissent'. They began to lose their congregations to the evangelical Independents, who combined Calvinist orthodoxy with Methodist-style preaching. Warley Chapel went over to the Independents in 1764 and Sowerby had followed suit by 1794. The Presbyterians at Eastwood dwindled to the point of extinction, until the cause was revived by the Independents, who appointed a new minister in 1807.[11]

When John Wesley began his mission in 1739 upper Calderdale had 6 Anglican churches and 6 dissenting meeting houses. At his death in 1791 there were, in addition to the 6 Anglican churches, 6 Baptist chapels (if Stone Slack is included), 4 Independent or Presbyterian chapels, a Quaker meeting house, and an Inghamite chapel (another evangelical sect). In addition the valley was dotted with Methodist chapels, some of them purpose-built, others converted buildings. Most of the people were now within easy reach of some place of worship. Moreover the growth of Methodism and of evangelical dissent meant that substantial numbers of people were actively involved in the business of their religious societies, as stewards, preachers, class leaders and Sunday school teachers, and so had a chance to exercise and develop their talents.

The Evangelical Revival had an economic impact. Hard work, persistence, sobriety and thrift were virtues which paid off materially as well as spiritually. The evangelical engine was driven by the boundless energy of the reformed individual, his belief in his own potential powerfully enhanced by the pursuit of the Wesleyan ideal of 'Christian perfection'. The same energy could drive the industrial engine on to spectacular business success. John Wesley's compassion, as demonstrated in his attitude to slavery, to prisoners and to the sick, did not extend to any general theory of social obligation. In his writings, economic distress is largely the consequence of individual failings, a convenient view of the world for a thrusting industrialist (although Wesley warned of the spiritual dangers of material success).[12] It is no coincidence that many of the leading millowners of the upper Calder Valley were active Nonconformists, to use the term which emerged to embrace Methodism and the older dissenting sects.

Religious Life in the Nineteenth Century

The first half of the nineteenth century saw three main developments. More and bigger chapels were built to cater for the growing population, especially in the valley-bottom towns, while converted accommodation was replaced by new chapels in the upland

The original Todmorden Unitarian Chapel.

settlements. Secondly, Methodism split into several competing connexions. Thirdly, the Church of England began to fight back, to recover some lost ground especially by building churches in the new centres of population.

The disputes in Methodism, about such issues as lay participation in decision-making and whether open-air evangelism should continue, generally took the form of collisions with the increasingly conservative and ecclesiastical leadership. The first group of dissidents, expelled in 1797, only two years after the formal separation from the Church of England, formed the Methodist New Connexion. They became strong in Halifax and as far up the valley as Midgley.[13]

In 1806 Joseph Cooke, a Wesleyan minister, was expelled for unorthodox teaching. A few years later some of his followers in the Rochdale area formed the Methodist Unitarians, whose combination of Methodist style with Unitarian openness in doctrine found support in Todmorden. John Fielden, who had been successively a Quaker and a Wesleyan Methodist, joined their ranks. A chapel was built in 1823-4. Fielden became the formal owner of the chapel in 1828 to clear its debts.[14]

The Primitive Methodists (1811-12) became established in upper Calderdale from 1821. They used women preachers, a practice disavowed by the Wesleyan Conference in 1803. There was often a social class difference between Wesleyan and Primitive congregations. Where the industrialists were dominant amongst the Wesleyans, the Primitives often had strong working-class support.

A new round of expulsions and secessions in 1835-6 produced the Wesleyan Methodist Association, and in 1849-50 the Wesleyan Reformers broke away. These two groups merged in 1857 to form the United Methodist Free Churches.[15]

One feature of the work of the Baptists and Independents was the colonisation of valley-bottom settlements from older hillside chapels. The General Baptists at Shore started services in Naylors Mill, Lydgate, in 1815, which led to the building of Bethel Chapel, Lineholme, in 1818-19. Some Shore members who lived in Todmorden set up a separate congregation there in 1845, in temporary premises until the chapel in Wellington Road was built in 1859. The Independents at Booth provided services at

Denholme, Luddenden Foot, which led to the building of a chapel, financed by Whitworths the worsted spinners, in 1859. Other millowners supported chapel building, for example, three members of the Rawdon family when the Independents at Eastwood built a new chapel in 1840. The most striking example of employer paternalism is provided by the Wilson family, bobbin manufacturers at Cornholme, who held a daily service lasting for fifteen minutes in the works for all their employees.[16]

Until the early nineteenth century the number of Anglican churches remained the same as in the reign of Henry VIII – six – of which only two, Sowerby Bridge and Todmorden, were in the rapidly-growing valley bottom towns. In 1815 the church of St John in the Wilderness was built amongst the textile mills of Cragg Vale. Between 1832 and 1848 new churches were built in Hebden Bridge, Mytholmroyd and Walsden; Cross Stone was rebuilt; and St Marys Church, Todmorden, was replaced by the much larger Christ Church. The work was financed partly by subscription, and partly by grants from a church-building fund established by Parliament. The fabric of the oldest church, Heptonstall, was neglected for a considerable time until part of the tower collapsed in a storm in 1847. The ratepayers of the chapelry, mainly Nonconformist textile workers, would approve only a derisory church rate of a farthing in the pound for the repairs. The leading local Anglicans were stung into action and raised a subscription to build a new church, opened in 1854, alongside the old one.[17]

On the 30th March 1851 a census of religious worship was taken, at the same time as the decennial population census. The original returns survive for the Todmorden registration district (the valley from Wadsworth and Erringden westwards), but for the Halifax district (including Midgley, Warley and Sowerby) only the less informative printed returns are available.[18] Different formulae can be used to translate attendance figures at two or three services into numbers of people attending at least once, but they produce very similar percentage figures, which can be consolidated as follows for the Todmorden district:

	Number of places of worship in use on census day	*Percentage of attenders*	
Church of England	7	18.1	
Methodists			
Wesleyan	11	21.8	
Wesleyan Methodist			
Association	8	12.2	
Primitive	4	8.7	42.7
Baptists			
General	8	18.7	
Particular	4	8.8	27.5
Independents	3	7.3	
Inghamites	1	2.5	
Unitarians	1	1.8	
Quakers	1	0.1	

The above calculations contain a small margin of error, but the statement that two-fifths of the worshippers were Methodist, a quarter Baptist and nearly a fifth Anglican

The Victorian church tower at Heptonstall, seen through the ruins of
the old church.

The new Unitarian church at Todmorden (1869).

is reliable. In the Halifax district the Independents were much stronger and the Baptists weaker than further up the valley. Amongst the Methodists the Wesleyan Methodist Association (WMA) was not represented, but the New Connexion and Reformers together had substantial numbers. Taking upper Calderdale as a whole, Nonconformists outnumbered Anglicans by at least three to one.

In the Todmorden district the estimated numbers attending came to about half of the 1851 population of 29,727. It was thought at the time that about a quarter of the population – young children, the old, the sick, those at work – would be unable to go to church or chapel on census day. On that assumption, and allowing for the provision of second and third services, the 18,000 seats available would be adequate in total. However, 11,000 of the sittings were appropriated, nearly all bought or rented. Pew sales and rents represented a major source of income for some chapels. The large chapels in the towns usually had a reasonable number of free seats, eg York Street, Todmorden (Wesleyan) had 300 free and 578 appropriated, and Cross Lanes, Hebden Bridge (WMA) had 203 and 458. Birchcliffe (General Baptist) had 700 seats, all appropriated, and at Wainsgate (Particular Baptist) there were only 40 free seats out of 295. Over forty per cent of Anglican seats were free, and the Unitarian chapel in

Booth Independent (Congregational) Chapel, now demolished.

Todmorden was entirely free. Even where the number of free seats was adequate, the system of appropriation increased the sense of alienation of poorer people, already inhibited by their shabby appearance.

The second half of the nineteenth century was the heyday of local Nonconformity. Old chapels were enlarged, or more frequently replaced by new and larger buildings. The major buildings included Hope Chapel, replacing Ebenezer in Hebden Bridge; Shore, an impressive chapel and a school building containing a lecture room and five classrooms; Booth, a large new Gothic chapel, the old chapel being converted into a Sunday school; and an imposing basilica, with a classical Italianate facade, at Birchcliffe. The three sons of John Fielden financed the building, in his memory, of a magnificent Gothic Unitarian church. The tower, topped by an elegant spire, was furnished with a peal of bells and a carillon to strike the hours. In Ken Powell's words, this church 'eclipses the undistinguished parish church and expresses the dominance of dissent'.[19]

The Particular and General Baptists merged in 1891. The move was strongly opposed by the General Baptists at Heptonstall Slack, and their minister wrote in 1907 that they still objected to the inclusion of a Calvinist creed in the *Yorkshire Baptists*

Year Book. The United Methodist Free Churches (WMA and Reformers) joined with the New Connexion in 1907 to form the United Methodist Church.[20]

As the cathedrals of Nonconformity were rising to dispute the dominance of the urban landscape with the mills and the mill chimneys, their societies were extending their role into secular affairs. The temperance movement grew in strength and Bands of Hope were formed all over the area. Nearly every chapel had a mutual improvement society attached, to provide both basic and general adult education, especially for young men. They went under a variety of names, including the Heptonstall Slack Reading and Mutual Improvement Society, the People's College at Vale Chapel, and probably the longest-lived, the MIS at Shore. Most of the larger Sunday schools had lending libraries, originally to serve the small army of Sunday school teachers, but developing into a resource for the whole chapel or church community. The books covered mainly religious topics, but the Unitarian library included such works as Tennyson's poems and Smiles's *Self Help*. It is convenient to call these buildings Sunday schools, but they were often in use on every weekday evening, for a variety of religious, educational and social activities, the latter including dramatic societies and chess clubs. Chapels often had football and cricket teams attached to them, although not usually confined to their members, as part of a strategy to satisfy as many as possible of the social needs of their adherents within the chapel community.[21]

Some Nonconformist ministers were active in public life. For example, Rev J K Archer, minister at Heptonstall Slack between 1895 and 1903, was chairman of the Hebden Bridge School Board, president of the Band of Hope Unions of Hebden Bridge and Colden, and a busy worker for the Liberal cause, apparently with radical leanings.[22]

One change which took place within the chapels was in their attitude to music. In the early nineteenth century they relied on unaccompanied choirs, or lead singers, or both. The idea of introducing organs, or the instrumental groups common in Anglican churches at the time, was frowned upon, and about 1830 the choir at Mount Zion (Heptonstall Slack) threatened to strike if instruments were brought in. In 1857, however, an organ was installed in the same chapel and accompanied music gradually became the general rule. There was a strong musical tradition in the valley, and the Wainsgate choir won the first prize at the Nonconformist Choirs Festival held at Crystal Palace in 1908.[23]

Education

The early records of educational provision in upper Calderdale are sparse. School-masters at Heptonstall and Luddenden are recorded in the 1560s. Heptonstall Grammar School was founded in 1642 by Rev Charles Greenwood, lord of the manor of Heptonstall. In the early nineteenth century the endowment paid for a free classical education for seventeen pupils. In 1711 Paul Bairstow left £16 a year to the master of Sowerby Grammar School to teach twelve poor children. Richard Clegg, vicar of Kirkham, whose family came from Stone House in Walsden, founded a more modest school in Todmorden in 1713. A few years later Cross Stone chapelry school was established, mainly by the initiative of a man of local origin called Pilling. The school was maintained by the chapelry, and the interest on the small endowment paid for free instruction for 6 poor children out of the 30 to 40 attending in the middle of the eighteenth century.[24]

The chapel in the moor: Blakedean Baptist Chapel at the head of the Hebden Valley.
The row of cottages has now been demolished.

An enquiry into the state of education in England and Wales in 1833 gives the first detailed picture of local provision.[25] Out of 271 children enrolled in endowed, subscription or boarding schools, only 22 were receiving free elementary instruction and 17 more had free classical tuition at Heptonstall. All other teaching was paid for by the parents, the only information about charges being the 2d per week at Sowerby subscription school. 'Dame' schools for infants had 245 enrolments, and 1,277 older children were in other private enterprise schools. Overall boys outnumbered girls by two to one.

Most children were in full-time work, either in a mill or in a domestic workshop, by the age of nine – some earlier – and for them day schooling meant at best a few years between the ages of five and nine, subject to interruptions when bad trade made it impossible for parents to find the weekly school pence. As a substitute or a supplement there was always the (free) Sunday school. The unpaid volunteers who taught at the Sunday school found that they could not make much headway in teaching the scriptures to pupils who could not read, and therefore gave elementary instruction in reading. A few Sunday schools taught writing as well, but this practice was suppressed by the Wesleyan Methodists as a profanation of the Sabbath. The schools normally opened for several hours, breaking off tuition for attendance at the morning and afternoon services.

The earliest recorded Sunday schools in the upper Calder Valley were established in the 1780s (when the Sunday school movement was just beginning) at St Thomas's Church, Heptonstall (1782), and John Fawcett's Ebenezer Baptist Chapel, Hebden

Bridge (1786). By the 1820s most chapels had Sunday schools attached.[26] In 1833 forty-nine Sunday schools, with a total of nearly 10,000 enrolments, were in operation. Nearly half of the pupils were in Methodist schools, and the sexes were fairly evenly balanced.

It is unlikely that the 1833 figures are completely accurate – some Sunday schools may have been overlooked, and some of the enrolment figures may be rough estimates – but assuming that they are reliable, twenty-two per cent of the 1831 population of the upper Calder Valley went to Sunday schools. Even allowing for the presence of some adults, that would mean a high proportion of the children of the area being taught religion and the rudiments of reading on Sundays. This arrangement was convenient for the upholders of the prevailing work ethic of the industrial society, which put sloth and not pride as the first of the seven deadly sins. It was an excuse for not providing more day school places, and also for keeping children at work for the other six days of the week. Sunday schools kept children out of mischief, and trained them to be diligent and obedient.

The first effective Factory Act, passed in 1833, provided that children aged nine to twelve inclusive employed in textile mills were to be restricted to nine hours work a day and to have two hours schooling in addition. Children under nine were not to be employed. The educational clauses did not apply to silk mills, in which the lower age limit for employment was eight. Some millowners gave one or more of their workers the task of 'teaching' the children in two hour shifts in some corner of the mill. Fielden Brothers gave a better example: they already had a school, opened in 1827, at their Waterside works in Todmorden, and provided a second at Lumbutts Mill in 1837.[27]

The 1844 Factory Act reduced the work limit to six and a half hours a day, and raised the educational requirement to three hours, this time including silk mills. The minimum age for starting work was reduced to eight. Henceforth the mill children under thirteen were half-timers, spending either the morning or the afternoon in school. This greatly increased the demand for school places. Three National (ie Church of England) schools were established in the Todmorden area, at Todmorden (1845), Cross Stone (replacing the old chapelry school, 1847) and Walsden (1848). In the same decade other National schools were opened at Sowerby, Sowerby Bridge and Luddenden. The Church school at Scarbottom, Mytholmroyd, had been founded in 1842 by William Sutcliffe of Bath, owner of Scarbottom Mill, who also built St Michaels Church nearby.[28]

The rapid growth of Anglican schools must have caused concern to the numerically dominant Nonconformist interest, and schools under the auspices of the British and Foreign Schools Society (formally non-denominational but in practice Nonconformist) were founded at Bolton Brow in Sowerby Bridge and at Lineholme in Cornholme. The 1844 Act also stimulated the development of factory schools, as at Foster Mill, Hebden Bridge, and Lumb Mill near Heptonstall.[29]

In March 1851 an educational census was held at the same time as the population and religious censuses. The returns have survived for the Todmorden registration district.[30] Sixty schools made returns, including 21 'dame' schools which taught reading only. Some of the teachers were incapable of teaching writing, as five signed their returns with a cross. There were 25 private elementary schools, which taught reading, writing and arithmetic. Other subjects, eg grammar, mathematics and geography, were available at some of them at extra cost. The remaining 14 schools consisted of 3 maintained by factory owners; 4 private 'academies' with some post-elementary teaching, eg book-keeping; Heptonstall Grammar School, with forty children in attendance including five girls; and 4 Church schools, with an average of 130 pupils per school, most of them half-timers, on census day.

To summarise the figures of attendances:

	Number of Schools	Boys	Girls	Total
Dame Schools	21	199	208	407
Private Elementary Schools	25	724	553	1,277
Other	14	686	536	1,222
Totals	60	1,609	1,297	2,906

The estimated total of *enrolments* is 3,240, compared with 895 eighteen years earlier. The population of Todmorden registration district had increased by only four per cent between 1831 and 1851, as the earlier rapid growth had been checked by the decline of handloom weaving and the depression of the 'hungry forties'. The main cause of the 260% increase in enrolments, and the increased proportion of girls, was undoubtedly the half-time system.

The fee charged by most Dame schools was 2d a week. At the larger Church schools the fee for basic subjects was 2d (1d at Mytholmroyd) with up to 6d for a broader curriculum. The private schools usually had a sliding scale according to curriculum. Joseph Dobson at Birchcliffe charged 3½d a week for reading, 5½d for reading and writing, and 7½d if arithmetic and grammar were taught as well. No school gave separate information about the fees paid by part-timers.

There were 7 evening schools, 4 of them provided by private day schools, with 110 male and 46 female pupils, nearly all studying the 'three Rs'. Over 7,000 pupils, no doubt nearly all children, were enrolled at 46 Sunday schools. With the population relatively static, the enrolment had increased by only eight per cent since 1833. All of the schools which gave full details taught both religious knowledge and reading. No other subjects were taught on Sundays except at three General Baptist schools – writing at two and singing at one. However, seven schools taught other subjects, mainly writing, on a weekday evening, apparently all free of charge. The schools reported a total of about 1,700 teachers, an impressive voluntary effort.

A few years before the 1844 Act the earliest national movement concerned with the education of adults had reached the upper Calder Valley. Mechanics institutes were founded in Todmorden in 1836 and in Sowerby Bridge in 1838.[31] The mechanics institute movement began in the early 1820s in the main industrial towns, with the aim of educating skilled workers in the scientific principles underlying their craft. There was often the additional ideological motive of conditioning the skilled workers to be reliable and sober employees. They achieved only limited success with scientific classes for artisans. Some could not take advantage of them because of their lack of basic education, and others would not because they resisted conditioning by the middle class sponsors of the institutes. Elementary classes for young people were therefore started and received better support.

At the same time the middle classes were keen to learn something about the scientific and technical achievements of the age, and well-presented, popular lectures on, for example, the steam engine or electricity often drew good audiences. Early in its life the Todmorden Institute stimulated interest and enlarged its membership by holding an exhibition of arts and sciences. Sowerby Bridge followed suit in 1839 with an exhibition which lasted for seven weeks, attracted 29,000 admissions and made a profit of £142.

Of the 153 Sowerby Bridge members in 1840, 55 were in specifically textile occupations, including 16 piecers who were presumably youths. There were also 10 mechanics, 5 bookkeepers, 4 warehousemen and packers, 12 metal workers and 12 wood workers. In 1842, when the Todmorden Institute had only 79 members (as compared with 153 in 1839-40), 30 were definitely in textiles (including 13 weavers and 6 overlookers) and 12 were mechanics and craftsmen.

The two local institutes were badly hit by the depression of the early 1840s. The Todmorden committee bemoaned the 'almost incredible apathy' of the artisans. 'Alienation' would have been a more appropriate word, as many of the politically-conscious workers were involved in the agitations and educational programmes of Chartism. By 1843 the membership at Todmorden had fallen to fifty-two, and soon afterwards the institute closed. It was replaced in 1846 by the Athenaeum, which was essentially a social club and library. Sowerby Bridge carried on, with declining support for lectures and classes, until about 1850. For the time being the mechanics institute movement in the valley had foundered.[32] Its subsequent revival is described in Chapter 14.

The factory inspectors' reports show the National schools steadily growing in size during the 1850s, probably at the expense of the less effective or more costly private schools, but reflecting also the expansion of factory employment. The schools which took half-timers received occasional grants, mainly to buy books, out of the money paid in fines for breaches of the Factory Acts. In 1858-9 five National schools had 652 half-timers out of a total enrolment of 1,022, and received £65 from the factory fine fund. Other half-timers went to private schools; for example, Hollinrakes School in Hebden Bridge had 120 half-timers out of a total of 140 pupils in 1861, and was also helped from the factory fine fund.[33]

The factory inspectors operated, in effect, as inspectors of schools. In 1858 the inspector annulled certificates of school attendance granted by Edward Henry Horsfall, schoolmaster of Mytholmroyd, for 'not having the books and materials necessary to teach children reading and writing'. Horsfall could therefore no longer enrol half-timers.[34]

The Factory Acts of 1847-53 shortened a little the working half-day of the textile mill children, but major developments took place in the 1860s. The Bleaching and Dyeing Works Act of 1860 and the Factory Acts Extension Act in 1864 brought finishing works and fustian-cutting shops respectively within the system of regulation, including the half-time system for the under-thirteens. Two further Acts passed in 1867 extended the half-time system to a wide range of manual trades. The factory inspector responsible for the upper Calder Valley referred to 'the [educational] success which has attended the Factory half-time system for so many years', and commented that the industrial districts now had 'the nearest approach to a compulsory system of education'.[35]

The standards achieved by the half-timers varied. Three constraints were the organisational problems of half-time attendance, the size of classes, and the age range in them. Mytholmroyd Church School had, in 1851, 159 children ranging in age from under five to thirteen, more than half of them half-timers, taught by two teachers. The Church schools were in general better than the private ones. The factory inspector

Roomfield Board School, Todmorden.

responsible for the Burnley-Rochdale-Hebden Bridge area commented in 1876 that only about half of the half-timers in Hebden Bridge had reached the fourth standard by the age of thirteen, 'owing to the imperfect methods' of the private schools which many of them attended, compared to about two-thirds in the rest of his area.[36]

The Wesleyans had established two day-schools by the 1860s, in Hebden Bridge and at Bolton Brow in Sowerby Bridge (the latter presumably replacing the British school), but most of the religious schools were Anglican. The Elementary Education Act of 1870 provided for the election, by the ratepayers, of school boards, which would provide schools, paid for out of an education rate, where the existing provision was inadequate in quantity or quality. In board schools any religious teaching had to be undenominational, which suited the Nonconformists but not the Anglicans. Voluntary school organisations had six months' grace to plan new schools, for which they could claim a building grant from the government. The Anglicans moved quickly to fill a major gap in the provision of National schools in Hebden Bridge by building a school next to St James's Church, with accommodation for about 300 children. It opened in January 1871.[37]

A school board was formed to cover the six townships of the Todmorden Poor Law Union, ie the area from Todmorden to Mytholmroyd. The election in 1874, as was invariably the case in the industrial districts, was fought on sectarian lines. The nine successful candidates were: a Wesleyan Liberal and a United Methodist Free Church Liberal; two other Liberals; a Baptist; two Unitarians, Rev Lindsey Taplin and Mrs

Stubbings Board School, Hebden Bridge.

Samuel Fielden, the only woman on the board; and only two 'Church Conservatives'. By 1878, board schools had been built in Hebden Bridge (Stubbins) and Todmorden (Roomfield), and in the following year the board took over Lanebottom School, Todmorden.[38]

Lower down the valley, school boards were established on a township basis – Midgley and Warley in 1874, but Sowerby not until 1884. Parts of Midgley and Warley were already served by Luddenden National School. The Midgley board built new schools at Midgley (1877) and Burnley Road, Mytholmroyd (1880), the latter a joint effort with the Todmorden District Board. Warley set up temporary schools at Wainstalls, Warley Town, Luddenden Foot and Tuel Lane in 1877-9, replacing them by new buildings during the next decade. In Sowerby township the existing schools at Brearley and Cragg Vale had been condemned by the school inspectorate, and the board replaced them with Scout Road and Cragg Vale Board Schools in 1887.[39]

The main issue of the 1890s was the half-time system, once an educational benefit when the alternative for many children was no school at all after the age of eight or nine, but now seen as a great barrier to educational progress. The minimum age was raised to eleven in 1893, but a further increase to twelve in 1899 was bitterly opposed by the textile unions: a weaver aided by two half-time child 'tenters' could run six plain cotton looms instead of four, so the removal of cheap child labour threatened a reduction in earnings. The half-time system was eventually abolished by the 1918 Education Act, but it was not until 1922 that the last half-timer in upper Calderdale reached the school-leaving age of fourteen.[40]

When the Borough of Todmorden was created in 1896, the Todmorden District Board was replaced by two boards, one for the borough, the other for Hebden Bridge and Mytholmroyd. The 1902 Act replaced school boards by local education authorities in the form of county boroughs, such as Halifax, and county councils. Todmorden Council became responsible for elementary education only, the West Riding County Council taking over all other public educational provision. Under the Act, Church schools received aid from the rates, much to the annoyance of local Nonconformists. County secondary schools were built in Todmorden, Hebden Bridge and Sowerby Bridge in 1905-12.[41]

The Age of Agitation

The Luddites and Parliamentary Reform

The industrial developments which brought fortune and power to families such as the Fieldens, and extra profits from land transactions to local landowners, were a mixed blessing to the industrial population at large. New opportunities were offered to some, as mechanics or foremen. The complex economic structure of the local textile industry meant that there were often openings for men with enterprise and a little capital to try their hand as 'small masters'. Some families gained a measure of independence and security from the occupation of a farm or smallholding. An increasing proportion of the population, however, had nothing but labour to sell. They were vulnerable to fluctuations in trade, which were increased by the distortions of demand and interruptions to exports caused by the long wars with France (1793-1815). In addition the mill workers and handicraftsmen had their own particular worries and grievances.

Moving from the cottage or the workshop into the mill meant not only longer hours, but relentlessly regular hours. Handicraft workshops usually worked a ten hour day, and this was probably regarded as the normal stint for a handloom weaver or wool comber working at home. The latter groups were, however, free to stop when they felt like it, to take time off one day and make it up later in the week. The mill worker was confined to his place of work, and subject to the rhythm of the machines, from 6 am to 7.30 or 8 pm on five days a week, with a little less on Saturdays. Such working days must have seemed endless to the children who were employed from the age of nine, eight or occasionally even younger, as 'doffers' (who replaced full bobbins on the spinning frames with empty ones) or pieceners.

Outside the mills, the two most vulnerable groups in the early years of the nineteenth century were the skilled craftsmen whose livelihood was threatened by machines – first the croppers in wool, later the combers in worsted – and the handloom weavers. The main threat to the living standards of the latter did not come for some time from the power loom. The first cotton power looms recorded in the upper Calder Valley were installed in 1829, and it was not until the middle of the century that power looms made much headway in woollens. The Achilles heel of the weaving trade was the relative ease with which the simpler kinds of work were learned, and the impossibility of controlling entry into the trade. The rapid expansion of cotton spinning led to a great demand for weavers, which gave them a 'golden age' of high wages in the period from about 1788 to 1803. It was presumably during this period that some of the weavers in the upper Calder Valley switched from woollen or worsted to cotton. The continued influx of new workers into cotton weaving turned the shortage of labour into a surplus and caused a sharp decline in earnings. Substantial wage cuts in depressions were only partially restored in the next boom, to be followed by further severe cuts in the subsequent downturn in trade. Weavers of better-quality cottons fared better, and the whole process developed later in woollens and worsteds.

The possibility of defending or improving their situation by forming trade unions was open in practice only to skilled workers. Mule spinners were the first major group in the mills to combine effectively, and the croppers and wool combers had old-established organisations. They faced serious legal obstacles, however. Even before trade unions were outlawed by the Combination Acts of 1799 and 1800, their members could be prosecuted for conspiracy, for administering illegal oaths, or under laws which forbade workers leaving pieces of work unfinished. The croppers and weavers petitioned Parliament for the enforcement of ancient legislation on such matters as apprenticeship and the regulation of wages and the price of bread, but Parliament responded by repealing the laws.[1]

The discontent of the croppers, who saw their livelihood threatened by the steady increase in the number of gig mills and shearing frames, rose to an explosive climax in 1812, against a background of general distress resulting from high food prices and the closing of overseas markets by wartime blockades. Bands of Luddites, so called after a mythical leader Ned Ludd, destroyed gig mills and shearing frames in the West Riding in a series of attacks at night during the period February to April 1812. A millowner of Marsden near Huddersfield was murdered. In January 1813 seventeen Luddites, including two Sowerby men, were executed, and six Halifax men were transported for administering illegal oaths. They included John Baines, a veteran radical, and had probably been involved in the organisation set up in 1812 to agitate for parliamentary reform.[2]

The campaign for parliamentary reform was not to bear fruit for another twenty years. It was supported both by workers who hoped that a reformed parliament would be more responsive to their pleas than had been the case in 1802-8, and by the industrial and commercial middle classes who argued that their interests were grossly under-represented. Yorkshire had thirty MPs, of whom two represented the county at large, and the remainder fourteen ancient boroughs. In the West Riding, which had 800,000 people in 1821, the five boroughs returning MPs had a combined population of 15,637. In most of the latter, a majority of the burgages (borough houses) which carried the right to vote had been bought up by powerful landowners, who nominated the MPs themselves. Very few people in upper Calderdale owned a freehold property worth forty shillings a year, the qualification for the county vote, but this was no great deprivation. Because of the high cost of fighting an election in a county as large as Yorkshire, the Whigs and Tories usually avoided a contest by naming one candidate each. There was, therefore, no great excitement in radical circles when Yorkshire was given two extra members in 1822.

The level of political agitation, over the general question of parliamentary reform and particular issues such as a minimum piece rate for handloom weavers, rose and fell with the state of the economy, with peaks caused by economic distress in 1819 and 1826. The reform campaign entered its decisive stage in 1830. The next two years saw a parliamentary struggle between the Whig majority in the House of Commons and the Tory-dominated House of Lords. 'Political Unions' in support of reform were established in many industrial towns, including Hebden Bridge and Todmorden. John Fielden and his brother James were leading lights of the latter.[3]

The Todmorden Political Union held frequent meetings and submitted addresses to the government, supported by petitions from the three constituent townships, Langfield, Stansfield and Todmorden with Walsden. As well as reciting the sufferings

'Honest John' Fielden.

of the local people, with many textile workers 'absolutely in a state of starvation', these statements included the threat that the denial of reform 'would inevitably produce great dissatisfaction in the manufacturing districts and consequences might follow which it is awful to contemplate'. The crisis was finally resolved when King William IV agreed to create as many new peers as were needed to override the opposition of the Lords. The threat sufficed, and the Third Reform Bill became law on the 7th June 1832.

Todmorden celebrated with an open-air banquet for 350 people, with John Fielden presiding, followed by a procession which included several friendly societies (Oddfellows, Foresters, Druids and Loyal Free Mechanics) and two which may also have been craft unions (Whitesmiths and the Mechanics Trade Society). Each society had its own band and banners, and a flag carried the slogan 'Union has conquered and will conquer'.

The 'conquest' did not in the short term amount to very much. There was a modest redistribution of seats, which still left gross inequalities. Four West Riding industrial towns, including Halifax, were given two MPs each, and two others one each; but Thirsk (1831 population 2,835) was still as well-represented as Huddersfield (19,035). In place of the four members for the county of Yorkshire, each of the three Ridings was allocated two seats. In the county areas, adult male copyholders with property worth £10 a year and tenants of £50 a year could vote, as well as the 40s freeholder, but most of the supporters of the local political unions were still disfranchised.

The radicals of Todmorden and district had, however, three reasons to be pleased. First, the reform, however inadequate, was a step in what they regarded as the right direction. Secondly, their leader John Fielden and his friend William Cobbett were elected Radical MPs for the newly-created constituency of Oldham at the general election held in December 1832. Thirdly, they had tried out a powerful political weapon – an organised mass movement, the leaders of which could warn that discipline could give way to disorder if no concessions were made to the popular will.

Factory Reform: the Ten Hours Campaign

The political unions of Todmorden and Hebden Bridge did not dissolve themselves after the enactment of reform, because they had become involved in a parallel campaign for a statutory limitation of working hours in textile mills. There was already some legislation, dealing with pauper apprentices and children in cotton mills, but it was almost completely ineffective.

The leaders of the campaign included John Fielden and two Tories, Michael Sadler MP and Richard Oastler. In September 1830 Oastler wrote a letter to the *Leeds Mercury*, in which he argued that the conditions of children in the textile mills were worse than those of negro slaves in the West Indies. The aim of the campaign was a reduction of working hours to ten a day. The battle was fought over the hours of children, but it was well known that most mills would find it difficult, if not impossible, to keep working for longer than ten hours a day if all their workers under the age of sixteen, or eighteen, were limited to that time. In the Sowerby Bridge area the campaign was orchestrated by a trade union, apparently of mule and jenny spinners.

Sadler introduced a Ten Hours Bill in the House of Commons in December 1831. A select committee under his chairmanship was appointed in the spring of 1832 to collect evidence. It interviewed many operatives and paid particular attention to stories of physical cruelty to children. A more systematic investigation by the Factories Inquiry Commission in 1833 built up, mainly out of the testimony of employers, an irrefutable case for new legislation.[4]

Twenty-nine mills in the upper Calder Valley answered the commission's questionnaire, or otherwise volunteered information. The majority of firms, including Fielden Brothers, made no return. The regular hours of work of the cotton mills in the sample ranged between 68 and 72 per week, and the woollen mills worked 72 hours, in both cases exclusive of mealtimes. The longest hours were worked in the worsted spinning mills. The largest of these, Walker and Edmondson's Mytholmroyd Mill, worked from 6 am to 8 pm on weekdays and until 7 pm on Saturdays, with an hour's break for dinner, a total of 77 hours. Peel House Mill in the Luddenden Valley (R Whitworth and Co) worked a 78 hour week when a full water supply was available. Water mills often worked overtime (at standard rates of pay) to compensate for time lost through drought, frost or 'backwater' (when the water of a river in spate backed up the mill race). In winter some mills started operations at daybreak and went on until 9 pm, to avoid having to light up at both ends of the day.

Nearly all of the twenty-nine mills employed children aged nine years or less. Walker and Edmondson had seventeen children under the age of eight. Stansfield Mill, Sowerby Bridge (cotton) was the only one which took a strong line against the beating of children, who were most vulnerable towards the end of the day when, as a result of exhaustion, they made mistakes which annoyed the spinners or other adults for whom they worked. According to George Crabtree, an associate of Richard Oastler who toured the Calder Valley in 1833 to coordinate the Ten Hours Campaign, some employers themselves used a strap to keep the children in order. He quoted Rev

Devine, an Anglican minister, as saying that he had recently buried an eleven year old boy who had died from overwork, '. . . in his grave with the black marks of the strap buckle upon him . . .'[5] Only one set of employers, John and James Greenwood who had a cotton mill at Lumbutts, said that corporal punishment was tolerated in their mill. Most were content to state that they did not sanction it. John Sutcliffe, a cotton spinner of Midgehole Mill, Hebden Bridge, who said that there was no corporal punishment in his mill, thought that too much fuss had been made about the whole subject, '. . . as in no mills that I ever worked in had a tenth of the corporal punishment been inflicted as is to be found in the best schools of our land.'

John Fielden's main argument, expressed with the authority of a very successful businessman with forty years' experience of cotton mills, was that even without any positive ill-treatment, long hours of work for children represented in themselves an intolerable cruelty. Fielden had started work at the age of ten in his father's mill, which was then in the 'jenny' and 'billy' stage, with much of the machinery hand-driven. The hours of work were only ten a day, but Fielden wrote that he would 'never forget the fatigue I often felt before the day ended and the anxiety of us all to be relieved from the unvarying and irksome toil . . .' John Fielden considered that the burden upon factory children had increased since his own childhood because machinery ran much faster, and mills worked longer hours than ten a day. His father had lengthened the working week to seventy-one hours when he had 'introduced the machinery that is now used', presumably spinning mules. 'This he was obliged to do in his own defence' as other manufacturers with the same machinery were working their hands from 77 to 84 hours a week.[6]

The 1833 Factory Act followed closely the recommendations of the Factories Inquiry Commission. The employment of children under nine years of age was prohibited in all textile mills except silk, for which the minimum working age was to be eight. Children under nine were to work no more than 9 hours a day and 48 a week. 'Young persons' from 13 to 17 inclusive were restricted to 12 hours a day and 69 a week. Neither group was to work at night. The under thirteens were to have two hours' schooling each day. Watermills were allowed to use children and young persons for a limited amount of overtime to make up for stoppages to the flow of water. Four inspectors were appointed to secure the observance of the Act. By the employment of three children for every two jobs, the mills could keep running for 69 hours a week, instead of the 58 hours proposed by Sadler's Ten Hours Bill.

Resistance to the New Poor Law

The battle lines of a new campaign were laid down when the recommendations of the Poor Law Commission of 1832-4 were incorporated in the Poor Law Amendment Act of 1834. The commission was set up to investigate what were considered to be serious deficiencies in the administration of the poor laws, and particularly any form of relief to the able-bodied which might lessen the will to work.[7] In the upper Calder Valley there had been no fundamental changes in the system of poor relief described in Chapter 9: allowances in money or kind, the occasional purchase of a loom for an unemployed man, assistance with the rent of paupers in most townships, and the use of the township workhouses mainly for shelter and not as places where the poor were put to work. Some inmates of the workhouses lived there with their own furniture.[8]

The local townships made only limited use of the practice of supplementing inadequate earnings, normally when there were three or more children in the family.

The commission was told that the townships could manage their own affairs well enough (except that Stansfield people had long wanted to subdivide their township for more efficient administration) and that the burden of poor relief was not excessive. The annual cost per head of the population averaged 3s 1d in the upper Calder Valley, compared with 5s 7d in the West Riding as a whole and 18s 3d in Suffolk.

The Poor Law Amendment Act laid down that the responsibility for the relief of poverty was to be taken away from the townships, which were to be grouped into Unions, governed by elected Boards of Guardians. The township overseers were reduced to the role of rate-collectors for the union. Outdoor relief for the able-bodied was to cease. Except for the old and unfit, there was to be a simple choice between managing without relief and going into a union workhouse, in which conditions were to be made, quite deliberately, 'less eligible' than those of the poorest employed workers outside. A permanent Poor Law Commission, with three members, was established in London with power to issue orders to the unions and to standardise procedures throughout the country.

The Act did not immediately affect the Calder Valley because the officials of the commission busied themselves at first with the organisation of unions in the South and Midlands. There was, in any case, much less poverty to relieve, because the boom which built up from 1834 to 1836 caused a shortage of labour in the local textile industries.[9] As the boom gave way to a depression in 1837, the commission prepared to organise the North of England. John Fielden warned the House of Commons that the new poor law would be resisted in Oldham and Todmorden 'and I do not mind telling you frankly that, if such resistance takes place, I would lead it'.[10]

The commission assigned Midgley, Warley and Sowerby to the Halifax Union which contained a total of twenty townships, and grouped the other six townships (Erringden, Heptonstall, Langfield, Stansfield, Todmorden with Walsden, and Wadsworth) into a union based upon Todmorden. Guardians were elected from four townships, but in Langfield and Todmorden with Walsden all the nominees withdrew, allegedly as a result of intimidation. A public meeting in Todmorden with Walsden resolved that the township would pay no poor rates to the union, but would continue to relieve its own poor in defiance of the new law. The resolution gave two reasons, the harshness of the new system and the need to defend 'that self-government which we have had handed down to us by our forefathers'. These two considerations were inseparably linked throughout the poor law controversy.[11]

The opposition to the new poor law was orchestrated by the Todmorden Working Men's Association, established in March 1838. There was probably a good deal of continuity of membership between the Todmorden Political Union and the Working Men's Association, but the adoption of a new name was significant. The London Working Men's Association, formed in 1836, which published demands for democratic reforms in the 'People's Charter' in 1838, sent missionaries to the north of England in 1837-8, whose work led to the establishment of a large number of Working Men's Associations. The Todmorden WMA declared firmly that its principal object was 'to obtain the repeal of the Poor Law Amendment Act', although it later adopted the full Chartist programme. The membership fee was one penny per month, and weekly meetings were held in the schoolroom attached to Fielden Brothers' Waterside Mill. As will be seen, the other anti-poor law/Chartist organisations in the valley generally followed the style of name of the Halifax Radical Association, formed in August 1836.

The Todmorden Working Men's Association used a combination of tactics – public meetings and processions, posters, petitions and, most effective, a boycott of all tradesmen who showed any sympathy with the new law. The Halifax Poor Law Union met much less opposition, and in 1838 the board of guardians took over responsibility for relief and planned a large workhouse. The Poor Law Commission ordered the Todmorden Union to follow a similar path, despite arguments that the board of guardians was not legally constituted because two townships were wholly or partially unrepresented. A meeting of the guardians was called for the 6th July 1838 to pass the necessary resolutions to take over the administration of poor relief from the townships.

John Fielden responded with a threat to close his mills on the 6th July unless the guardians resigned. His intention was to wreck the new system by throwing 3,000 workers and their dependants on to poor relief. A mass meeting was called for the same day. The guardians, declaring that they feared for their lives, postponed their meeting but refused to resign. The Fielden mills were closed on the 6th July, a Friday, but the guardians kept their nerve. The two local magistrates, John Crossley of Scaitcliffe and James Taylor of Todmorden Hall, who were the first and second chairmen of the board of guardians, swore in fifty special constables and called in a squadron of cavalry from Burnley. Disorder was prevented and on Monday the 16th July the Fielden mills reopened.

If the rebels had lost a battle, they had not yet lost the war. The board of guardians formally took over the administration of poor relief on the 12th August 1838, but both Todmorden with Walsden and Langfield refused to hand over their poor rates. They continued to pay outdoor relief to their paupers on the old system. The overseers were fined and, when they refused to pay, distress warrants were issued against them. Attempts to execute the warrants were met by force, and two constables from Halifax who tried to seize goods from a Langfield overseer in October 1838 were beaten up by workers from the Fielden mills.

In November, a mob, or mobs, attacked the houses of several guardians, including James Taylor. Windows were broken, furniture and pictures destroyed and Taylor's new carriage was wrecked. John Fielden sent the Waterside Mill fire engines to Taylor's house (Todmorden Hall) and one of the others to deal with the threat of arson. John Crossley again summoned the cavalry, which restored the peace, but it was thought prudent to quarter a force of infantry in Todmorden, in an old handloom weaving workshop.

Eighteen men were arrested for involvement in the October and November disturbances. The Todmorden Working Men's Association raised a subscription to help the accused men at their trial – 'Poor and innocent individuals . . . dragged in chains of iron, from their affectionate Fathers, Mothers, Wives and Children' – and to support their dependants. The men were eventually bailed out by John Fielden, and only one of them was sentenced to imprisonment, for nine months. The judge at the York Assizes commented that there were parties more deserving of punishment than the misguided men who stood before him for sentence.

Meanwhile the opposition to the poor law had begun to vary its tactics. Appeals against convictions for refusing to work the new system were entered on various legal technicalities, eg that the auditor of the union had been improperly appointed. It was found that the wording of the Poor Law Amendment Act provided that fines imposed for breaches of the Act were to be paid over to the overseers of the township concerned. William Crossley, the overseer of Todmorden with Walsden, meekly brought £20 worth of goods to be distrained for a fine of that amount, bought them himself and then claimed the money back. Because of the presence of the military, large demonstrations and overt violence were avoided, but the Working Men's Association

Todmorden Hall, the home of James Taylor.

carried out a very successful policy of boycott and intimidation. Similar pressures were kept up in the Hebden Bridge area. Three guardians – Thomas Sutcliffe of Stoneshey Gate, Crossley Sutcliffe of Lee near Hebden Bridge and one of the Hinchliffes of Cragg Vale – resigned, alleging threats of murder. At the elections in March 1839, according to the assistant overseer of Heptonstall, 'the occupiers of small cottages (which are numerous here) succeeded in returning two Guardians who live a distance of four or five miles from the Township merely because they were Chartists and opposed to the New Poor Law'.

This combination of intimidation, infiltration and 'the law's delays' paralysed the board of guardians. The remaining members decided that they had put up with public scorn and vilification, without adequate support from the law, for long enough. The board therefore began to evade or ignore the directives of the Poor Law Commission. It was decided in 1840 that, instead of having a relieving officer for the whole union, one man would be appointed in each township to act as both relieving officer and rate collector, at a salary to be fixed by the township. This meant, in effect, restoring the old township system, but the commission dare not take a strong line for fear that all the guardians would resign.

In September 1842, Assistant Commissioner Mott reported to the commission on the 'very unsatisfactory state' of Todmorden Union: 'The whole of the proceedings of the Guardians are irregular and at variance with the Law and the directions of the Commissioners'. The supervision of relieving officers by the guardians was only a formality, and the six township workhouses were still managed by the overseers. By 1843 all the legal cases had been decided against the rebel townships, but there was no longer anything to rebel against. The guardians from Langfield and Todmorden with Walsden took their seats and co-operated happily with the new policy, which may be described as using the board of guardians as a shield behind which the townships enjoyed their cherished independence.

In January 1844, Assistant Commissioner Clements visited the six township workhouses – 'one confused mass of squalid filth and wretchedness' – which were used merely to lodge homeless paupers. When the commission pointed out that all the workhouses in the union were legally the responsibility of the guardians, the latter officially declared them closed. The townships continued to operate them as before, the only difference being that as they did not officially exist, the workhouses could not be maintained out of the poor rate and were destined to grow worse rather than better.

The Halifax Union opened its workhouse in 1841. The master and matron received £80 a year and their keep. The schoolmaster, whose working hours were 9 am to noon and 2 pm to 5 pm five days a week, with mornings only on Saturdays, received £26 a year, without lodgings or food – about half the earnings of a mule spinner. The workhouse diet consisted of one and a half pints of oatmeal porridge – the notorious workhouse 'skilly' (gruel) – with half a pint of milk for breakfast and supper every day, and the following for dinner:

Sunday, Wednesday	2 pints soup, 5oz. bread
Monday, Thursday, Friday	1¾ lbs. lobscouse (stew), 3oz. bread
Tuesday, Saturday	5oz. meat, 1¼ lbs. potatoes

Coarse and monotonous as the diet was, it was no worse than that of many poor families outside. (The local townships told the Poor Law Commission of 1832-4 that the labouring classes lived off oatmeal, potatoes and milk, with occasionally a little bacon, and meat a rare treat.) The forbidding features of workhouse life were strict prison-like discipline which shut the workhouse paupers off from the rest of the local community, and the frequent separation of men from their wives and parents from their children.

It was not, however, possible to maintain the principle of relieving the able-bodied only in the workhouse during periods of acute depression, such as that of 1841-2. The commission urged boards of guardians in such circumstances to require some work, eg stone breaking in the workhouse yard, but many boards in industrial districts dismissed this idea as impracticable. The Halifax Guardians reported that there was no alternative to considerable outdoor relief, as forcing partially-employed men with families into the workhouse would be both impracticable and expensive. In the third quarter of 1842, 82 people from Sowerby, Warley and Midgley were relieved in Halifax workhouse, but 1,812 people from the same townships received some form of outdoor relief. In Stansfield only thirty per cent of men workers were fully employed in the summer of 1842, but most of the remainder had some work, if only weaving an occasional piece of cloth at starvation wages. The normal condition of textile districts when trade was depressed was under-employment rather than massive unemployment. The theory behind the principle of 'less eligibility', that the threat of the workhouse would force the able-bodied to find work somewhere, made no sense in such communities. The local response in Stansfield was to form a relief committee, which gave over six tons of oatmeal to the needy in a two month period. In December 1842 other relief in kind was given to 468 families, mainly bedding, cotton cloth and clogs.[12]

The Todmorden Board of Guardians continued to fight off the intermittent attacks of the Poor Law Board, which replaced the commission in 1847. Small money payments were made to large families with low earnings. Eventually the Local Government Board, which took over the functions of the Poor Law Board in 1871, struck at the Achilles heel of local patriotism. It threatened to divide the Todmorden area between the Halifax and Rochdale Unions, which already had union workhouses, unless a workhouse was built in Todmorden. The guardians reluctantly decided, in 1874, that a local workhouse was the lesser evil. Curiously enough, the site chosen in Langfield was commonly known as 'Beggarington'. Work progressed at a leisurely pace, and there were no celebrations when the building opened in 1879.

All was not lost, however. The Todmorden Board of Guardians knew that other unions with workhouses had contrived to maintain selective outdoor relief to the able-bodied, including assistance to those in work. The Local Government Board admitted in 1881 that 'the old abuse of relief in aid of wages' was still widespread.[13]

The success of the struggle against the new poor law in the Todmorden-Hebden Bridge area had several interlocking causes. One was the bitterness and sense of betrayal felt by the politically-conscious workers when their support for the cause of parliamentary reform in 1830-2 was rewarded by the principle of 'less eligibility' and the hated symbol of the 'Bastille' workhouse. The strength of their local organisation, already tested in the reform agitation and in the Ten Hours movement, sustained a campaign of persuasion and intimidation which twice spilled over into violence. Although some of the guardians resisted this pressure, the local board as a whole was able to use the obvious and dangerous disaffection of the district as a justification for refusing to enforce the orders of the national poor law authority. There is little doubt that in the long run the 'Union workhouse' was resisted more because it symbolised the victory of central bureaucracy over local independence than because of tenderness towards the poor. The attitude of the local guardians was summed up in a letter to the Poor Law Board in 1852:

. . . this board also again strongly protests against the recent attempt (still persisted in) by the Poor Law Board to destroy the exercise of all judgement and discretion on the part of the Guardians . . . [We] cannot . . . consent to be made mere tools in carrying out rules and orders which we conscientiously believe to be illegal, impracticable and unjust.

The central body was told that, if it persisted in its policy, it must find some other instrument for carrying it out. But there was no other instrument. The 1834 Act had created a centralised bureaucracy which could operate locally only with the consent and support of the propertied and professional classes. In Todmorden and district this co-operation was lacking. The two resident magistrates, James Taylor and John Crossley, were prepared to resist both popular agitation and the massive influence of the Fieldens, but they received insufficient support. The Home Office expected the troops sent into the district to be accommodated 'at the expense of those persons for whose protection a military force is stationed at Todmorden'. John Crossley commented: 'From the well known disaffection of this neighbourhood, you will readily believe that few will be found to contribute . . .'

The Chartists

The printed address in which the Todmorden Working Men's Association thanked 'the inhabitants of Todmorden and its vicinity' for their 'very liberal support' of the rioters tried in March 1839, went on to announce a collection 'for the support of the National Convention'. The latter was an assembly of delegates elected by Chartist groups all over the country which was meeting to promote the six-point 'People's Charter' – annual parliamentary elections, votes for all adult men, equal electoral districts, abolition of the property qualification for MPs, payment of MPs and vote by secret ballot.[14]

In the industrial West Riding, Chartism grew directly, in both spirit and organisation, out of the anti-poor law movement, which often involved also the activists of the Ten Hours campaign. In upper Calderdale this continuity reached back to the agitation for parliamentary reform. In Halifax, by contrast, the alliance between working-class Radicals and middle-class Whigs had not survived the achievement of the 1832 Reform Act. Most of the prominent industrialists, led by the Akroyds, opposed factory legislation and supported the new poor law.

One of the dominant figures of Chartism in Yorkshire was Feargus O'Connor, who launched the weekly journal the *Northern Star* in Leeds in November 1837. It was avidly read (and read from, by the literate to the illiterate) and eagerly discussed by working men in the upper Calder Valley. It appealed particularly to handloom weavers and wool combers, whose plight was discussed at some length in its columns, and to groups of politically-conscious mill workers, such as the men in the silk mills at Mytholm, near Hebden Bridge. The *Northern Star* reported fully on the activities of radical organisations, large and small. For example, it gave an account of a meeting of the Midgley Radical Association on the 26th December 1837, addressed by Benjamin Rushton of Ovenden, a handloom weaver and a Methodist New Connexion lay preacher, who became one of the most respected and influential of local Chartist leaders. From the columns of this journal, it is clear that nearly every town and village in the upper Calder Valley had a Radical organisation.

The Chartists developed the technique of procession and mass meeting on a regional scale, with huge rallies at Peep Green on Hartshead Moor, which was roughly equidistant from Bradford, Halifax and Huddersfield.[15] The first such meeting in October 1838 attracted marching contingents, each with its own banners and many led by a brass band, from all over the Riding. Several townships of upper Calderdale were represented. The speakers included O'Connor, John Fielden and William Thornton of Skircoat, another Methodist local preacher. At a similar rally on Whit Monday, the 21st May 1839, brass bands led contingents from Hebden Bridge, Heptonstall, Mytholmroyd, Luddenden and ten other places in the Halifax area. Frank Peel said that it took several hours for all the detachments to march on to the common.[16]

Violent language was used, both at mass rallies and at local meetings, including frequent references to arming and 'self defence'. The Hebden Bridge Radical Association resolved 'that we are confident of the justice and right of the people to possess arms in their own defence, against home as well as foreign enemies'. There were already 100 infantry soldiers in Todmorden to deal with the poor law riots, and in December 1838 a detachment of dragoons arrived in Halifax. Fears were expressed in local newspapers that an armed insurrection might be launched if the Chartist petition was rejected. On 30th March 1839 the *Halifax Guardian* stated that 700 local Chartists, mainly in the upland hamlets of upper Calderdale, were armed with muskets. There is some evidence of the possession of firearms, but the same newspaper was probably nearer the truth with a later report of Chartists with pikes and knives.

In July 1839 the first Chartist petition, with over 1,200,000 signatures, was rejected by the House of Commons. The local Chartist groups remained active. The presence of the military prevented any overt violence – in August the cavalry force in Halifax was replaced by infantry – but cases of intimidation were reported. Rev W H Bull, parson of Sowerby, who may have felt personally threatened because of his opposition to the Ten Hours campaign, wrote to the Home Secretary that the Chartists were demanding contributions from innkeepers and shopkeepers with threats of violence:

> They went yesterday to Mr. Joseph Broadbent, a grocer at Sowerby Bridge, and threatened to put down his name in *Red Ink*, as one of the first to be attacked when they rise . . .

'When they rise' – but was an armed insurrection ever seriously planned in the upper Calder Valley or elsewhere in the West Riding? When John Frost led an armed attack on Newport, South Wales, on the 4th November in which fourteen Chartists were killed, there was some expectation of supportive action from Lancashire and the West Riding. A shadowy conspiracy, apparently including the Chartists of the Halifax area and involving armed attacks in three West Riding towns, led to the arrest of many leading Chartists. Frost and seven associates were transported, and twenty-two Yorkshire Chartists were imprisoned for terms of one to four years. In May, O'Connor was sentenced to eighteen months in York Castle for seditious libel in the *Northern Star*.[17] None of the Halifax/upper Calder Valley men were imprisoned, however, and unlike most Chartist centres the local organisation remained intact. Money was raised for the defence of the 'martyrs', and later petitions organised for their release. A campaign was carried on against the Anti-Corn Law League, in which the Akroyds were prominent figures. This antipathy was partly a result of the influence of Oastler, who was a protectionist Tory, although the reason given was that cheap bread was being sought as a means of reducing wages. In April 1840 a league meeting in Halifax was broken up by Chartists.

A new form of Chartist organisation emerged in 1839-40 copied from Methodism. The basic unit was the 'class', and Chartist 'localities' were federated into 'districts'. The Halifax district included Chartist groups in Sowerby, Warley and Midgley. Local magistrate John Crossley complained to the Home Secretary that because the Todmorden Working Men's Association was using the class system, with only ticket holders admitted, he could not find out what was going on. The plagiarisation of Methodism went further. Some Chartist districts organised timetables of lecturers' visits to Chartist groups, on the lines of Methodist preachers' plans.

In April 1842 the second Chartist National Convention met in London, and the following month presented to Parliament a new petition, which, it was claimed, had 3,300,000 signatures. It received no more support than the first petition, but the rebuff was not followed by any militant action. A Chartist district meeting at Luddenden resolved:

> . . . we are not at all disappointed . . . being persuaded that those interested in the present monopolising system will never render to labour its just reward, namely equality before the law.

This relatively peaceful period in local Chartist history was ended abruptly by the outbreak of the Plug Riots in August 1842. A serious trade depression had caused wage cuts, short time and unemployment for both factory and out-workers. Conditions were difficult in the West Riding, but were worse still in the Lancashire cotton towns. The cotton handloom weavers, rapidly losing ground to the power looms, were in a pitiable condition. Early in August, mill workers began to come out on strike against further wage cuts, and desperate mobs marched from mill to mill, forcing them to stop work; if they refused to do so, they pulled the plugs out of the boilers. The Chartists had not initiated this movement, but they were quick to identify with it.

John Crossley and James Taylor, the Todmorden magistrates, were warned early on Friday the 12th August that a mob was approaching from Rochdale. They swore in 100 special constables and secured a troop of cavalry from Burnley. They offered protection to the leading manufacturers 'but they all seemed disposed at once to give up working rather than run the risk of continuing their works in operation'. At about one o'clock a crowd of people estimated by Crossley and Taylor to number between 15,000 and 20,000 arrived, mainly along the Rochdale and Bacup roads. Many of them were carrying sticks. According to the local magistrates:

> . . . the whole of the works in the neighbourhood have been visited by them and the workmen turned out at their request with a strong intimation given at a meeting held this afternoon that in case any of them resume work until the entire demands of the mob have been complied with throughout the manufacturing districts the properties will be destroyed or burnt. These demands professedly are 12 hours' wages upon the scale in 1840 for 10 hours' work. No disturbance whatever took place and the troops returned to Barracks in the afternoon.

In fact what the strikers were demanding was the 1840 wage scale with no reference to a reduction in hours. According to Police Sergeant William Harrison, the mob returned home later in the same day.[18] One would not expect several thousand people from east Lancashire to camp out in the upper Calder Valley, and there is no evidence of any further Lancastrian involvement in the local agitation. The assumption that all the mills in the West Riding which were forced to shut down did so in the face of 'the ragged hordes who swept over the Pennines' is unfounded.[19] It was a relay race, not a marathon.

Another large crowd assembled in Todmorden on Saturday the 13th August and moved down the valley, closing the mills as far as Hebden Bridge. Sunday offered a breathing space which allowed the local Chartists to take stock of the situation. They called a mass meeting for five o'clock on Monday morning on Skircoat Moor. It was addressed by Ben Rushton, who urged his hearers to support the strike but avoid violence. The people moved off up the valley, stopping mills on the way, until at Hawksclough they met the contingent which had started out at Hebden Bridge. Joseph Greenwood, later a pillar of the Co-operative movement and a Hebden Bridge councillor, described the scene he witnessed as a boy:

> . . . it was a remarkably fine day . . . The broad white road with its green hedges and flanked on one side with high trees, was filled with a long, black, straggling line of people, who cheerfully went along, evidently possessed of an idea that they were doing something towards a betterment . . .[20]

After another speech by Rushton, the united procession then moved off towards Halifax, with some parties diverging into the tributary valleys to stop the mills there.

According to John Waterhouse, a Halifax magistrate, they levied 'contributions on many of the respectable inhabitants in the shape of provisions'.

They were joined in and around Halifax by another 4-5,000 who had come from Bradford. The streets were cleared by the cavalry, apparently without any injuries, but about eighteen men were arrested at Akroyds Mills at Haley Hill. They had 'pulled the plugs' and were trying to let the water out of the mill dam.

On the following day the prisoners were taken to Elland railway station in two omnibuses, with a cavalry escort consisting of an officer and ten men. As the cavalry returned up Salterhebble Hill they were ambushed. Five soldiers were unhorsed by a volley of stones, and two were kicked and beaten. The rest of the detachment used both swords and firearms to scatter the rioters. Over thirty people were arrested. A list of eight rioters wounded on the 16th August was sent to the Home Office, including 'Samuel Bates, weaver, Cragg near Hebden Bridge, wounded by a sword cut in the head, in custody', and three others with bullet wounds.

There was no more violence and the strike collapsed after two weeks. Some Chartist leaders were arrested, including Rushton who was soon released, and Robert Brook, secretary of the Todmorden Working Men's Association, who had long been in the sights of Crossley and Taylor. He was committed for trial along with fifty-eight others, but they were all acquitted through an error in the indictment.

The 'Plug Plot' was a hopeless move by workers driven to desperation. A general strike in the textile industry had no chance of success when trade was depressed. For many employers, a fortnight's 'play' was very convenient. The Chartists, who tried to harness the movement, were weakened by its collapse and the arrest of their leaders. There was less damage in upper Calderdale. Ben Rushton, the 'beloved old veteran' or 'bald-headed rascal' according to political taste, was in great demand both locally and elsewhere in the West Riding, at camp meetings, demonstrations and classes. He was supported by younger men such as Benjamin Wilson of Salterhebble. If Crossley and Taylor had hoped to suppress the Todmorden Chartists, they were disappointed. They reported:

> . . . the Chartists are continually holding meetings, principally in the evenings after the hours of work, and have engaged lecture rooms in several places in which both on the Sabbath and on weekdays political sermons and lectures are delivered.

The Chartists and John Fielden saw the trade depression as a suitable opportunity for a new Ten Hours campaign. The idea of reducing the working hours of mills appealed also to handloom weavers, who hoped for an increased demand for their labour. Three factory bills were debated in the House of Commons in 1843-4. Lord Ashley and John Fielden fought hard for the Ten Hours principle, but the measure enacted in 1844 left all operatives over eighteen working a twelve hour day. The Act limited the hours of children under thirteen to six and a half per day, and raised their ration of schooling to fifteen hours a week. Henceforth these children were 'half-timers' at both mill and school. The restriction of hours was, however, taken as a justification for lowering the minimum age of employment to eight. Women were brought under the limit of sixty-nine hours a week previously applied to young persons.[21]

Good harvests and brisker trade in 1843-4 – building up towards the 'railway mania' boom of 1844-5 – took the edge off working class discontent for a time. In some West Riding towns, as already mentioned, Chartism was at a low ebb. Feargus O'Connor was absorbed in his scheme to settle working class families on the land, and set up the

Chartist Land Company in 1845. In the first year of the scheme, Halifax Chartists subscribed nearly £200 towards the purchase of land for settlement, while the secretary of the Sowerby Bridge Radical Association, Samuel Moores, collected 'several hundred pounds'.[22] The movement in the upper Calder Valley was still vigorous, and when O'Connor visited the area in 1844 and 1845 he seemed to have lost none of his popularity.

Another Ten Hours Bill was narrowly defeated in May 1846, but a new campaign was launched in the autumn. John Fielden and Richard Oastler addressed a well-attended rally in Halifax in November, with Ben Rushton in the chair. An industrial recession weakened the manufacturers' opposition, and an alliance of Whigs and Protectionist Tories carried the bill, which provided for a ten hour day for women and young persons. It became law in June 1847. There was great rejoicing in the textile districts, not least in the upper Calder Valley. Fielden's political base in Oldham had, however, been eroded by his frequent alliances with protectionist Tories and his lukewarm attitude to corn law repeal. At the election of July 1847 he insisted on having John Cobbett, son of his old colleague William Cobbett and his prospective son-in-law, as his running mate. John Cobbett, an Anglican of conservative views, had failed to hold his father's seat at the by-election caused by the death of William Cobbett in 1835, and was thoroughly disliked by Oldham Radicals. These tensions split the Liberal-Radical alliance and John Fielden lost his seat.[23]

The trade depression revived the general interest in Chartism, and the movement received a great stimulus from the overthrow of the French monarchy in February 1848 which touched off risings throughout Europe. Forty-nine delegates were elected to a new Chartist Convention, including Ernest Jones who had contested Halifax as a Chartist in the 1847 election. He was chosen at a huge gathering on Skircoat Moor on the 24th March. Banners proclaiming 'Liberty, Equality, Fraternity' and 'The Charter, peaceably if we may, forcibly if we must' were paraded frequently as the Chartists marched in military formation to their crowded meetings in Halifax, Ripponden, Hebden Bridge and other places. Signatures were collected for a new petition to Parliament.

When the convention met on the 4th April, many of the delegates openly advocated the use of force. Ernest Jones declared that his 'constituents' were 'to a man ready to fight' and 'if necessary . . . to rush down from the hills of Yorkshire and aid their brother patriots in London'. There were reports of widespread arming and drilling in the townships around Halifax, particularly Queensbury, Ovenden, Sowerby, Midgley and Todmorden. Benjamin Wilson, a comparatively moderate Chartist, 'purchased a gun, although I knew it was a serious thing for a Chartist to have a gun or a pike in his possession. I saw Cockroft [William Cockroft, a leader of the Halifax militants] who gave me instructions how to proceed until wanted . . .' Troops were moved into Halifax again, 500 special constables were sworn in, and the magistrates warned the people to avoid 'assemblages so dangerous to themselves and to the peace of the community'. Some of the 'more respectable' townspeople left Halifax in fear.[24]

The last Chartist petition to the House of Commons, in April 1848, was contemptuously rejected. As a national movement, Chartism was steadily disintegrating. As a local force it was still extremely strong. Mass rallies continued. In May 1848 the Halifax Chartists made a successful alliance with middle class nonconformist radicals in the first borough elections to be held after the incorporation of the town. Four Chartists were elected, together with seventeen Radicals, six Whigs and three Tories. In the following month a town meeting convened by the mayor carried a resolution in favour of the people's charter. Fresh reports of drilling led to the arrest and imprisonment of Chartist leaders, including Ernest Jones.[25]

In the following year the struggle for the Ten Hours Act, which the reformers thought they had won, was re-opened. The revival of trade in 1849 caused some millowners, led by John Bright MP of Rochdale, to look for loopholes in the factory laws. It had been the intention of the 1844 Act to prevent the working of women, young persons and children in shifts, but the wording was found by the courts to be ambiguous. Some millowners used children as assistants to men after the women and young persons had left work, so that the men, whose hours were not directly regulated, could be worked for more than ten hours. In 1850 Lord Ashley (formerly an ally of John Fielden) agreed to a compromise plan for a 10½ hour day for women and young persons – 6 am to 6 pm with 1½ hours for meals – but the loopholes were not all plugged and a new Act was required in 1853. The Fielden family never forgave Ashley (who became the earl of Shaftesbury in 1851) for his 'treachery'.[26]

John Fielden died on 29th May 1849, a few days after he and Ashley had led a deputation to the Home Secretary in defence of Fielden's Act of 1847. He was described in the *Annual Register* as 'essentially the advocate of the labouring classes . . . A member of the legislature, he was still in all his recollections and predilections a member of the labouring multitude'. Many thousands of that multitude followed him sorrowing to his grave in Todmorden Unitarian Chapel yard. His brothers James and Thomas, and his sons Samuel, John and Joshua, carried on his public work and organised 'Fielden Societies' to defend the Ten Hours Act.

Chartism in the upper Calder Valley did not fade out with the failure of the 1848 petition. It remained an active force for another ten years, before yielding place to new movements and crusades in which Chartist veterans played a prominent part. The years 1848-9 may be taken, however, as the end of an epoch in local history. They saw, as well as the death of John Fielden, the last occasion on which the magistrates nervously watched the massed ranks of the politically-conscious workers on the move and wondered how many of them possessed guns, and whether they would use them.

The underlying causes of the continuity and strength of working class radicalism in upper Calderdale lie deep in the history of a people struggling with a challenging, sometimes hostile, environment. What stands out in the 'Age of Agitation' is the combination of a spirit of independence and very strong group loyalties. Hundreds of meetings were held during this period, to sustain this sense of solidarity and to provide mutual education in political thought. Their ideology was one-sided and had obvious defects – it was backward-looking and it over-estimated the power of governments to control economic affairs – but it was no more distorted or subjective than the prevailing economic theories which included, for example, the idea that an employer and an individual workman had equal bargaining power. Nor was the ideology reduced to a few simple slogans, except for the manufacture of banners. Whenever an address had to be written, or a poster prepared, there was someone available to draw it up in lucid, and occasionally eloquent, English. This massive work of political education, and training in what the Co-operative movement later called 'the art of association', may be placed on the scale of positive achievements, along with factory reform and the resistance to the new poor law, to balance the failure to protect the out-worker and gain the charter.

13

Economic Life Between 1836 and 1914

Industrial Development, 1836-61

The first phase of the Industrial Revolution in the upper Calder Valley, dominated by the development of spinning mills, had been closely associated with improvements in transport. The turnpike road and especially the canal had opened up the valley to through traffic and cut transport costs. Cheap canal-borne coal encouraged the adoption of steam power.

The first trans-Pennine railway followed the same route as the Rochdale Canal. The Manchester and Leeds Railway, authorised by Act of Parliament in 1836, took a roundabout route between the two towns via the Calder Valley to Normanton, from where it had running rights over the ten miles of the York and North Midlands line to Leeds. The largest engineering work was the Summit Tunnel, 2,885 yards in length. The narrowness of the Walsden and Calder valleys, already accommodating the turnpike road and canal, made other tunnels necessary, the longest at Sowerby Bridge being 657 yards. Several viaducts were needed, the most dramatic one striding across the town of Todmorden fifty-five feet above street level.

The whole sixty miles of line opened on the 1st March 1841. The passenger trains took between 2 hours 45 minutes and 3 hours 20 minutes to make the journey between Leeds and Manchester. Travel was initially expensive, a second class return ticket between the two termini costing £1. Goods traffic grew steadily as the economy recovered from the depression of the early forties, from 196,000 tons in 1841-2 to 380,000 in 1843-4. In 1846-7 the Manchester and Leeds joined with several smaller companies to form the Lancashire and Yorkshire Railway.[1]

Halifax had been promised a link to the Manchester and Leeds Railway by 1839, but it was not until 1844 that a branch line was opened from North Dean station, later re-named Greetland, to Shaw Syke (the present goods depot). It was single track only until 1869. In 1850 better connections were provided for Halifax with lines to Sowerby Bridge in one direction and Low Moor in the other, the latter soon extended to Bradford. The completion in 1857 of a line from Low Moor to Leeds cut the distance from Manchester and upper Calderdale to Leeds by twelve miles.[2]

A projected line from Todmorden to Burnley was surveyed in 1841, when the main Calder Valley line was about to open. The surveyor, Henry Clarkson, described how, as he was trying to list the occupiers of houses adjoining the proposed line, 'a great, rough-looking woman' would admit to being the wife of 'Bill o' Jacks' or 'Tom o' Dicks', but would disclaim all knowledge of her 'proper' married surname.

The line was eventually built as far as Burnley between 1845 and 1849, and connected to the Colne-Preston line a year later. It was very much a mountain railway, with the spectacular North Wood viaduct at Lydgate harmonising with the rugged

Railway lines at Todmorden, from the south; the Burnley branch is in the foreground. The town hall is beyond the railway arch in the town centre.

scenery. The gradients on both sides of the summit at Copy Pit were steep, the most severe being 1 in 65 on the three mile climb north from Stansfield Hall. Tunnels were driven at Kitson Wood, Holme and Towneley. Originally single track, the line was doubled in 1859-60.[3]

The other local branch line was not, like the Burnley branch, a link in an extensive system, but was one of the many spurs pushed into the Pennines by the Lancashire and Yorkshire Railway. It was hoped that these would become 'feeders', bringing local traffic on to the main line, but most of them turned out to be 'suckers', expensive (per mile) to build and never recovering their costs. A Ryburn Valley branch had been projected as early as 1845, but the four mile line from Sowerby Bridge to Ripponden was not opened until 1878. It was extended to Rishworth in 1881.[4]

The development of cheap excursions and holiday travel widened the horizons of many people in upper Calderdale. The Burnley branch made the Isle of Man, via Fleetwood, relatively accessible, but Blackpool became the most popular destination. Excursionists also came into the upper Calder Valley, especially to visit Hardcastle Crags. On Whit Friday 1896 over 8,000 tickets were collected at Hebden Bridge station from people visiting the Crags. Todmorden's busiest day was probably Saturday the 22nd August 1896, when 12,000 people arrived by train to celebrate the granting of the town's charter.[5]

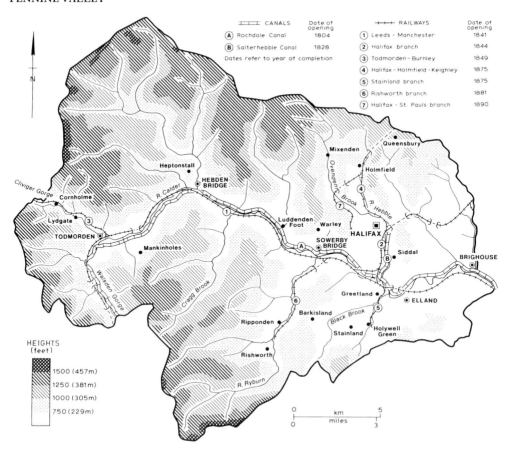

CANALS	Date of opening		RAILWAYS	Date of opening
(A) Rochdale Canal	1804		(1) Leeds – Manchester	1841
(B) Salterhebble Canal	1828		(2) Halifax branch	1844
Dates refer to year of completion			(3) Todmorden – Burnley	1849
			(4) Halifax – Holmfield – Keighley	1875
			(5) Stainland branch	1875
			(6) Rishworth branch	1881
			(7) Halifax – St. Pauls branch	1890

HEIGHTS
(feet)

1500 (457m)
1250 (381m)
1000 (305m)
750 (229m)

Canal and railway development in upper Calderdale.

Although great public events and throngs of excursionists made the headlines in local railway history, the benefits to industry were of much greater economic and social significance. For the transport of coal, where speed was not important, the canal was still competitive, but for the movement of textile materials in different stages of production, the railways offered relatively speedy transport through a network which honeycombed the industrial districts of East and South Lancashire and the West Riding. This facility encouraged the trend towards greater local specialisation within this textile region, a feature of the middle and late nineteenth century. Several of the larger enterprises, including Fielden Brothers at Todmorden, Whitworths at Cooper House and Boy Mills at Luddenden Foot, and Hollings Mill at Sowerby Bridge had their own sidings, as did Wilsons' bobbin mill near Todmorden and the Sowerby Bridge Co-operative Flour Mill.[6]

The rapid growth of the local textile industry in 1833-6 was part of a general economic expansion which culminated in the boom of 1836. The economy in the nineteenth century was subject to cyclical fluctuations, and the boom of 1836 was followed by a depression in 1837 and early 1838. A partial recovery over the next twelve to eighteen months gave way to a severe and prolonged depression lasting from late 1839 to 1843, the period known as the 'hungry forties'. A contributory factor was a run of bad or poor harvests from 1836 to 1841, which also meant higher food prices and increased distress to workers who were unemployed or on short time.

Although there were a few failures, the local textile firms weathered the depression of 1837-8 reasonably well. In 1839-43, however, at least seventeen bankruptcies occurred in the textile and ancillary trades, in addition to three corn mill failures. Some of the victims were 'small masters' employing worsted handloom weavers, who were up against the competition of power looms as well as the poor state of trade, but they included two firms prominent in cotton spinning since the 1790s. Crossleys of Knowlwood Mill went bankrupt in 1840, and three years later Buckleys of Ridgefoot Mill, the pioneers of 'gambroons', suffered a similar fate.[7]

Recovery began in 1843, with the cotton industry leading the way. In 1844 Fieldens extended the Waterside Mill complex to the opposite side of the Rochdale road. After the boom associated with the 'railway mania' of 1844-5, the cotton industry was affected by short-time working from early 1847, and 1848 was a poor year for the textile trades as a whole. The hardest hit were those handloom weavers who were in direct competition with power looms. This depression was, however, neither as severe nor as prolonged as that of the 'hungry forties'.

The period from 1850 to 1861 was generally, although not uniformly, prosperous. It saw a considerable expansion of factory industry in the upper Calder Valley. Twenty-eight new mills (including power-loom weaving sheds) were definitely built during these twelve years; 21 more were first recorded, a few of which could be earlier in date; and 9 mills were extended or provided with additional power. Most of these enterprises were concerned with cotton weaving, although the woollen and worsted trades also contributed towards the expansion.[8]

The 1851 census returns provide the first detailed picture of the occupations of local people.[9] The statistics from three townships, Sowerby, Warley and Stansfield, are unreliable in the main, because of a failure to distinguish between handloom and power-loom weavers, and the description of people as 'factory operatives' without any details of the type of factory. The other six townships contained 6,282 textile factory workers, about three-quarters of them in cotton. The balance of the 1,900 handloom weavers was quite different – approximately 1,300 worsted, including worsted/cotton

The railway viaduct at Lydgate on the Burnley branch.

mixtures, 400 cotton, 150 wool and 50 others including silk and carpets. Over 500 hand-woolcombers prepared wool for worsted spinning. Of the excluded townships, Stansfield was concerned mainly with cotton, but had some worsted weavers and a few silk weavers; Warley mainly with worsted; and Sowerby with wool. The net effect of their exclusion has been to understate the proportions of woollen spinners and weavers, and woolcombers.

Within the valley there were striking contrasts. The Todmorden area was nearly all cotton and factories. Less than 3% of the working population (excluding female domestics) of Langfield and Todmorden with Walsden were handloom weavers or hand-woolcombers. The comparable figure for Midgley, Wadsworth and Erringden was 31%. In Wadsworth those working at these two hand processes outnumbered the factory workers. Sixty years after the establishment of the first worsted spinning mills in upper Calderdale, the combing and weaving stages were still carried on mainly by hand.

In the area between Hebden Bridge and Sowerby Bridge there was another marked contrast, between the valley-bottom towns and villages, peopled mainly by factory workers and their families, and the upland settlements in which most houses had at least one handloom weaver or hand comber. However, only about a quarter of these households were dependent upon a single craft. Taking the six well-documented townships together, of 1,061 households containing at least one handloom weaver, 707 had one or more members working in textile mills, and 172 combined weaving with farming or both farming and mill work.

The census returns throw some light on a minor branch of textiles in the valley – silk spinning. The major concern was Binns Brothers, who were operating in the Sowerby Bridge area in the 1820s and moved later to three mills at Mytholm/Eaves Bottom on Colden Water. These mills, originally developed by King and partners for cotton spinning, were driven entirely by water until silk processing ceased there in the 1860s. Mules were used for spinning the silk, and about 200 people were employed in the 1850s.

The picture revealed by the 1851 census, of hand workers in wool combing and worsted and woollen weaving holding their own in numbers although not in earnings, was transformed during the 1850s. The trade of hand combing was virtually extinguished. Fifty years of experiment, beginning with Cartwright's 'Big Ben' in 1790, had failed to produce a successful combing machine. The traditional defences of the handcombing craft, once tightly-knit and well-paid, had, however, been undermined by the sheer growth in numbers necessitated by the expansion of worsted spinning. Combers were easily recruited from the ranks of youths turned out of spinning mills at the age of eighteen. The combers' union in Bradford was broken in 1825 by a long and unsuccessful strike. An effective trade union organisation survived for a time in the upper Calder Valley, and worsted spinning mills in Luddenden Dean told the Factories Inquiry Commission in 1833 that they had been forced by a combers' strike to give higher wages.[10]

In 1845 Samuel Cunliffe Lister at last developed a successful combing machine. It quickly became dominant in the Bradford area but was not immediately adopted in Halifax and upper Calderdale, partly because Lister charged high licence fees but also because handcombers' wages had fallen to a low level.[11] In 1851 only one worsted spinner in upper Calderdale, Robert Whitworth and Company of Cooper House Mill, Luddenden Foot, had definitely adopted machine combing. Ten years later there were few handcombers left. In Crimsworth Dean, for example, their numbers fell from 84 to 3.

In the same decade the number of handloom weavers in Wadsworth fell by three-quarters, and the workforce in cotton mills in the same area rose from 465 to 1,100. Many former worsted handloom weavers were now employed in cotton power-loom sheds, and the worsted trade had almost disappeared from the area west of Mytholmroyd. In the 1850s the power loom triumphed in worsted, and by the 1860s an efficient woollen power loom was in general use. At this time handloom weavers in general were used as a reserve army of labour for boom periods. When trade was slack they were laid off first, and the employers left their power looms running as long as possible to recover their capital investment. By the time of the 1871 census there were few woollen handloom weavers and hardly any in the other branches.

The victory of the factory system which was apparent by the 1850s, and the increasing amounts of capital needed in most branches of textiles, made it difficult for an intelligent and industrious worker to set his foot on the ladder of material success by becoming a small master. However, the greater prosperity experienced after about 1850, through better trade conditions in textiles and a fall in the cost of living, increased the possibility of working class families saving modest sums of money, particularly during the phase of the family cycle when all, or most, of the children were earning. Co-operative society dividends, savings banks and the strong local temperance movement were other positive factors. These savings could be mobilised collectively through joint-stock companies, or on a family basis through the room-and-power system.

Lee Mills, Hebden Bridge.

Legislation in 1855-62 gave the small investors the protection of limited liability. Between 1854 and 1861 ten joint-stock companies were formed, all in cotton. Most engaged in both spinning and weaving, the remainder in weaving only. Their nominal capital ranged between £5,000 and £70,000, and the shares could be bought by instalments, either by fixed monthly payments or by answering 'calls' when more capital was needed. The £70,000 capital of the Derdale Cotton and Commercial Company, set up early in 1861 to build a spinning mill, weaving shed and workers' cottages at the eastern end of Todmorden, was issued in £10 shares. They could be bought for a down-payment of 2s 6d and a minimum monthly contribution of 5s.

Small-scale investment could not have been made easier, but the system was not without its drawbacks. It took over three years for a share to be fully paid up through the minimum instalments, and as it was usual for only part of the nominal shareholding to be subscribed in the early days of these companies, there was often a shortage of money to pay for the building and development work. Secondly, if a shareholder's circumstances changed and he could not meet a call, he was still liable to the extent of the full cost of the share, and at best would probably lose his shares and the money already paid for them.[12]

Industrial development and modern housing in the valley bottom at Sowerby Bridge, overlooked by older houses on the terraces above.

The pioneer of the room-and-power system seems to have been William Clegg, a Todmorden shuttle maker. He began to build Vale Mill, in Stansfield Road, Todmorden, in 1854, 'because of the clamour in the district for room and power from people who had saved a little money and aspired to become manufacturers in a small way'. The practice of renting part of a mill building and a share of its power had been known for some decades, but the new system involved the building or conversion of mills specifically for this purpose. The owner provided space, engine power and shafting, and the tenant put in the production machinery, nearly always power looms. With a small outlay an ambitious weaver or overlooker could start off with a dozen second-hand looms, using family labour. If the enterprise failed, the family could return to its previous occupations, disappointed but not humiliated.

At least six more room-and-power sheds were built in the 1850s in the Todmorden/Cornholme area. Most of the entrepreneurs responsible were engaged in trades ancillary to textiles, eg bobbin making and warp sizing. Room-and-power ventures lower down the valley included Hanging Royd shed, Hebden Bridge (three occupiers in 1861) and Sowerby Bridge Mill (nine occupiers in 1862). Some of the joint-stock companies mentioned above went into the room-and-power business.[13]

The boom in the cotton trade in 1859-60, which created something of a joint-stock 'fever' in upper Calderdale, had been brought about by a particularly favourable combination of circumstances: an upturn in the British economy; a surge in exports to the Far East following the end of the Indian Mutiny and the war in China; and a plentiful supply of cheap cotton resulting from the extension of the plantations in the southern states of USA. Warning voices were raised locally about a reckless expansion out-running the supply of cotton. The real dangers at the time were over-production and over-stretched credit, but within a short time a mistaken forecast was turned into a tragically correct one.[14]

From the Cotton Famine to the 'Great Depression'

Before the outbreak of the American Civil War in April 1861, the southern states of USA supplied eighty per cent of the cotton used in Lancashire and the adjoining counties. The naval forces of the Union imposed a blockade, which was never completely successful – in four years, blockade runners brought out cotton equivalent to six months' British consumption on the eve of the war – but caused supplies to dry up from October 1861 onwards. By January 1862 most of the cotton mills in upper Calderdale were on short time and some were completely stopped. Soon afterwards three firms went bankrupt.[15]

The main source of additional cotton supplies was India, but much of it was of poor quality, and the very short staple cotton from the Surat district was difficult to work. 'Surat' became synonymous in the minds of the cotton operatives with the miseries caused by the cotton famine. Wild fluctuations in the price of raw cotton provided another problem for the manufacturers.

By September 1862, of the 1,790 people employed in cotton manufacture in Hebden Bridge, 942 were wholly unemployed and only 278 were working full-time. Some of the short-time working was, in effect, a welfare provision made by the employers. In the Todmorden area, Fieldens and Ormerods were at times paying for three days work a week when there was little or nothing to do. Many cotton workers and their families were at starvation level.[16]

The Todmorden Poor Law Union's bill for outdoor relief for the first half of November 1862 was £668, compared with £130 for the corresponding period in the previous year. Some distressed workers were reluctant to accept poor relief. In any case the board of guardian scales, at 6d to 1s per head per week, were too low. Relief committees were set up in Todmorden, Hebden Bridge, Luddenden, Sowerby Bridge and Halifax. They raised money locally, and also received allocations from funds set up nationally, in Australia and in the northern states of USA. In November 1862 the Todmorden committee assisted 560 people on outdoor poor relief with supplementary allocations of clothing and coal, and provided another 1,475 people with help, mainly in kind – flour, meal, coal, blankets, etc. In March 1863 the Halifax committee reported that it had raised to date £6,177. To find useful occupations for unemployed workers, educational activities were developed, funded mainly by relief committees and employers. They included sewing classes for women and girls, adult schools and full-time schooling for children under thirteen who would normally be attending half-time.[17]

Trade picked up in the spring of 1863, partly because of an improved supply of raw cotton. Several mills in Sowerby Bridge which had been closed, two of them for over a year, resumed work and the Sowerby Bridge Relief Committee was able to suspend

Oats Royd Mill, Luddenden, in its rural setting.

Oats Royd Mill: the weaving shed, 1971.

its distribution in April 1863. Woollen and worsted mills and ironfounders at the Sowerby Bridge end of the upper Calder Valley were busy during the summer, and in September all of the cotton mills in the same area were running full time. Conditions were by no means as good in Todmorden, which was more heavily dependent on the cotton trade. In early June 1863 only 2,254 out of 9,752 cotton workers in the Todmorden area were working full-time; 4,780 were on short-time, mainly three days a week; and 2,718 were wholly unemployed. However, the latter figure had fallen by nearly 900 in the previous month. As the worst of the distress was thought to be over, the relief committees reduced or suspended their activities.[18]

The main problems of 1864-5 were not the volume of cotton supplies, but the unstable pattern of the trade and a sharp narrowing of the gap between the average price of raw cotton and the price of cotton cloth. Fieldens told their agents in August 1864: 'We cannot dispose of our goods at anything like a price that will cover costs with present prices of cotton'. The underlying problem was that the cotton industry had not removed the excess capacity created by the boom which preceded the American Civil War. As John Kelly explains in his paper, 'The end of the Famine', this was because of the 'sophisticated network of credit allowing unprofitable manufacturers to stay in business'.[19]

An employment census taken in Sowerby Bridge in 1865 shows why the town had suffered less from the cotton famine than Hebden Bridge or Todmorden. Sixty-three per cent of the workforce was employed in textile mills, but most of these were in woollens or worsted:

woollens	1,918	ironworking	727
worsted	992	railway	85
cotton	721	corn milling	58
dyeing	297	building	270
chemicals	119	small trades, shops etc	532
		Total	*5,719*

The ironworking industry was concerned mainly with supplying equipment to the textile industry, on the prosperity of which depended also the livelihood of those in the building and retail trades.[20]

By the late winter of 1867-8 the local textile industry, including cotton, had returned to normal conditions. But 'normal' included an alternation of booms and slumps. A boom in 1873-4 boosted profits but also caused a wave of strikes in pursuit of pay increases, because one feature of the boom was a sharp rise in the price of food and other necessities. A downturn in the economy from 1876 brought the usual response of the textile industry – extended holidays (unpaid) and short-time working rather than complete closure. During this period industrial disputes centred on resistance to wage reductions, but none of the strikes was successful. At Oats Royd Mill, for example, the workers struck in 1878 against a wage cut of ten per cent. The mills reopened later at the reduced rates, with a promise to the workers of an increase as soon as trade improved.[21]

Trade did not improve, however. The economy as a whole was severely depressed in 1879 – which was also a ruinous year for arable farmers because of atrocious weather – ushering in the period of two decades known as the 'Great Depression'. During these years industry experienced the familiar ups and downs, but foreign competition became fiercer, profit margins were reduced and unemployment increased. In August 1879, 19 mills in Todmorden and Hebden Bridge were stopped altogether, 11 were working three days a week, 21 four days, and 3 five days. Between 1877 and 1882 nineteen local firms went bankrupt.[22]

The Ancillary Trades

The growth of a varied textile industry in upper Calderdale generated a demand for a wide range of supplies and services.[23] Three of the trades, fulling, dyeing and sizing, were part of the processes of textile manufacture. The others supplied equipment and materials for the industry.

Fulling, the process of shrinking and felting cloth, was applied only to woollens. At least thirteen firms engaged in this trade in the nineteenth century are recorded, all of them in the Sowerby Bridge/Luddenden Foot area where the woollen mills were concentrated. Eighty-one firms of dyers and finishers have been identified, but many of them had only four or five workers, and nearly half are recorded as being in business for no more than five years. The major development of dyeing in Hebden Bridge, associated with the rapid expansion of fustians and ready-made clothing, is described later. Lower down the valley, one of the outstanding firms was William Edleston and Company of Asquith Bottom Dyeworks, Sowerby Bridge, established in the 1820s.

The firm started manufacturing dyes in 1848, and made four extensions to the premises between 1853 and 1875. At the latter period they were dyeing and finishing between 20-30,000 pieces a year, mainly worsted and alpaca.[24]

Cotton warps required sizing, with a mixture of flour and china clay, to strengthen them for the weaving process. Fifteen firms in this business in Todmorden are recorded in directories. In 1868 Gledhill, Ashworth and Co employed twenty-four workers and sized 12,000,000 lbs of cotton warps that year.[25]

A few woollen card or comb makers were in business locally, the most important being James Walton of Sowerby Bridge Mills, who in 1834 invented a series of machines for raising the pile on woollen fabrics by means of wire cards in place of vegetable teazles. In the same year he patented the application of india rubber to the surface of the foundation of wire cards, which secured a greater elasticity and durability.[26]

The beginnings of the local textile engineering industry have been described in Chapter 10. Amongst the leading firms were Bates of Sowerby Bridge, later known as Pollit and Wigzell, whose main product was steam engines; Jacksons of Walsden, machine makers and millwrights; and Lord Brothers of Todmorden, who concentrated on the manufacture of textile machinery. An outstanding feature of Lord Brothers' activities in the 1850s and 60s was the large number of inventions and improvements which they patented. They related mainly to opening, cleaning and blowing machinery; drawing, spinning and doubling frames; and the design of looms. Twelve patents were registered in 1861-5, some of them apparently intended to deal with the technical problems of processing Indian cotton.

Pudsey Bobbin Mill.

Some cotton manufacturers also registered patents, eg for improvements to self-acting mules. The proliferation of local patents is historically important for two reasons. It underlines the point already made that invention was a cumulative process, and not a once-for-all affair. Secondly it demonstrates the current spirit of enterprise which showed itself in a constant search for small improvements, for quicker, cheaper or more reliable processes of manufacture.[27]

The larger engineering firms kept local foundries and machine shops busy making parts for them. One such firm, John Marland and Sons of Sun Vale Works, moved into power loom and other textile machinery production on their own account.[28] There were also many firms, mainly small, making equipment and spare parts for textiles, including reeds and healds, shuttles, spindles and flyers, and pickers, ie the leather straps which propelled the shuttle across the loom.

The largest in scale of the ancillary trades was bobbin making. As many as ten bobbins were needed for every spindle – the leading firm in spinning, Fielden Brothers, had 100,000 spindles in the late nineteenth century – and the bobbins needed replacement about once a year. The Lake District was a major centre of bobbin production, but upper Calderdale seems to have been able to meet its own needs. The main concentration of bobbin firms was found in the Cornholme area, and the largest was founded in 1823 by Lawrence Wilson. In 1830 he built Cornholme Mills, where 200 men were said to be out of work in 1859 as the result of a fire. At one stage Wilsons had their own saw mill at Athlone in Ireland, and later their own ships to carry wood from Ireland. In 1897 the enterprise was operating as a limited company with a capital of £120,000.[29]

Cornholme and Wilson Brothers bobbin works in 1905.

The extensive use of leather in textile mills, for belting, rollers and pickers, sustained a local tanning industry. Fifteen tanners and fellmongers (dealers in skins) are recorded in the upper Calder Valley at this time. The largest known tanneries were at Ellenroyd, Midgley (60 tanpits), Hoyle Green, Warley (46) and Hollings Mill Lane, Sowerby Bridge (30 tanpits, 9 limepits and 2 large soak pits). In the mid-nineteenth century, tanning took about fifteen months to complete, by long-established methods. Later technical developments in both chemical and mechanical processes more than halved the tanning time, and increased the optimum scale of operations. What had once been the most widely distributed of all English industries became concentrated into a relatively small number of specialist centres. The tanners of the upper Calder Valley could not compete, and only three local firms are recorded after the 1870s.

Another ancillary industry, which developed out of the needs of the dyeing processes, was the supply and manufacture of chemicals. Fourteen chemical manufacturers and drysalters (suppliers of dyestuffs) are recorded between the 1790s and the 1880s. William Norris, in business in Halifax since the 1790s, built Calder Chemical Works near Mearclough Bottom about 1815. The business continued in the same family until the twentieth century. There were several other enterprises in the Sowerby Bridge area, at Bank Ware Mill, Centre Mills and Mearclough Mills. Todmorden also had several chemical businesses.[30]

Agriculture

If a Calderdale man of the mid-eighteenth century had been allowed to revisit the valley a hundred years later, he would have marvelled at the revolution in transport, the industrial innovations and the bustling life of the valley-bottom towns; but he would have found a much more familiar landscape on the terraces and hillsides above the main valley. Some moorland had been enclosed by Act of Parliament, but this was just the culmination of a process of organised intaking which had been carried on for several centuries.

At the time of the 1851 census, about one in eight of the families in the upper Calder Valley had some involvement with farming. In the six townships analysed in detail earlier in this chapter (Midgley, Wadsworth, Heptonstall, Erringden, Langfield, Todmorden with Walsden), 612 households included farmers or farm-workers. Just over a quarter were dependent upon farming alone. The remainder combined farming with industrial activities, with more family members working in textile mills than at handloom weaving or hand combing.

For most farms the 1851 census gave the acreage. Of the 155 farms in Wadsworth, only 5 had more than 100 acres, 25 had fewer than 10 acres, and the average was just over 20, plus access to moorland grazing in some cases. The agricultural returns available from 1866 give a fuller picture of local farming.[31] In 1866, Wadsworth had only 10 acres of arable (8 oats, $1\frac{1}{3}$ potatoes, $\frac{1}{4}$ peas) out of 2,611 acres of enclosed land. Arable cultivation was relatively more important lower down the valley, but Sowerby had only 196 acres of arable (129 oats, the rest mainly root crops) out of almost 3,000 enclosed acres.

With arable cultivation on such a small scale, the first wave of agricultural depression, which began in the late 1870s, had only a marginal impact locally. The decline in oats cultivation accelerated, and the only arable crops in Wadsworth in 1880 were $\frac{1}{4}$ acre of rye and $\frac{3}{4}$ acre of potatoes. In Sowerby the arable acreage fell from

196 in 1866 to 34¼ (26¼ oats, 8 roots) in 1880. Warley township had 81¼ acres of arable in 1866 (nearly all oats), but by 1900 only 5½ acres were still under cultivation.

In the second phase of the agricultural depression, from the mid-1880s, the importation of wool and refrigerated meat, especially from Australia and Argentina, hit the local sheep farmers, but by way of compensation the milk producers had the benefit of cheaper feeding stuffs to supplement their own hay and pasture. The growth of the valley-bottom towns provided an expanding market for dairy farmers, who delivered their own milk in their one-horse traps, a familiar feature of the local scene right up to the Second World War. Cow-keepers who had no horse set off with churns strapped to their backs. The agricultural statistics show a steady increase thoughout the late nineteenth century in the number of cattle kept in the upper Calder Valley, and in the ratio of milk cows to other cattle. A striking feature of the late nineteenth century scene was the number of farms without any working horses; eg Warley with 176 returns in 1880 had only 43 working horses. Most of the farmers with 10-15 acres were managing without any horse power.

Large flocks of sheep were kept on only a few high-lying farms. Eight Wadsworth farms employed shepherds in 1851, all located on the moor edge in places such as Walshaw, Widdup, Alcomden and Baitings. The local sheep breeds were gradually improved during the second half of the nineteenth century, by the careful selection of rams. The aim was to produce a hardy but productive sheep, which did well on poor pastures and could survive severe weather. By the time W B Crump wrote *The Little Hill Farm* in 1938 the main local breeds were the Lonk and the Derbyshire Gritstone, as they are today.

There was some increase in the previously small scale of commercial pig rearing in the late nineteenth century. The returns from Sowerby show 202 pigs in 1866, 433 in 1880 and 895 in 1894. The rate of increase in the other townships was a little less.

The numerous small farms of the Calder Valley hillsides were never viable solely as farming units. Their survival depended upon the other, and usually stronger, side of the dual economy – cottage or factory industry. With the decline of handloom weaving and hand combing, the dual economy came to depend more and more on the availability of mill work for some members of the household. As the small mills in the tributary valleys gradually went out of business through the competition of the larger, more efficient firms, dual-economy farming was also undermined.

Crump noted that the last of the intakes from the moors were made in the 1860s. Soon afterwards the retreat from the moorland margins began. In 1850-5 the head of Luddenden Dean had thirty-one farms, mainly small, as well as about 100 people living in twenty-three cottages, making a total estimated population of about 280. In 1905 all of the cottages were uninhabited; some had been demolished and others were in ruins. Ten of the farmsteads were empty, and the population had fallen to ninety-six.

In 1937 local historian H W Harwood made another survey of the head of Luddenden Dean. Fifteen farms were still occupied and the population had fallen to seventy-one. At Upper Saltonstall, formerly a hamlet of several families, only Great House was still inhabited.[32]

The Changing Industrial Scene 1870-1914

The upper Calder Valley continued to be a transitional zone between Lancashire cotton and Yorkshire woollens and worsted. Cotton was dominant in Todmorden, and fustian

The sewing department at Nutclough Mill.

weaving had become established alongside cotton spinning in and around Hebden Bridge. Lower down the valley a rich variety of cloths was produced – worsted, woollens, cottons and several mixed fabrics.

The process of industrial evolution is well illustrated by the rise of a new industry in and around Hebden Bridge. During the middle years of the nineteenth century the remnants of the worsted trade here died out, leaving three tiers of textile activity – cotton spinning, fustian weaving (both factory processes), and fustian dyeing and finishing. Fustian cutting remained a hand process until the late 1890s. The pile on corduroy and similar ribbed cloths was cut with a knife, the only other equipment needed being a frame to hold the pieces in position. With virtually no capital involved, the work was done at home by cutters working for small masters who operated on commission for merchants and other dealers. There was hardly any social distinction between 'master' and 'worker'.

The development by Isaac Singer in 1851 of the first successful sewing machine, and subsequent associated inventions, opened the door to a ready-made clothing industry. Some fustian manufacturers began to produce ready-made garments. At first it was a domestic industry, but soon power was introduced. For some years the finishers, who were hand workers, were far more numerous than the machinists. Technical development, however, was rapid. Soon garments were cut out by machines; then followed the adoption of machines for making button holes and, later, machines for sewing on buttons. As a result the industry became entirely factory-based.

Hebden Bridge had at least one firm making sewing machines, Gibsons who are recorded from 1866 to 1876, but their scale of operations was small, and this ancillary trade did not take root in the valley.

In the 1890s, 32 clothing manufacturers were recorded in Hebden Bridge, together with 1 at Pecket Well, 5 in Mytholmroyd and 4 in Todmorden. Twenty-two of these firms were also fustian manufacturers. One of the largest concerns was the Hebden Bridge Fustian Co-operative Manufacturing Society, which produced a range of fustian cloths including corduroys, twills, velveteens and moleskins (the last-named being a smooth not ribbed material). The story of the 'Fustian Co-op' is told in Chapter 14. The largest firm was probably Redman Brothers, which in 1890 employed between 600 and 700 people at Salem Mill, Hebden Bridge, turning out 15,000 fustian garments per week, and another 100 people at Vale Mill, Todmorden, making slippers.[33]

As the processes of fustian weaving and finishing and clothing manufacture expanded, the spinning side of the trade gradually died out, although some enterprises, including the Fustian Co-op, did their own 'doubling' (taking two single yarns and twisting them together). Increasing numbers of fustian pieces were brought in from other weaving centres. Local manufacturers found it profitable to expand their clothing side and buy additional fustian pieces, either finished and ready to make up, or, very often, 'in the grey' so that they could be dyed to their own orders.

These developments led in turn to a great expansion in dyeing capacity. The Hebden Bridge dyeing firms built up a considerable trade in commission work for Manchester exporters, as well as dealing with the local output. An example of a rapidly-expanding enterprise was the Crimsworth Water Dyeing Company, of Midgehole Mill, founded by James Worrall who bought the mill for £9,700 in 1861. The firm employed about fifty workers in 1868, and the number had doubled by 1872.[34]

At first the local clothing firms dealt exclusively with ready-made garments, but later a large made-to-measure trade developed. Thousands of garments were made to order every week and sent off by post or on the railways. Some firms expanded into cotton fabrics other than fustians for the ready-made trade. Some of the larger producers built up a substantial trade with wholesale houses in London and other big cities, and also with the multiple stores which were becoming increasingly important in retailing. The large export trade, especially to South Africa but also including South America, Australia and other markets, was handled almost exclusively by London agents working on commission.

In the late 1890s, machines which cut the pile on cords in an effective manner were at last developed. Hundreds of hand cutters were displaced, and with them went the small masters who had employed them. The cutting machines were set up on the premises of the dyeing and finishing firms – Worralls being one of the first to use them – and there was no longer any branch of the fustian/clothing trade which did not require a considerable amount of capital. It is a striking illustration of the uneven character of technical progress in textiles that the introduction of cropping frames in the woollen trade provoked the Luddite disturbances in 1812, but the corresponding invention in fustian cutting did not succeed until the end of the century.

By about 1900 Hebden Bridge, although not the main centre for the weaving of fustians, had become the leading town in Britain for the finishing trade and the making

Sam Moore, c1914, by the display cabinet which Nutclough Mill used to advertise
their goods at trade fairs.

of fustian clothing. The biggest merchant-finishers and clothing manufacturers in the
trade were located in Hebden Bridge.

Sam Moore, who was a traveller for the Fustian Co-operative, surveyed the problems
of the fustian/clothing trade in a long paper, the substance of which appeared as articles
in the *Economic Journal* in 1911 and 1913. Export growth had slowed, and the home
demand was fairly static. Fustians were seen essentially as hard-wearing working
clothes, and with a gradual rise in living standards they were going out of favour with
the skilled worker in the towns. Recently they had suffered competition from dungaree
overalls, a trade which grew out of shirt making, used lighter machinery and probably
paid lower wages. Moore argued that fustians should move up-market, especially into
'high-class corduroys for ladies' costumes'.

Todmorden, only four miles from Hebden Bridge, was only marginally affected by
the growth of the clothing industry, as a few firms expanded into the neighbouring
town because of a local shortage of plant or labour. It remained a cotton spinning and
weaving centre, with the largest firms engaged in both stages. The leading enterprise

was, of course, Fielden Brothers Ltd of Waterside and Lumbutts Mills, who had about 100,000 mule spindles in the 1890s. The other large firms, on the spinning side, were Ormerods with 44,000 mule spindles, Maden and Hoyle with 30,000, and S and A Barker Ltd, listed in textile directories as having 25,000 mule spindles in 1893 and 30,000 in 1897. Barkers were apparently in the spinning business only, but the other firms also had weaving sheds. By 1895 B Hoyle had become the sole owner of Maden and Hoyle, and in the years 1905-13 the firm is credited with 60,000 mule spindles. Ormerods went out of business at some time between 1901 and 1905.[35]

In the 1890s and the first decade of the twentieth century, ring spinning began to replace mule spinning. Unlike the mule, the ring spinning frame had no moving carriage. It was, in fact, similar in principle to the throstle or roller frame described in Chapter 10, except that in place of the flyer the revolving part was a little hook of steel, called the traveller, which moved around a metal ring surrounding the spindle and bobbin. The great advantage of the cotton ring frame was its speed – around 8,000 revolutions per minute, depending upon the type and thickness of the yarn. It was particularly good at producing heavier yarns with a hard twist, but could be adapted for a wide range of yarns.

The ring spinning frame was an American invention, dating from 1831-2. It was not given a serious trial in England until the 1870s, and was accepted only gradually in face of doubts about the quality of its yarns. The change from mule spinning to ring spinning meant the displacement of highly-skilled men workers by machine minders who were normally women or girls. The changeover can be traced through the descriptions of local firms given in Worrall's *Directories of Cotton Spinners and Manufacturers*. W Dugdale, a spinning and weaving firm, had the following:

	mule spindles	ring spindles
1893-1901	8,000	nil
1905	5,000	11,000
1909	3,000	13,000
1913	nil	13,000

W Barker Ltd (also a weaving firm) had 8,000 mule spindles in 1901 and 8,000 ring spindles in 1905-13. Fieldens changed over between 1901, when they had 100,000 mule spindles, and 1905 when the figures were 94,000 ring and 6,000 mule. The firm of W Greenwood seems to have changed back again, being credited with 9,000 mule spindles in 1897, 7,000 ring and 3,000 mule in 1901 and 1905, but 11,000 mule in 1909 and 1913.[36]

Joshua Holden, in his *Short History of Todmorden*, published in 1912, described Fieldens as being still the leading local cotton firm, with 100,000 spindles and 1,600 looms. Caleb Hoyle of Derdale and Walsden had 60,000 spindles (the type is not specified) and 1,600 looms, and corresponding figures from Luke Barker and Sons were 7,500 and 1,406. Joshua Smith of Cornholme was a weaving-only enterprise with 1,760 looms. There were also many smaller weaving concerns, as well as several room-and-power sheds.[37]

On the eve of the First World War, water power made a diminished but still useful contribution to industry in upper Calderdale. Some of the wheels had been replaced by turbines, as at Calverts Mill, Wainstalls. They were more efficient and allowed for better speed control of the main drive to the mill machinery. At Old Sowerby Bridge Mill, however, water wheels still provided the only power; there was no steam engine.

Both the Calder and Ryburn rivers were harnessed, through four mill races, to drive four wheels, of about 15 to 16 feet in diameter, in parallel. The last wheel stopped in 1942.[38]

This chapter ends as it began, with developments in transport. In 1914 most goods were still carried on the close network of railways which covered the industrial West Riding and the neighbouring areas of Lancashire. Until late in the nineteenth century the same lines had a monopoly of all but the most local of passenger traffic, for which horse buses were used. In 1900 Halifax station handled about 140 passenger trains each weekday. Leeds had steam trams as early as 1880, but the steep hills around Halifax delayed development there for nearly two decades. Eventually Halifax Corporation chose electric traction, which was becoming dominant. The first tramway section opened in 1897 and, during the next few years, lines were extended to Sowerby Bridge and Hebden Bridge. Todmorden Borough Council, formed in 1896, never ran a tram service, but introduced a motor bus service to Walsden and Cornholme in January 1907.[39]

14

The Age of Improvement

The 1830s and 1840s have been described as the 'Age of Agitation' for two reasons. First, they were dominated by popular campaigns: for parliamentary reform; for legislation to restrict working hours in textile mills; against the new poor law; and finally, subsuming all the earlier movements, for the People's Charter, which was intended to create a popular democracy (for men at least) through which the people's will could prevail in economic as well as political matters. Secondly, the method used in each case was agitation – through pamphlets, meetings, petitions, mass processions and rallies, and at times the threat of force – in the hope of securing, repealing or amending parliamentary legislation.

Although Chartism remained a strong force in Halifax and the upper Calder Valley during most of the 1850s, the years 1848-9 saw the effective end of the Age of Agitation. A major cause was greater economic stability and prosperity. Three good harvests in 1850-52 brought down food prices. Although the economy was still subject to marked cyclical fluctuations, the valley never again experienced (except in the very special circumstances of the cotton famine) the acute distress of the 'hungry forties'. Popular agitation had also been fuelled by the desperation of men in declining trades – wool combing and handloom weaving. Although the numbers of handloom weavers in woollens and worsted remained considerable until the late 1860s (some of them surviving by combining their craft with farming), the growth of the textile industry – particularly the cotton branch – during the 1850s caused a significant shift in the balance of employment from declining to expanding occupations.

This did not mean that the upper Calder Valley was settling contentedly into a system in which the highest aspiration for the great majority of the people was to have steady employment at adequate wages. In the first place there were still considerable numbers of small masters, eg in fustian cutting and some of the trades ancillary to textiles, whose lifestyle and social position were not very different from those of the skilled worker. Secondly the 1850s saw the birth of both the joint-stock company with large numbers of working class and lower-middle class shareholders, and the room-and-power system, which gave skilled men who had saved a little money the chance to become independent producers on a small scale within the factory system. In addition to these features of local economic life, which have been discussed in Chapter 13, there were important long-term social forces at work.

The local Chartists – that is to say, the great majority of politically-conscious working men in the valley – began to explore alternative means of realising their dreams of social reform. One of these was the establishment of consumer Co-operative societies modelled on the Rochdale Equitable Pioneers Society, started in 1844. This was not, it must be emphasised, the beginning of Co-operative trading, which had been going on for several decades. Todmorden had a society in 1832, which paid dividend in proportion to share capital, the general practice at the time. There were five pre-Rochdale societies in the Hebden Bridge area, most of them trading in a few basic commodities such as flour.[1]

The Rochdale principle was to pay interest on share capital, but distribute profits in the form of a dividend on purchases. This spread the benefits of Co-operation much more widely. Societies on this model were formed in Todmorden in 1847, Hebden Bridge in 1848 (by a group of Chartists who took over an existing Co-operative store in High Street) and Walsden in 1849. Two years later the Bridge End Equitable Progressionists Society, which served the Walsden end of the town of Todmorden, separated from the Todmorden society. The movement later spread to Heptonstall and Luddenden Foot (both founded in 1860), Blackshaw Head, Pecket Well, Mytholmroyd, Midgley, Wainstalls, Cragg Vale and Sowerby Bridge.[2]

At first the Co-operative stores opened in the evening only, staffed by volunteers, but it soon became the practice to open during the day, employing a shop man. At Bridge End in 1854 the latter was paid sixteen shillings for an eighty-six hour week – no 'Ten Hour Day' for the employees of the millworkers! In the 1850s the Bridge End dividend was usually in the range of 1s 2d-1s 6d in the £.[3]

Several young men who pioneered Rochdale-style Co-operation in upper Calderdale rose to prominence in local affairs later in life, with the result that their biographical details are well known. They were nearly all Chartists – the epithet 'an old Chartist' was worn like a battle honour at the end of the nineteenth century – brought up as Baptists or Methodists, who saw Co-operation as the centrepiece of a new social order, one built by the workers themselves from the bottom upwards. The other elements were thrift, practised through savings banks and especially friendly societies; temperance – every local town and village had a temperance society; and adult education. Joseph Greenwood, already mentioned as an observer of the Plug Riot/ Chartist marches of 1842, and Joseph Craven – both destined for key roles in the Co-operative movement – were members of a temperance friendly society, the Rechabites.[4]

Greenwood and two other young men who were active in the Hebden Bridge Temperance Society founded a new mechanics institute in Hebden Bridge in December 1854. By 1857 it had 149 members, most of whom were working men paying a subscription of twopence per week. Control of the institute remained firmly in working class hands, but there was nothing radical about the programme. The institute concentrated on 'systematic instruction in evening classes', including arithmetic, writing, grammar, elocution, vocal music, drawing and phonography (ie shorthand). The founders of the institute were able to draw not only on their recent experience of political education, but also on a strong local tradition of workmen-scholars, who included geologists, botanists and poets. The success of the Hebden Bridge venture may have helped to revive the moribund Sowerby Bridge institute, which was active again by 1858. In the following year the Todmorden institute was re-founded, mainly on the initiative of the local Unitarian minister. Other ministers, both Anglican and Nonconformist, took the lead in establishing the Luddenden Foot Mechanics Institute in 1866.[5]

Consumer Co-operation grew steadily, apart from the setback caused by the cotton famine, but those who dreamed of a 'Co-operative Commonwealth' argued that Co-operation must also extend to the workplace. In 1869 and 1870 Joseph Greenwood, then a fustian cutter who was a member of the committee of the Hebden Bridge Co-operative Society, was deeply impressed by arguments in favour of Co-operative

Nutclough Mill.

production which he heard at Co-operative Congresses. In 1870 a group of fustian cutters in Hebden Bridge formed a producer's Co-operative society, with Joseph Greenwood as secretary. One of its objectives was to educate its members 'in the causes which operate for and against them in their daily employment, and in the principles that will tend to their elevation and improvement'.

In July 1873, with the aid of a loan from the Co-operative Wholesale Society, the Fustian Co-operative bought the Nutclough estate in Hebden Bridge, which included a small four-storied mill, with a good supply of water for both the water wheel and industrial use, and a steam engine. The business already involved garment making as well as fustian cutting, and a dyeing department was added. By 1875 the operating principles of the Co-operative were clearly established. Dividends were paid both on purchases, mainly by retail Co-operative societies, and on labour, the latter one shilling per pound of wages in a good year. A fixed rate of interest was paid on capital, at first $7\frac{1}{2}\%$, reduced in the 1880s to 5%, by which time the amount of any individual shareholding was limited to £100. To quote Joseph Greenwood, for many years manager of the enterprise, the idea was 'that labour ought to hire capital', not the other way round.

After the depression of 1877-9, the Fustian Co-operative began a series of extensions to Nutclough Mill which left the original structure as no more than the kernel of a large five-storey building. In 1886 winding, doubling and weaving departments were added, and the society now dealt with the whole range of productive activities from doubling to finishing and clothing manufacture. By 1900 the workforce was nearly 400, large by upper Calderdale standards. The capital of over £28,000 was held as follows: employees £9,216; purchasing Co-operative societies £11,191; individual shareholders £8,259. The affairs of the society, including the election of the management committee, were the concern of the first two groups. The non-working shareholders had no rights of participation.[6]

A second producer Co-operative started in 1892, when an ailing 'clog iron and sundries' factory in Walsden was taken over by the newly formed Calderdale Co-operative Clog Sundries Manufacturing Society. It too paid a fixed interest on capital and a dividend on labour as well as sales. The buildings were extended in 1903, but it was never a large concern, having sixteen workers in 1914.[7]

A third kind of Co-operative society concentrated on corn milling, and was usually owned collectively by the retail societies which it supplied. The Sowerby Bridge Flour Society, formed in 1854, operated Union Mill in Sowerby Bridge and Brecks Mill in Hebden Bridge. There were two successive flour-mill societies in Todmorden.[8]

The growth of consumer Co-operation accelerated in the late nineteenth century. In 1868, twenty years after its foundation, the Hebden Bridge society had 1,043 members and sales of £18,000 a year from its various departments, including grocery, drapery, hardware and footwear. By 1898 it had 2,658 members and sales of £79,000. The Todmorden society was larger, with sales in excess of £130,000 a year in 1891-2. The average dividend for all the Calderdale societies in 1903-4 was 3s 2½d in the £, on average purchases of over £35 a year. The typical Co-operative family therefore received dividends of about £6 a year, or six weeks' wages for a weaver.

The 'divi' was often used to buy children's clothes, especially for Whitsuntide, which saw the Pennine version of the Easter Parade, but it was also invaluable for tiding families over periods of slack trade and short-time working. Another use for the dividends was the house purchase schemes developed by some societies, including Hebden Bridge and Todmorden. After saving a certain amount, a member could secure a housing loan.[9] An important step in the development of Co-operation as a social movement came in 1883, when the Women's Co-operative Guild was founded. The first branch to be established, in September 1883, was Hebden Bridge. By 1888 there were branches also at Todmorden and Bridge End. Nearly all of the important positions in local Co-operative societies were held by men, but the Women's Co-operative Guild gave the women in the movement a taste of responsibility, if not of much actual power.[10]

The loyalty and sense of fellowship of Co-operators were strengthened by the organisation of purely social activities – concerts, galas, sports days for children, and excursions. In July 1900 Walsden's gala attracted 600 children, who enjoyed themselves to the accompaniment of the Walsden Temperance Brass Band.[11]

One feature of the Rochdale Pioneers' policy which other societies were slow to adopt was the allocation, from 1852, of 2½% of the net profits to an educational fund. Education committees were established in local societies from the 1870s, and in 1873 Hebden Bridge voted 1½% of the profits to its committee. However, in 1892-93 less than ½% of the profits of all the societies in the Calderdale District Association was given to education. Furthermore the latter was defined to include not only libraries, lectures and classes but also promotional activities which were social rather than educational.[12]

The urge to preach as well as to practise the principles of Co-operative production, and the belief that its success depended upon having an educated membership, made the 'Fustians' keener than most Co-operative societies on education. In 1886, with the support of the Hebden Bridge consumer society, they began to sponsor university extension lectures. The extension system was started by Cambridge in 1873, and Oxford took it up seriously in 1885. One of the aims of the extension movement was to break down the barriers of social class and attract substantial numbers of working class students. The response was disappointing. One reason was financial: the lecture courses had to be locally self-supporting, and the fee for an unsubsidised course was beyond the pockets of most working people. A second problem was the sense of alienation and suspicion of the motives of those who wanted to educate the workers. Both problems could be solved if a working class organisation took on the financial responsibility and charged the students a low fee, or even no fee at all. The most consistent success was achieved by Oxford in partnership with three Pennine strongholds of Co-operation, Oldham, Todmorden and Hebden Bridge.[13]

After the Oxford courses had been running in Hebden Bridge for four years, Todmorden took up the work, with the Todmorden Co-operative Society providing the main subsidy. In both towns, admission was normally free. Thirteen courses, usually of six fortnightly lectures, were held in the two centres, in the Co-operative halls, during the next decade. The 'Fustians' had hoped to develop courses relevant to Co-operative ideology, but found that their members and the general public were more interested in historical topics. Courses on 'The Age of Elizabeth', 'The Puritan Revolution' and 'The Expansion of England' drew average audiences of 400. Most of these people went for uplift rather than serious study, but a small minority stayed behind after the lectures for a discussion class, wrote essays and entered for a certificate examination at the end of the course. 'The Puritan Revolution' was also offered in Sowerby Bridge under the auspices of an *ad hoc* committee. Over 500 people attended, but the experiment was not repeated.[14]

The committed students had an influence out of all proportion to their numbers. Some of them won essay prizes which paid for their attendance at the extension summer schools, which were normally held in alternate years in Oxford and Cambridge. In the 1890s most churches and chapels had mutual improvement societies attached, and it became the practice for one or two enthusiastic members of each to attend an extension course, and feed back the knowledge so gained to the mutual improvement society. An attempt was made in December 1890 to federate the twenty or so societies in the Todmorden area into one large students' association to provide a local base for extension work. There was a similar proposal at Oldham, but these efforts, which foreshadowed the formation of the Workers Educational Association, were a little ahead of their time. However, some of the keener extension students established an intermediate layer between university lectures and local society meetings, in the form of discussion classes which met regularly to consider the current extension topic, sometimes under the leadership of local ministers of religion. The same students also played a major part in founding or reviving local cultural societies, including the Hebden Bridge Literary and Scientific Society and the Todmorden Literary Society.[15]

The value of university extension work to these activists, and the quality of their contribution to local society, can be illustrated by the careers of two weavers from the Fustian Co-operative, Samuel Fielding and Robert Halstead.

Nutclough Mill workers' houses: two storey houses at the front...

Fielding began work in a mill at the age of eight, and finished his half-time schooling when he was thirteen. He was an active Anglican (although he often attended Nonconformist chapels as well), a choir member, Sunday school teacher, an ardent temperance worker, a local Co-operative leader and a Liberal in politics. A self-taught botanist, he became a part-time science teacher. A keen extension student, he gained a distinction in the examination following an extension course on physical geography. Later he had a period of residential study at Ruskin College, Oxford, founded in 1899. Another of his enthusiasms was poetry, and in 1915 he was instrumental in founding the Calder Valley Poets Society. He was president of the Hebden Bridge Adult School, part of an adult education movement with a religious basis. He often lectured to mutual improvement societies, and published pamphlets and articles on a wide range of subjects. Samuel Fielding is one of the finest examples of the Pennine workman-scholar, all of whose activities in learning, teaching and the promotion of good causes had to be fitted into the spare time of a weaver, until he retired a few years before his death.[16]

Robert Halstead (1858-1930) was also a half-timer from the ages of eight to thirteen. As a youth he attended evening classes, and later became one of the most dedicated of extension students. He won a succession of certificates and essay prizes which took him to most of the extension summer meetings held in Oxford and Cambridge in the 1890s.

. . . at the back, an extra storey below street level plus an attic.

In the early 1890s he became a four-loom weaver at the Fustian Co-operative mill, where he was once observed by a visitor in the classic pose of the workman-scholar, with a book (John Ruskin's *The Crown of Wild Olive*) propped open on one of his looms. He put his learning to good use as an eloquent advocate of Co-operative production, Co-operative education and university extension. He became secretary of the Lancashire and Yorkshire Centre of the Labour Copartnership Association, formed in 1897, and was prominent in the Co-operative movement at national level.[17]

His ideas on economic and social issues were set out in a series of articles, where he attacked what he saw as the fundamental inhumanity of industrial capitalism, and warned that the workers would not always 'sharpen sickles for those who reap the golden grain'. He was, however, in common with most of the Fustian Co-operative activists, equally hostile to state socialism. The idea of a 'centralised collectivism' directing 'a well-drilled, well-conditioned, wage-earning labour population' was to him 'morally repulsive'. Industrial democracy had to grow from within the community of workers, and sharing responsibility was as important as sharing profits. For this work, adult education was essential.

Halstead advocated in 1897 the establishment of a residential Co-operative College (eventually achieved three decades later) and the creation of a Co-operative wing to the extension summer meetings. The only result of the latter initiative was the creation of a few more scholarships for Co-operative students, but Halstead organised a party of them each year and himself lectured amongst the dreaming spires. Although he emphasised the social purpose of adult education, he saw learning also as an end in itself:

> Fortunately for the poor, the highest pleasures of life are not inseparably connected with material possessions . . . those who are poor in worldly goods need not succumb to the greater curse of poverty of ideas . . .[18]

At the foundation conference of the 'Association to Promote the Higher Education of Working Men', held at Oxford in August 1903, Robert Halstead (who had left Hebden Bridge in 1900 to become full-time secretary of the Co-operative Productive Federation) made the keynote speech. He became one of the national leaders of the new movement, renamed the Workers Educational Association in 1905.[19]

The first local branch of the WEA was formed at Todmorden in 1907. It was known as the Todmorden Education Guild, a style of name adopted by Rochdale in 1905 and favoured in some Co-operative-dominated Pennine towns. The guild put a labelled collection of wild flowers in the town library; promoted a short course of lectures on the use of the library; organised natural history rambles; and arranged an extension lecture course on 'The Study of Animal Life'. There was at first no indication that the WEA would be anything more than a useful coordinating body for existing adult learning activities. In 1908, however, the WEA persuaded Oxford University to set up a joint committee to provide tutorial classes, lasting for seventy-two meetings over three years, and secured grant aid from the Board of Education. Other universities soon followed Oxford's lead.

This scheme at last offered the earnest student, keen to learn for social purposes as well as personal development, an opportunity for serious study. There was a quick response in Hebden Bridge. In September 1909 the WEA branch was formed, and at the same time a tutorial class in economic history and economics was launched. The tutor was Henry Clay, later (as Sir Henry) one of the country's leading economists. The twenty-six students, aged 19 to 37, were nearly all men, predominantly textile workers. They included a traveller for the Fustian Co-op, Sam Moore, who maintained the workman-scholar tradition by writing articles in the *Economic Journal*. Moore was the first president of the WEA branch; was chairman of the Hebden Bridge Literary and Scientific Society, which had been refounded in 1905; and is described in the local press as active in Christian affairs. Unlike the older generation of Co-operative activists, who were nearly all Liberal in politics, Moore was a socialist. In 1909 he declined, for personal reasons, an invitation to become the Labour parliamentary candidate for the Sowerby Bridge division.

The Hebden Bridge branch arranged public lectures, on subjects as diverse as 'The Calder Valley in the Ice Age' and 'Labour Exchanges'. WEA members lectured free of charge to organisations affiliated to the branch, especially church and chapel societies, and the working men's clubs at Hebden Bridge, Midgehole and Mytholm-royd.

Todmorden did not begin tutorial classes until 1912 – in the early years, classes had to be rationed by university-WEA joint committees for financial reasons – when a three year course on English literature was started, with 28 men and 8 women enrolled. In the same year the Sowerby Bridge branch was formed, with the support of a range of local organisations including the Sowerby Bridge Literary Society. A tutorial class in industrial history, which began in 1913, drew its students mainly from the mutual improvement societies attached to local churches and chapels.[20]

Victorian housing in Hebden Bridge, seen from above Stubbing Lock.

The relatively strong adult education movement of upper Calderdale had grown out of the culture of 'Co-op and chapel'. The experience of running Co-operative societies, chapels, and the large number of local organisations dedicated to moral improvement, proved to be useful training for participation in local government. (Two aspects of the latter, the poor law guardians and the school boards, have been discussed in Chapters 12 and 11 respectively.) The modern system of local government began to develop from the 1850s, the main driving force being a concern for public health. The sanitary conditions of the hillside settlements were far from ideal – in 1843-4 a polluted water supply caused 51 cases of typhus, with 8 deaths, at Slack near Heptonstall – but the growth of the valley-bottom towns created new and serious health problems.[21]

The response was the formation, under Acts of Parliament passed in 1848 and 1858, of elected Local Boards of Health, usually known simply as the local boards. They dealt with drainage, highways and pavements, street lighting and building regulation, and levied a rate. The General Highway Act of 1835 had replaced compulsory 'statute labour' on the roads by a highway rate, which facilitated the transfer of responsibility from the townships. The first local board to be established, in 1856, covered the urban area of Sowerby Bridge. The people of the latter had the example on their doorstep of

Halifax, incorporated as a municipal borough in 1848, where a new system of drains and sewers was being developed.[22]

In 1860 the Todmorden Local Board was formed, covering parts of the townships of Stansfield, Langfield and Todmorden with Walsden. The footpaths along the main roads were widened and paved at a cost of £3,000, the streets in the town were lit by gas, and work started in 1868 on a sewerage system. In 1875 the board's area was extended to include all of the three townships except for part of Stansfield, and also Cornholme in Cliviger township, which had been given its own board in 1868, but was increasingly linked to Todmorden by industrial and urban development.[23]

Wadsworth township set up a local board in 1862, but townships stretching from the moor top to the valley bottom were no longer convenient units. Hebden Bridge, Mytholmroyd and Sowerby Bridge were each, like Todmorden, made up of segments of at least three townships. In 1866 a new board was established for the whole urban area of Hebden Bridge, including a small part of Mytholmroyd. The latter did not secure its own board until 1891. Local boards were formed for Luddenden Foot and Sowerby in 1868 and 1869 respectively.[24]

The Halifax-Rochdale-Burnley turnpike road became the responsibility of the local boards and townships when the turnpike trust was wound up in 1878. As a result of the development of the railways, the traffic on the turnpikes was now mainly local, and it was more convenient to maintain these roads from a rate rather than tolls. The other, minor, turnpike roads from Mytholmroyd via Cragg Vale to Blackstone Edge, and from Hebden Bridge to Keighley, had already been handed back to the local highway authorities.[25]

The rationalisation of local government began in 1888 with the creation of county councils, which took over responsibility for the maintenance of the main roads. (In Yorkshire, each of the three Ridings became a separate county authority.) Under the Local Government Act of 1894 the local boards became Urban District Councils (UDCs), and the rural areas formed rural districts, based upon the poor law unions minus the UDC areas. The remaining highway powers of the townships were transferred to the rural district councils, but the townships, outside the urban areas, had limited power of self-government restored under (civil) parish councils. Todmorden UDC petitioned for borough status, which was granted in 1896.

The Todmorden Local Board had already bought out the three local gas producers, the Todmorden Gas Company, and Fieldens and Wilsons, the two industrial firms with their own gas works which had supplied their surplus to parts of the town. The borough council started its electricity undertaking in 1905. The UDCs of Hebden Bridge and Mytholmroyd joined forces in 1895 to buy the local gas works, and Hebden Bridge opened its electricity works in 1904. The oldest public gas undertaking in the area was at Sowerby Bridge, where the local board bought out the Sowerby Bridge Gas Company in 1861. The supply was extended in 1886-7 to Luddenden Foot (which had been partially supplied by Whitworths Mill), and to Luddenden and Midgley in 1897.[26]

The leading lights of local government were often men who were prominent in the Co-operatives and chapels. In 1896-7 the Todmorden Co-operative Society handed over its library of 8,000 volumes to the borough council to become the town's public library. Several of the donating committee and the receiving council were the same people. The integration of Co-operative activity, the chapel ethos and municipal service is well-illustrated by the life of Joseph Greenwood (1833-1924): manager of the Fustian Co-op, he was prominent in national Co-operative affairs, for thirty-three years a member

The directors of the Fustian Co-operative Society about 1900. Joseph Greenwood is fourth from the left on the front row; on his left is John Hartley, an active Chartist as a young man.

and several times chairman of the Hebden Bridge Local Board/UDC, member of local school boards and chairman of the governors of Hebden Bridge Secondary School, a JP, a Liberal in politics, a General Baptist in religion and a worker for the temperance cause.[27]

Trade unionism made limited progress in upper Calderdale until the end of the nineteenth century, mainly because of the substantial proportion of women and girls in both the textile and clothing trades. The mule spinners, who were men, were organised in local spinners unions. In the 1860s a union of fustian cutters in the Manchester area and Hebden Bridge was in operation. There are records of the Todmorden Power Loom Weavers Association from 1882. The absence of a union did not mean the absence of strikes. Some disputes affected a single firm, where the workers could easily form a temporary organisation.

In July and August 1906 a marathon strike of fustian weavers in Hebden Bridge began when their union, the Todmorden and District Weavers Association, demanded that their pay should be based on the 'Bury list' – wage rates being higher in Lancashire. Nearly all of the weavers, with the exception of those in the Fustian Co-op who were paid on the Bury list and had the labour dividend as well, came out. Settlement was reached with three of the five firms in November 1907, but the two largest held out by using non-union labour until the strike finally ended in January 1909. The workers were paid 6½% more than in 1906, but still less than the current Bury list.[28]

Eaves Self-Help Manufacturers Society, 1907.

Some of the striking workers, with the support of Hebden Bridge Co-operative Society, set up the Eaves Self-Help Manufacturing Society Ltd (chairman Joseph Greenwood) as a workers co-operative. The society bought two old silk mills at Eaves Bottom to develop for cotton weaving. It was a brave effort, but by the time the mills were repaired and the second-hand looms ready to run in March 1908, trade was depressed. The enterprise limped on, exciting much sympathy in the Co-operative world and stubbornly supported by Joseph Greenwood, until it closed down in 1911.[29]

There were some successes for the trade union movement in 1912-13. A dyeworkers union recruited nearly all of the 650 workers (including 50 women) in the business in the Hebden Bridge district, and won an increase in pay and a shorter working week – although the latter was still 55½ hours. The Clothing Operatives Union had recruited most of the men workers by 1913, but they numbered only about 300 out of 2,800 employed in the trade. Most of the men earned 20-23s a week. Girl machinists were often earning 20s a week before they were out of their teens, and a few highly-skilled women piece workers could take home 30s for a 58 hour week. Not surprisingly the women and girls showed little interest in trade unionism. Legislation achieved what the union could not. When the Trade Boards Act came into force in February 1913, minimum wages of 6d an hour for men and 3¼d an hour for women had to be paid. The employers cut the working week to 52 hours, which meant a minimum weekly wage for men in full work of 26s. The women's rates were already far above the minimum, but their working week was also cut by 6 hours. Apparently they maintained the same level of output and therefore the same earnings.[30]

At the end of the nineteenth century some of the veterans of the Co-operative movement looked back nostalgically to the days when cloth was woven at home, on a handloom owned by the weaver, who was depicted as master of his own destiny.[31] However, to find a true golden age for handloom weavers it would have been necessary for recollections to reach back as far as about 1815. The doctor who wrote an account of the typhus outbreak in Heptonstall and Slack in 1843-4 described the conditions of the handloom weavers, deteriorating 'physically and morally' for twenty years because of the relentless decline in their earnings. They lived in 'cold, damp and dreary' cottages, wore heavily-patched fustian clothes, and survived on a diet of oatmeal and potatoes.[32]

In material terms the workers were much better off at the end of the Victorian era. The main problem was the relatively low wages earned by men in occupations such as weaving, which were open equally to, if not dominated by, women. A family of four or five wholly dependent upon one weaver's wage, averaging 23s 6d a week in Mytholmroyd and Hebden Bridge in 1913, lived in poverty even during periods of full employment. Family earnings lifted a majority of families well above the poverty line and, to quote Sam Moore, 'there is an absence of the miserable, sordid, dirty-looking houses that are so common in larger towns'. The rate of pauperism in the Todmorden Poor Law Union was about half the national average.

Hebden Bridge had a special housing problem. As a consequence of the narrowness of the main and tributary valleys, about half of the 1,800 houses existing in 1913 had been built literally one on top of another. Streets were laid out parallel to the valley sides, the buildings between them having four storeys on the low side and two on the high side. All the 'bottom houses' were built into the hillside, and most were damp and dark. Some of the 'top houses' went straight over the bottom house, with windows facing both streets. In others the living room of the top house backed on to a bedroom of the bottom house. In a few cases, by using a gallery on the low side, pairs of back-to-back houses could be put on top. Some of these structures had been built in the early nineteenth century; many more were erected in the late Victorian period when the town was growing rapidly.[33]

The workers of the upper Calder Valley had made a major contribution to their own well-being and self-esteem by building up the Co-operative movement. In parts of the area there were more Co-operative members than families. To all members the 'divi' was a great boon; some had bought their houses through Co-operative schemes; and many more had some capital in the Co-operative society or savings bank. The enthusiastic few were confident that, with the help of adult education and the moral discipline of chapel and temperance, their goal of a Co-operative Commonwealth could be achieved.

Upper Calderdale was known nationally as a powerhouse of Co-operative ideology, with a strong input from the Fustian Co-op, which occupied the same position in producer Co-operation as the Rochdale Pioneers in the consumer field. When the International Co-operative Congress met in Manchester in 1902, the delegates were taken in pilgrimage first to the original store in Toad Lane, Rochdale, and then to Nutclough Mill. In 1918, however, the Fustian Co-op became insolvent. To save the jobs of the workers, it was bought out by the Co-operative Wholesale Society. Joseph Greenwood, who had retired as manager in 1909 but was a member of the Fustian board, vainly opposed the deal, as the CWS did not share profits with its workers.[34]

Producer Co-operation had never taken off as its advocates had hoped, and the loss of its national flagship was a serious setback. Consumer Co-operation, however,

Hebden Bridge housing: above, two or three stories on the upper side; below, four or five stories on the lower side.

continued to grow in strength. Throughout the valley in the interwar period, retail trades and services, including hardware, clothing, footwear, furniture, coal and the funeral service, were dominated by the Co-operative societies. As the Co-operative veterans went to their rest, even the coffin earned a 'divi'.

15

Twentieth Century Transformation

A Calder Valley Rip van Winkle who fell asleep at the end of the First World War and awoke in the last decade of this century would see profound changes etched on the landscape, especially in the valley-bottom towns. On the terraces above he would find more familiar scenes. The pre-Industrial Revolution character of the villages and lines of hillside houses are still evident, although there has been some modern housing development, eg at Heptonstall and Blackshaw Head. Old houses have been restored after a period of neglect, and some barns no longer needed for farming have been converted into dwellings. The ruined cottages and crumbling walls near the edge of the moor, and the former intakes invaded by moorland vegetation, mark the retreat of cultivation which has been going on since the late Victorian period. Some farms have grown in size by the purchase or renting of fields separated from houses where farming has been abandoned. A form of dual economy survives. A survey made in 1958 showed that only half of the farms were full-time holdings. The rest were supported by income from another source.[1]

There is little doubt that our re-awakened observer would be struck most of all by the disappearance of many of the mill chimneys and Nonconformist chapels which were such dominant visual features in 1918. Not much remains of the textile and clothing industries which formerly employed many thousands of people. In the Hebden Bridge area, some firms make specialist clothing for sport and recreational activities, but there are no textile or clothing factories with as many as 100 workers. The streets of the Hangingroyd area of the town, which used to echo to the clattering clogs of hundreds of workers going to and from the mills there, have fallen quiet. The Pecket Shed near Hebden Bridge is the only factory still making fustians.

Thomas Sutcliffe and Sons of Mytholmroyd, clothing manufacturers employing 250 people, now rank as one of the major employers of upper Calderdale. In the Todmorden area, NR Components Ltd of Der Street Mill produce caravan awnings, waterproofs and sportswear with a workforce of about 150. Walsden Printing Company, with about 200 workers, still operates at Ramsden Wood Mill. Bottoms Mill, Walsden, is an example of a firm still producing heavy cottons, eg for sheets, but it has only about thirty-two workers.

The much-transformed engineering industry – no longer linked to textiles – has fared rather better. For example, Mons Mill in Todmorden is now home to the Volex Group, which makes wiring harnesses for the motor industry and employs about 600 workers; Warman International Ltd, with nearly 300 employees, produces heavy duty pumps in the premises of the former Sandholme Iron Company. An example of industrial diversification is provided by the firm of Alan Cooper, which employs about 160 people making office furniture in the former textile mill of Joshua Smith at Cornholme.

Foster Mill, Hebden Bridge, being demolished in 1985.

Since Crossley Carpets of Halifax closed in 1984, the largest employers within the Borough of Calderdale have been the borough council and the Halifax Building Society. For most people, 'going to work' used to mean walking to a local mill. Now it usually involves a journey by car, bus or train to work in service industries rather than manufacturing.

Some industrial buildings have been split up into smaller units, to be rented by high-technology firms or those starting up in a small way. Longbottom Mill in Luddenden Foot, previously making heavy woollens, is now the Tenterfields Industrial Estate. The Moderna Blankets site in Mytholmroyd has been converted to a similar role. Parallel developments have taken place in Todmorden, eg on Salford, but Waterside Mill, after being used for a time for plastics manufacture, stands derelict, awaiting redevelopment.

After the Co-operative Wholesale Society closed Nutclough Mill in 1967, special efforts were made to preserve the building because of its importance in the national history of Co-operation as well as in the story of Hebden Bridge and the fustian trade. The building was listed, and eventually it was acquired by Pennine Heritage, a charitable trust set up in 1979 to promote the economic and social regeneration of the

Modern houses spreading up the hillside at Mytholmroyd.

South Pennine region. After restoration it was opened as accommodation for industrial units in the winter of 1987-8. One floor was taken by Calrec Audio, a company making sound equipment for recording and broadcasting which began as the spare-time activity of a few enthusiasts in Hebden Bridge. By the end of 1991 the company, which exports over half of its output, had expanded to occupy three of the five floors, at which point it bought the mill from Pennine Heritage.

Some of the sites of the mills are now housing estates, notably at Eaves Bottom where the Mytholm silk mills used to stand, and at Cornholme, where the address Bobbin Mill Close is all that survives of Wilson Brothers bobbin works. Council housing estates developed since the Second World War have been located mainly on the lower hillsides because of the shortage of suitable valley bottom land, eg the Kershaw estate, Luddenden; the Banksfield estate, Mytholmroyd; the Dodnaze and Fairfield estates, Hebden Bridge; and Higher Ashenhurst, Carr House and Longfield in Todmorden.

In 1929 the boards of guardians were abolished, and their responsibilities transferred to county and county borough councils. During the interwar years, Sowerby Bridge Urban District Council amalgamated first with Sowerby UDC and later with Luddenden Foot UDC, the enlarged authority also being known as Sowerby Bridge UDC. Hebden Bridge and Mytholmroyd UDCs joined to form Hebden Royd UDC.

Mons Mill, Todmorden. The chimney has now been demolished.

In 1974 the four local authorities of upper Calderdale – the two UDCs, the Hepton Rural District Council and Todmorden Borough Council – were merged with five others, including the County Borough of Halifax, to form the Borough of Calderdale. This is technically a metropolitan district, and was one of five in the Metropolitan County of West Yorkshire. Since the abolition of metropolitan counties in 1986, the Borough of Calderdale, which is roughly co-extensive with the ancient parish of Halifax plus the parts of Todmorden which were originally in Lancashire, has been an all-purpose authority, dealing with planning, housing, highways and education. New-style parish councils, known in urban areas as town councils, have been established for Todmorden, Blackshaw, Heptonstall, Hebden Royd, Wadsworth and Erringden. They have limited powers, but can promote useful initiatives such as the minibus service to hillside housing estates started by Hebden Royd Town Council in 1978.

A new school building at Mytholmroyd, begun in 1938 as a senior school but never used as such because of the war, became the first comprehensive secondary school in the West Riding of Yorkshire when it opened its doors as Calder High School in 1950. The subsequent reorganisation of secondary education produced two more comprehensives, at Todmorden and Sowerby Bridge. The former secondary school at Hebden Bridge (known as the grammar school from the late 1920s) became Riverside Junior School in 1964.

The canal in decay: a lock at Brearley, 1971.

The canal restored, but the mills in decay: Hebden Bridge, 1992.

Hope Baptist Chapel, Hebden Bridge. In 1992 the noticeboard proclaimed: 'We are open on Sundays and have been for 215 years'.

The culture of 'Co-op and chapel' has died. The success of Co-operation as a social movement rested upon the practical benefits of membership, particularly the generous dividend. The Victorian Co-ops were in competition with private traders operating with large profit margins and sometimes supplying adulterated food or other substandard goods. The growth of multiple stores and discount supermarkets after the Second World War undermined the commercial basis of the Co-ops. Although nationally they still have a considerable share of retail trade, the days when Co-operative shopping was dominant in upper Calderdale, and provided the resources for libraries, education and social activities, have gone. The Todmorden Co-op is now part of Norwest Co-operative Ltd, with a supermarket, decorating, furniture and electrical departments, all at Dale Street. The Hebden Bridge Co-operative Society, with a proud record of material and social achievement, came to a sad end in 1968, when the embezzlement of £23,000 by an employee forced the society into bankruptcy. Its property was sold. The ground floor of the main block in the town centre is now occupied by shops, and the upper two stories form the Carlton Hotel. A Co-operative supermarket in Market Street is operated by Yorkshire Co-operatives Ltd.

A decline in the membership of local Nonconformist chapels was evident by the end of the First World War. One cause was the heavy loss of life amongst young men – thirty-seven were killed from the Todmorden Unitarian congregation alone[2] – and the carnage may have contributed to a loss of faith. Church or chapel going ceased to be

The interior of Todmorden Unitarian Church in 1975.

a normal activity of the respectable inhabitants. This trend accelerated after 1945, leaving a huge over-capacity in the chapels and schoolrooms. Buildings erected for several hundred worshippers had to be maintained by a few dozen. In 1932, partly in response to the decline in membership, the Wesleyans, Primitives and United Methodists came together in Methodist Union. There were now, in several parts of the upper Calder Valley, two or three chapels of the same organisation within a short distance of each other.

Between 1953 and 1967 four Baptist chapels in a two mile stretch of the valley between Cornholme and Todmorden – Vale, Lydgate, Lineholme and Wellington Road – were demolished.[3] Currently services are held in the schoolroom at Vale, which, since the closure of Shore Baptist and Cornholme Methodist chapels, is the only surviving Nonconformist place of worship in the Burnley Road valley. On or near the main road from Halifax to Todmorden twelve chapels, mainly Methodist, have closed. Ken Powell's book *The Fall of Zion*, published in 1980 by SAVE Britain's Heritage as a *cri de coeur* against the wholesale destruction of Nonconformist chapels in Lancashire and Yorkshire, has on the front cover a photograph of the Congregational (known earlier as Independent) chapel at Sowerby, which then had just been demolished. In the same year the 1869 Congregational chapel at Booth in the Luddenden Valley, which had dominated the village like a miniature Gothic cathedral, was pulled down, together with the 1824 chapel which had been converted into a Sunday school.

The 1898 Birchcliffe Chapel.

When the Todmorden Unitarians celebrated the centenary of their magnificent Gothic church in 1969, they could no longer afford a minister of their own, and launched a centenary appeal for £5,000 to pay for urgent repairs.[4] The church still stands, but the small congregation, which had been meeting for some time in the church lodge, disbanded in April 1992. Another treasure of Calderdale Nonconformity, the octagonal chapel at Heptonstall, is still in use.

The Church of England has also suffered some losses. For example, St Johns Church in Hebden Bridge, which opened in 1931 in a central location, more convenient for the townspeople than St James's Church at Mytholm, was closed in 1984 and converted into dwellings.

The decline in religious observance has affected the local Roman Catholic churches, but to a lesser extent than in the case of most denominations. The Catholics were relatively late arrivals in upper Calderdale. The 1851 religious census recorded no Catholic churches above Halifax. A gradual build-up of support, mainly as a result of Irish immigration, led to the establishment of churches in the five main valley-bottom settlements. All five are still in use, but only three now have resident priests.

Birchcliffe Baptist Chapel in Hebden Bridge, after being threatened with demolition, was converted by the Joseph Rowntree Trust into the Birchcliffe Centre. A floor was inserted at the base of the gallery level to create a concert/lecture hall, with meeting rooms, offices and other facilities for local and regional organisations underneath. One of the latter is Pennine Heritage which, in addition to promoting economic development, has published booklets, maps and a magazine dealing with the history and socio-economic problems of the Lancashire and Yorkshire Pennines south of the Aire Gap. The building was opened for its new uses in 1978, and in 1981 the adjoining Sunday school was converted into a residential study centre.

Another study centre is nearby, at Lumb Bank in Heptonstall, where the Arvon Foundation runs courses on the craft of writing. The house was given for the purpose by Ted Hughes, co-founder of Arvon, who was born in Aspinall Street, Mytholmroyd, and attended school locally before his family moved away from the area. Ted Hughes, who lived for some years at Lumb Bank, is a prolific poet and was appointed poet laureate in 1984. The founders in 1915 of the Calder Valley Poets Society can hardly have dreamed of such an honour linking upper Calderdale to the wider world of poetry.

If we are to look in this secular age for the impulse towards collective self-help and social improvement which in the past was an expression of the culture of 'Co-op and chapel', we will find it in a concern for the heritage and environment of upper Calderdale. This attitude can be traced back to before the Second World War. Several reservoirs for water supply were already in existence on high-lying sites, eg at the head of Luddenden Dean, when a proposal was made to dam the Hebden Valley and flood the intimate grandeur of Hardcastle Crags. The protests against this threat to one of the most famous and popular beauty spots in Yorkshire were successful; and twice more, in 1949 and 1970, similar schemes were rejected.

In 1965 the Calder Civic Trust was formed, a voluntary society which aimed not only to protect the local environment but also to promote harmonious development, including the potential of the upper Calder Valley as a recreational area. In 1967 the trust proposed the creation of a Pennine Park, located between the existing National Parks in the Yorkshire Dales and the Peak District, 'an underused area situated adjacent to large populations whose leisure activities are causing serious congestion elsewhere'. The Pennine Park Association was established in 1973 to foster the idea and had attracted sixty-three member organisations by 1979.[5] The PPA has now become the South Pennines Association, working with the Standing Conference of South Pennines Authorities to develop the South Pennines as a Heritage Area – a kind of homespun, low-cost version of a National Park.

The tourist potential of the area has been enhanced by the efforts of both local authorities and voluntary organisations to improve the environment, as for example in the riverside walk at Hebden Bridge. In 1973 the Sowerby Bridge Civic Trust, the Calder Civic Trust, the Todmorden Conservation Group and five similar organisations within the new Borough of Calderdale began work on defining and describing a fifty mile circular routeway exploring the most interesting and visually striking features of the area. With the support of West Yorkshire Metropolitan Council and the Countryside Commission, the Calderdale Way was opened in 1978. In the first year, 15,000 copies of the guidebook published by the Calderdale Way Association were sold.

The recent reopening for recreational use of the Rochdale Canal, effectively closed since 1939, including the creation of a marina in a former loading bay in Hebden Bridge, is one example of the 'recycling' of resources no longer needed for their original purpose. Another is a conversion into an hotel and restaurant respectively of Scaitcliffe Hall and Todmorden Hall, the former homes of the embattled JPs in the 'Age of Agitation', John Crossley and James Taylor.

What is now called 'the heritage approach to economic recovery', involving both the rescue of historic buildings for appropriate modern uses and the enhancement of the

The canal marina, Hebden Bridge.

Stoodley Pike, topping the 'barren and unfruitful hills'.

attractions of the area for residents and visitors alike, seems to be working. Between 1971 and 1981 the population of Hebden Bridge grew by 2%, reversing a period of decline, and the proportion aged 25-45 rose from 22% to 32%.

An economic future heavily dependent on tourism, and on the attractions of upper Calderdale as a dormitory for people working in the conurbations of West Yorkshire and East Lancashire, could have a negative side. This is depicted by Glyn Hughes as 'tradition mocked by the glitter of gentility': chapels turned into 'homes for atheists'; antique shops selling plain 1890s articles at fancy 1990s prices; the houses of the yeomen clothiers occupied by people who are part of the global village of television watchers but make no contribution to the life of the local village.[6] It need not be so. In some other parts of the Yorkshire Pennines the 'incomers' are as active in community life, and as respectful of local tradition, as the natives.

Perhaps the conflict is not, as Glyn Hughes suggests, 'between gentility and tradition', but between nostalgia and heritage. Nostalgia sees the past as a collection of interesting old tales, as snapshots rather than a film with a well-developed plot and strong characters. There is no intellectual nourishment, no social inspiration, in nostalgia. Heritage is our social and cultural inheritance, preserved, analysed and made accessible through historical research and the selective defence of key sites and buildings. Furthermore the technology which could flatten local differences into a bland uniformity can also be made the engine of decentralisation, as more people and

Five centuries of Calderdale history in Hebden Bridge town centre:

1. Stubbings School (Board school, 1878)
2. Carlton Hotel; originally the Hebden Bridge Co-op main buildings
3. The new road to Halifax of 1806, bypassing the town centre
4. Hope Baptist Chapel (1858)
5. Bridge Gate (1772)
6. Hebden Bridge (1772)
7. A646 to Todmorden
8. Old Gate leading to Old Bridge
9. Old Bridge (1510)

10. The Buttress; the old way to Heptonstall
11. The White Lion (1657); known in the eighteenth and nineteenth centuries as 'Kings Farm'
12. St Georges Bridge (1893)
13. Bridge Mill (now a restaurant and shops) was the original site of the manorial cornmill for Wadsworth
14. River Hebden
15. Keighley Road
16. St Johns Church, 1929-84; now converted to dwellings

organisations whose product is either information or high-value goods have a wider choice of location for their work. Shorter journeys to work, as well as the trend towards shorter working hours and earlier retirement, would leave people with more time and energy to devote to collective voluntary effort for social, cultural and environmental causes. The culture of 'Co-op and chapel' cannot be revived, but there is still plenty of scope for what the Co-operative movement used to call 'the art of association'.

This has been demonstrated by the Birchcliffe-Nutclough story. Birchcliffe Chapel and Nutclough Mill are symbols of two Calder Valley creations which made a national impact: Dan Taylor's General Baptist New Connexion, and the flagship of producer Co-operation. The modern link between them is a voluntary organisation, Pennine Heritage, which is housed in the Birchcliffe Centre, and succeeded in the face of many obstacles in rescuing Nutclough Mill, which now accommodates an outstanding example of local enterprise in the field of modern technology.

A continuing theme of this book has been the influence of the landscape on the lives of local people, directly through shaping the economy, indirectly through encouraging particular attitudes. One of the slogans used by Pennine Heritage is 'The hills are alive . . .' In the sixteenth and seventeenth centuries the Calderdale hills were alive with the sound of the Puritan yeomen clothiers proclaiming their economic and moral triumph over a hostile environment. The hills are 'alive' today in a different sense, recognised as a major asset for living and for livelihood. The gorges, crags, hillsides, moors and vistas now make up a benign environment, a recreational treasure for both residents and visitors. The 'barren and unfruitful hills' are fertile at last.

Glossary of Medieval Terms

Assart	Virgin land cleared for cultivation.
Berewick	Outlying part of a manor.
Bondage	Restrictions on personal freedom, the nature of which varied from manor to manor, exceptionally within the same manor. A bondman could not take legal action against his lord over matters relating to rents, tenure and services. In the manor of Wakefield he could not hold freehold land.
Bondhold land	Land held by the rules, relating to rents, tenure and obligations which applied to tenants in bondage, but which could be held by freemen.
Bovate	See *oxgang*.
Demesne	Land used directly by the lord, and not occupied permanently by tenants.
Entry fines	Payments for entry to land on clearance, purchase, leasing or inheritance.
Grave	A peasant officer of a manor.
Heriot	A death duty/inheritance payment payable in respect of bondhold land.
Moldbrest	'Soil exhausted': the description of land abandoned by tenants, apparently through loss of fertility.
Oxgang	The basic peasant holding, ranging locally between 10 and 18 acres in size. Bovate is the equivalent term of Latin origin which appears in the written records: *bos*, genitive *bovis* = ox.
Ploughland	Eight oxgangs.
Relief	A death duty/inheritance payment payable in respect of freehold land.
Royd land	The vernacular term for assart, ie virgin land cleared for cultivation, in active use until about 1400.
Tourn	Major meeting of the court of the manor of Wakefield, held twice yearly.

Bibliography and References

Sources and Abbreviations

Newspapers and Periodicals

CN	*Co-operative News*
HC	*Halifax Courier*
HG	*Halifax Guardian*
HBT	*Hebden Bridge Times*
TA	*Todmorden Advertiser*
TAHBT	*Todmorden Advertiser and Hebden Bridge Times*
THBA	*Todmorden and Hebden Bridge Advertiser*
OUEG	*Oxford University Extension Gazette*
UEJ	*University Extension Journal*

Other Publications

EYC	*Early Yorkshire Charters* (YASRS)
FIC	Factories Inquiry Commission 1833, Supplementary Report Part II, C1, *PP Vol XX 1834*
HAS	*Halifax Antiquarian Society*
PP	*Parliamentary Papers*
VCH	*Victoria County History*
YAJ	*Yorkshire Archaeological Journal*
YASRS	*Yorkshire Archaeological Society Record Series*

Wakefield Court Rolls

The first five volumes, published in YASRS and covering the years 1274-1331, are cited as *WCR I-V*. The new series published by the YAS, not in date order, is cited as *WCR* followed by the dates of the volume. Detailed references are given when the material presented cannot be traced by using the indexes to the above volumes. The MS court rolls (YAS Library) are cited as WCR followed by the date of the court meeting.

Manuscript Sources

BIHR – Borthwick Institute of Historical Research, University of York
  Wills and inventories
  Archbishop Drummond's Visitation Returns 1764
  Dissenting certificates
Calderdale District Archives, Halifax
  Upper Calderdale township records
  School board records
  Rochdale – Halifax Turnpike Trust minutes 1827-48
  Murgatroyd MSS
Guildhall Library, London
  Insurance policies: RE (Royal Exchange) and Sun
HBLHS – Hebden Bridge Literary and Scientific Society, Local History Section
  Unpublished papers and copies of documents listed below
LCA – Leeds City Archives
  Saville MSS
  Sutcliffe MSS
  Class TN, Temple Newsam MSS
Nottinghamshire County Record Office
  Class DDSR, Savile MSS
Public Record Office
  Classes DL, E, HO, MAF, PL, SC
West Yorkshire Archive Service, Wakefield
  WRRD – West Riding Registry of Deeds
  West Riding Quarter Sessions Records
  Calendars of Wakefield House of Correction
  Todmorden Churchwardens accounts
  Fielden Brothers MSS
Yorkshire Archaeological Society, Leeds
  Wakefield Court Rolls, MS 759
  Foster-Greenwood MSS, DD 99

Other MSS locations are given in the References.

References

The place of publication is London unless otherwise stated.

Chapter 1

The account of the geology of the area is based upon P F Kendall and H E Wroot, *The Geology of Yorkshire* (1924), especially pp 727-30; W Edwards and F M Trotter, *British Regional Geology: The Pennines and Adjacent Areas* (3rd ed, 1954); D A Wray and others, *The Geology of the Country around Huddersfield and Halifax* (Memoirs of Geological Survey, Sheet 77, 1930); W B Wright and others, *The Geology of the Rossendale Anticline* (Memoirs, Sheet 76, 1927).

Chapter 2

1 M L Faull and M Stinson (eds), *Domesday Book Yorkshire* Part 1, 299 c,d (Phillimore, Chichester, 1986); *VCH Lancashire* Vol I, p 287.
2 *HAS Record Series II, 1914*, Extent of Sowerby Graveship 1309.
3 T A M Bishop, 'The Norman Settlement of Yorkshire', in E M Carus-Wilson (ed), *Essays in Economic History* Vol II (1962), pp 1-11; A Raistrick, *The Pennine Dales* (1968), pp 82-4; D Hey, *Yorkshire from AD 1000* (1986), pp 25-8.
4 A H Smith, *The Place Names of the West Riding of Yorkshire* Parts 3 and 7 (Cambridge, 1961-62).
5 WCR 25 May 1347.

Chapter 3

1 *EYC VIII*, pp 4-18; R Somerville, *History of the Duchy of Lancaster Vol I 1265-1603* (1953), pp 26, 33; YASRS 101, *Wakefield Manor Book 1709*, pp 2-3.
2 *EYC VIII*, pp 235-6; J Watson, *History and Antiquities of the Parish of Halifax* (1775), pp 106, 108, 123; *Calendar of Charter Rolls II*, p 476; *WCR I*, pp 136, 141, 146, 209; Extent of Sowerby Graveship 1309; DDSR 1/18/2,3, 1/19/3-26, Box 26.
3 *VCH Lancashire* Vol V, pp 187-92, 222. Hundersfield was not finally broken up until 1801.
4 Record Society Lancashire and Cheshire, *Vol 41*, p 145, *Vol 48*, pp 38-40; Somerville, p 35; Chetham Society New Series 71, *Survey of the Manor of Rochdale 1626*, pp 138-45, 150-3; DDSR 28/1/37, 209/10; Christopher Towneley's MSS, British Museum Additional MS 32104.
5 DDSR 1/18/2,3, 1/19/3.
6 WCR 6 Dec 1336.
7 WCR 1 Oct 1337.
8 *EYC VIII*, pp 234-6.
9 WCR 3 Oct 1336.
10 *Cal. Patent Rolls 1361-64*, pp 72, 149, 525.
11 WCR 3 Oct 1376.
12 WCR 7 Oct 1336.
13 WCR 25 Aug 1335, 15 April 1336.
15 YASRS 12, *Yorkshire Inquisitions I*, pp 102-3.

Chapter 4

1 Extent of Sowerby Graveship 1309.
2 *WCR I*, pp 93-7.
3 WCR 3 Nov 1332, 19 Feb 1333, 26 Nov 1339.
4 *WCR V*, p 163; SC6/1145/21.
5 C Spencer, *The History of Hebden Bridge* (Hebden Bridge, 1991), pp 3-5.
6 Chetham Society New Series 86, G H Tupling, *The Economic History of Rossendale* (1927), pp 6-27.
7 Extent of Sowerby Graveship 1309.
8 *EYC VIII*, pp 215-6, 233-5; *WCR I*, p 117, *II*, p 176.
9 YASRS 39, *Yorkshire Deeds I*, pp 115-6.
10 DDSR 30/10; *HAS 1904-05*, pp 45-6.
11 Upper Smallshaw Deeds A, copy in HBLHS.
12 DDSR 30/48.

13 C Towneley's MSS.
14 Extent of Sowerby Graveship 1309.
15 H S Lucas, 'The Great European Famine of 1315-17', *Essays in Economic History* Vol II, pp 49-72; I Kershaw, 'The Great Famine and the Agrarian Crisis in England', *Past and Present* 59, pp 3-50; *WCR IV*, p 208.
16 I Kershaw, *Bolton Priory: the economy of a northern monastery* (Oxford, 1973), pp 38-42.
17 SC6/1091/6, 1145/21, 1148/6.
18 WCR 15 April 1336, 28 April 1337, 19 June 1338.
19 Kershaw, *Bolton Priory*, pp 38-42; E Miller and J Hatcher, *Medieval England: Rural Society and Economic Change 1086-1348* (1978), p 216.
20 WCR 19 June 1338.
21 *WCR IV*, pp 178-80.
22 A H Thompson, 'The Pestilences of the Fourteenth Century in the Diocese of York', *Archaeological Journal* Vol 71, 1914, p 105.
23 Ibid, pp 112, 135-7; B Jennings (ed), *A History of Nidderdale* (2nd ed, York, 1983), pp 86-9.
24 E Lipson, *An Introduction to the Economic History of England, Vol I, The Middle Ages* (9th ed, 1947), pp 114-7; B H Putnam, *The Enforcement of the Statute of Labourers* (New York, 1908, new ed 1970), pp 2, 73; *WCR 1350-52*, pp 91-2.
25 Ibid, pp 54-5.
26 YAS DD 99 B2/1.

Chapter 5

1 SC6/1145/21; *HAS 1922*, pp 203-16; *Yorkshire Inquisitions I*, p 103; DDSR 26/42, 1/15/44-49.
2 *HAS 1914*, p 200.
3 DDSR 1/18/2/, 3.
4 Watson, *Halifax*, pp 144-5; H R Schubert, *History of the British Iron and Steel Industry to 1775* (1957), p 342.
5 H Jewell, D Michelmore and S Moorhouse, 'An Oliver at Warley, West Yorkshire, AD 1349-50', *Historical Metallurgy* Vol 15, 1981, p 39; Schubert, p 138.
6 J Holden, *A Short History of Todmorden* (Manchester, 1912), pp 10, 23, 109; W B Trigg, 'The Halifax Coalfield', *HAS 1930*, pp 117-8; *HAS 1918*, pp 101-13; TN HX/E; DL43/11/25.
7 E M Carus-Wilson, 'An Industrial Revolution of the Thirteenth Century', *Essays in Economic History* Vol I (1954), pp 45-6; *Pipe Roll 32 Henry II*, p 70.
8 WCR 25 May 1347; *HAS 1903*, p 34.
9 H Heaton, *Yorkshire Woollen and Worsted Industries* (2nd ed, Oxford, 1965), pp xiii-xiv, 68-72; *Cal. Inquisitions Miscellaneous VI*, pp 242-9.
10 E179/17, 30, 47.
11 Heaton, pp 50-9; L Toulmin Smith (ed), *Leland's Itinerary* (1907), p 82.
12 WCR 14 Jan 1472, 24 Aug 1492, 21 Oct 1502, 24 Nov 1503; DL29/560/8899; DL42/11/23, 25; SC6/Henry VII/1019, Henry VIII/4099; DDSR 1/21/1; LCA Sutcliffe MSS 44.
13 *HAS 1904*, pp 84-5; *HAS 1922*, pp 72-80; *HAS 1933*, p 111; *Halifax Wills II*, p 136; DL4/43/92, 44/41; *TAHBT* 13 Sept 1901.

14 The wills referred to below are printed in J W Clay and E W Crossley, *Halifax Wills*, 2 vols (Leeds, no date).

15 Heaton, pp 108-9.

16 Ibid, pp 133-5, 379; M Garside, 'The Halifax Piece Hall', *HAS 1921*, pp 169-208; E101/345/25.

17 Surtees Society 77, *Yorkshire Diaries II*, pp 26 et seq.

18 Heaton, pp 94, 118-21.

19 YAS DD 99 B2/1; SC11/991.

20 Jennings, *Nidderdale*, pp 162-9; *VCH Yorkshire* Vol III, p. 451; Surtees Society 53, *Testamenta Eboracensia IV*, p 137.

21 Heaton, p 77.

22 E179/207/130, 186, 196; Thoresby Society Vols 9, 11; R B Smith, *Land and Politics in the England of Henry VIII* (Oxford, 1970), pp 264-6.

23 SC11/991; Surtees Society 92, *Yorkshire Chantry Surveys II*, pp 297-8, 423.

24 *HAS Record Series I*.

25 WCR passim; SC6/Henry VII/1019, Henry VIII/4099.

26 Heaton, p 77.

Chapter 6

1 *Wakefield Manor Book 1709*, p 3; Somerville, *Duchy of Lancaster*, pp 302, 506, 519, 523; *VCH Lancashire* Vol V, pp 190-1; *Survey of the Manor of Rochdale*.

2 M J Ellis, 'A Study in the Manorial History of Halifax Parish in the Sixteenth and Early Seventeenth Centuries', *YAJ* Vol 40, pp 256-8; DDSR 1/7/5, 6, 28/1/43; TN/HX/A 19, 30-2, 37.

3 DDSR 1/14/6; *Survey of the Manor of Rochdale*.

4 WCR passim; DL43/18/2, 44/355.

5 *Survey of the Manor of Rochdale*; SC11/760; DL5/27; DDSR 1/15/1-26, Box 10 243-7, 250-4, 26/109 A and B.

6 TN/HX/B4/4.

7 DL5/26, 28/33/32, 43/18/16; DDSR 1/7/6.

8 DDSR 9/140/8, 26/235-6, Box 10 247, 250, 252, 254.

9 H P Kendall 'Old Heptonstall', *HAS 1922*; DDSR 30/48.

10 WCR 12 June 1472.

11 Watson, pp 335-44.

12 DL44/131; WCR 26 April – 9 August 1560.

13 DDSR 1/21/2-17, 23/1, Box 10 243, 245/6.

14 DDSR 26/120-1, 127-130A, 134-40, Box 10 264-97.

15 DL4/49/53, 5/27, 44/973.

16 *Survey of the Manor of Rochdale*; B Jennings (ed), *A History of Harrogate and Knaresborough* (Huddersfield, 1970), p 57.

17 DL44/1178.

18 The following account is based upon WCR passim, and especially on the draft rolls prepared for the tourns. The latest of these to survive is for 1737-38.

Chapter 7

1 The wills referred to in this chapter are printed in *Halifax Wills*.

2 *Calendar of Papal Registers: Papal Letters I*, p. 350; Watson, pp 342-7; Record Commission, *Taxatio Ecclesiastica* (1802), p 298.

3 J Murray, *Handbook for Travellers in Yorkshire* (1867), p 421; T W Hanson, *The Story of Old Halifax* (Halifax, 1920), p 37.

4 G C Ramshaw, *Concerning Todmorden Parish* (Todmorden, 1911), p 4; Watson, pp 425-8, 442-6.

5 Ibid, p 433-7; *Letters and Papers Henry VIII* Vol 13(1), pp 138-9, 431, 492.

6 Ibid, Vol 3(1), p 34; Watson, p 364.

7 *Yorkshire Chantry Surveys II*, pp 297-8, 423; *Valor Ecclesiasticus*, Vol V, p 70.

8 Hanson, pp 99-100.

9 A G Dickens, *Lollards and Protestants in the Diocese of York* (Oxford, 1959), pp 148-50.

10 Cross Stone deed in the possession of Mr J Chadwick of Todmorden; R A Marchant, *Puritans and Church Courts in the Diocese of York* (1960), pp 113, 226, 246.

11 Holden, *Todmorden*, Chapter 13.

12 Marchant, pp 113, 226, 246, 270, 291.

13 Hanson, p 140.

14 M. Campbell, *The English Yeoman under the Tudors and Stuarts* (Yale, 1942), Chapter 2 and p 218; Hanson, pp 137-8.

15 J T Cliffe, *The Yorkshire Gentry from the Reformation to the Civil War* (1969), pp 291-2, 304-5, 317-8; Hanson, pp 138-9.

16 Heaton, *Yorkshire Woollen and Worsted Industries*, pp 178-84, 197-203.

17 Ibid, pp 183-4, 201-2.

18 *Yorkshire Diaries II*, pp 19-23.

19 Hanson, pp 145-50.

20 *Yorkshire Diaries II*, pp 9-18; Hanson, pp 149-50.

21 Ibid, p 160.

22 Ibid, p 161.

23 Watson, pp 487-90; Hanson, pp 167-8.

24 B. Dale, *Yorkshire Puritanism and Early Nonconformity* (Bradford, 1910), pp 43-5, 127-9, 156-8; A G Matthews, *Calamy Revised* (Oxford, 1934), pp 135, 259, 489-90.

25 Ibid, p 417; Dale, pp 130-1.

26 J H Turner (ed), *Oliver Heywood's Diaries* (Brighouse, 1881-85), Vol 2, pp 260-1; Matthews, pp 234, 417, 421; Dale, pp 130-5.

27 W C Braithwaite, *The Beginnings of Quakerism* (Cambridge, 1961), Chapters 1-4; N Penney (ed), *The First Publishers of Truth* (1907), pp 291-2; *The Journal of George Fox* (1902), Vol 1, pp 189, 195-7; W P Thistlethwaite, *Yorkshire Quarterly Meeting 1665-1966* (private, Harrogate, 1979), pp 2-3, 403-4.

28 Ibid, pp 244, 275.

29 J Besse, *A Collection of the Sufferings of the People called Quakers* (1753), Vol II, pp 136-7, 143, 152-3, 168.

30 Dale, pp 17-18, 48-9; *Oliver Heywood's Diaries*, Vol 2, pp 260-1.

31 Ibid, Vol 4, pp 89-91.

32 H Wood, *Congregationalism at Eastwood* (Todmorden, 1940), pp 13-16; J H Turner (ed), *Northowram Register*, pp 138-54.

33 Yorkshire Baptist Association, C E Shipley (ed), *The Baptists of Yorkshire* (1912), pp 73-86.
34 Lambeth Palace MSS, Notitia Parochialis, Nos 748, 908.

Chapter 8

1   The wills and inventories referred to in this chapter are from the Deanery of Pontefract, BIHR, indexed by name, with the exception of reference 11.
2   W H Long, 'Regional Farming in Seventeenth Century Yorkshire', *Agricultural History Review*, Vol VIII, 1960, pp 103-14; and an unpublished survey of 1720-22 by the Yorkshire Agrarian History Group.
3   *WCR 1664-65*, pp 124, 177.
4   Cornholme WEA Branch, *Shore in Stansfield* (Cornholme, Todmorden, 1986), pp 8-9.
5   Heptonstall Township accounts 1754-9; DDSR 26/238, 31/411-22, 1/19/27.
6   See reference 2 above.
7   D Defoe, *A Tour through England and Wales* (Dent, 1928), Vol 2, p 195.
8   Heaton, pp 264-71; F Atkinson (ed), *Some aspects of the eighteenth century woollen and worsted trade in Halifax* (Halifax, 1956); Jennings, *History of Nidderdale*, pp 163-4; A P Wadsworth and J de L Mann, *The Cotton Trade and Industrial Lancashire* (Manchester, 1931), p 13.
9   Heaton, p 297.
10 M Dickenson, The West Riding Woollen and Worsted Industries 1689-1770, Nottingham PhD 1974, p 74.
11 *HAS 1962*, p 46.
12 Royal Commission on Historical Monuments, West Yorkshire CC, *Rural Houses of West Yorkshire 1400-1830* (1986), pp 27, 109.
13 *J D Purdy, Yorkshire Hearth Tax Returns* (University of Hull, 1991), pp 107-8.
14 Defoe, p 195.

Chapter 9

1   Township constables accounts.
2   The following account is based, unless otherwise stated, upon the constables accounts for Heptonstall, Midgley, Sowerby, Wadsworth and Warley, and T Sutcliffe, 'Warley Township Accounts', *HAS 1907* and H P Kendall, 'Sowerby Constables Accounts', *HAS 1906*.
3   Calendars of Wakefield House of Correction, 1825, 1832, 1834.
4   C Spencer, *The Coiners of Cragg Vale* (Halifax, 1984); H Ling Roth, *The Yorkshire Coiners 1767-83* (Halifax, 1906); T W Hanson, 'The Cragg Coiners', *HAS 1909*; C B Webster, 'Robert Parker, attorney', *HAS 1966*; *Leeds Mercury* Nov – Dec 1769, April – May 1770, July – Aug 1774, 18 April 1775.
5   The following account is based, unless otherwise stated, upon the churchwardens accounts for Heptonstall and Wadsworth.
6   *Halifax Wills I*, p 28.
7   The following account is based, unless otherwise stated, upon H W Harwood, 'Midgley Township

Records', *HAS 1940-42*, E W Watson and B Gledhill, 'Wadsworth Township Accounts', *HAS 1951-55*, Heptonstall surveyors accounts and West Riding Quarter Sessions records.
8   *Halifax Wills I*, pp 36, 38, 46-7, 49-52, 55, 58, 63, 69, 72, 98, 185-6.
9   The account of the turnpikes is based upon J L Hanson, Transport Development in West Yorkshire from the Industrial Revolution to the present day, London PhD 1949, and an unpublished paper by Mr B Gledhill, 'A Pennine Turnpike', copies held by HBLHS and Todmorden Antiquarian Society. Mr Gledhill used the minute books of the Halifax – Rochdale – Burnley Turnpike Trust, the present location of which is unknown, with the exception of the minutes for 1827-48 which are in Calderdale Archives, Halifax.
10 The following account is based, unless otherwise stated, upon the overseers accounts for Heptonstall, Midgley and Wadsworth.
11 Todmorden churchwardens accounts, 1722-3.
12 Holden, *Short History of Todmorden*, p 151.

Chapter 10

1   J James, *History of the Worsted Manufacture in England* (1857), pp 253, 293-4, 312, 324; Hanson, pp 199-204.
2   James, p 356; Wadsworth and Mann, pp 451-70; Heaton, pp 340-1, 356.
3   H Catling, *The Spinning Mule* (Newton Abbot, 1970), Chapter 1, pp 40, 151; W English, *The Textile Industry* (1969), pp 45-53; E Baines, *History of the Cotton Manufacture in Great Britain* (1835), pp 172-86.
4   R G Wilson, *Gentlemen Merchants* (Manchester, 1971), pp 20, 245; Calderdale Archives RP 932; RE 157243; Holden, pp 158-60.
5   WRRD CS 752; LCA Savile 1/140, 206; Sun 22/672162, 65/774103, 391/607866.
6   Crompton MSS, Bolton Public Library.
7   James pp 321-8, 355-6; RE 145015, 146645, 157479.
8   Valuation of the township of Warley, 1805; RE 95667, 130856, 143311, 156708, 158794.
9   RE 181456. General statements about the textile industry and other local industries are based, unless otherwise stated, upon a large databank, covering hundreds of firms and mills, maintained on behalf of the group by Mrs Sheila Wade of Holling Hall Farm, Luddenden Foot. To give all the detailed references here would be impractical.
10 RE 181456.
11 RE 148237, 98928.
12 *HAS 1967*, pp 40-1; WRRD CS 958.
13 LCA Savile MSS II/111.
14 G R Binns, 'Water Wheels in the Upper Calder Valley', *HAS 1972*.
15 B F Duckham, 'Canals and River Navigation', in D Aldcroft and M Freeman, *Transport in the Industrial Revolution* (Manchester, 1938), pp 100-13.

16 B R Law, 'The Calder Millowners and the Rochdale Canal', *HAS 1954*; *Rochdale Canal Act 1794* 34 George III, c. lxxviii; J Becket, 'A History of the Rochdale Canal', unpublished, Rochdale Reference Library; C Hadfield and M Biddle, *The Canals of North-West England* Vol 2 (Newton Abbot, 1970), pp 280, 290.

17 Boulton and Watt MSS, Engine Book Nos 16, 298, 311, Birmingham Public Library; *HAS 1908*, pp 127-8.

18 *FIC*, pp 26-37, 64-6, 71-5; J Fielden, *The Curse of the Factory System* (1836, 2nd ed 1969), pp 61, 65.

19 *HC* 22 Feb 1862.

20 Baines, *Cotton Manufacture*, pp 235-6; E Baines, *The Woollen Manufacture of England* (1875, new ed Newton Abbot, 1970), pp 70-1, 110.

21 *PP 1836 Vol XLV*, pp 148-57; James, p 445; W Dodd, *The Factory System Illustrated* (1842, reprinted 1968), p 145.

22 Fielden, pp 32-3, 69; Catling, Chapter 8; Dodd, p 145; G Crabtree, *A Brief Description of a Tour through Calderdale* (Huddersfield, 1833), pp 10-17; *FIC*, pp 71-5.

23 *HAS 1927*, pp 68 et seq; J Travis, *Notes on Todmorden History* (Todmorden, 1901), passim.

24 Watson, *History of Halifax*, p 69; Calderdale Archives Box 103.

Chapter 11

1   YASRS 71, 72, 75, 77, *Archbishop Herring's Visitation Returns 1743*, Vol I, pp 131-2, Vol II, pp 31-9, 149-50, Vol III, pp 49-51, Vol IV, pp 226-9.

2   F Baker, *William Grimshaw 1708-1763* (1963); J W Laycock, *Methodist Heroes in the Great Haworth Round 1734-84* (Keighley, 1909), pp 36-41; J U Walker, *A History of Wesleyan Methodism in Halifax and its Vicinity* (Halifax, 1836), p 24; N Curnock (ed), *The Journal of John Wesley* (8 vols, 1938).

3   W Darney, *A Collection of Hymns* (Leeds, 1751); F Baker, *Charles Wesley, as revealed by his letters* (1948), pp 82-7.

4   *Journal of John Wesley*, Vol 3, p 293.

5   Archbishop Drummond's Visitation Returns 1764, BIHR; J Fawcett, *Letters to his Friends by Rev John Parker* (Leeds, 1794), pp 32-3.

6   *Journal of John Wesley*, Vol 5, p 475; A Taylor, *Memoirs of Rev Dan Taylor* (1820), p 9; Walker, p 106; J Horsfall Turner, *Halifax Books and Authors* (Brighouse, 1906), pp 83, 95-6.

7   Taylor, pp 10-17, 31-2, 76-8.

8   *Journal of John Wesley*, Vol 5, pp 179-80; Baker, *William Grimshaw*, p 244; C. Stell, 'Calderdale Chapels', *HAS 1985* for 1984, p 23.

9   Taylor, passim; A Taylor, *Memoirs of Rev John Taylor* (1821), pp 21-5; W B Wilson and W S Davies, *A History of the Halifax and Calder Valley District of Baptist Churches* (Halifax, 1968), p 28-9.

10 J Fawcett, junior, *An Account of the Life, Ministry and Writings of Rev John Fawcett*, passim; Shipley (ed), *The Baptists of Yorkshire*, p 101.

11 Archbishop Drummond's Visitation Returns; Turner, pp 100-8; Stell, p 19.

12 M Edwards, *John Wesley and the Eighteenth Century* (1955), pp 150-61, 180-2.

13 Turner, p 238; R Currie, *Methodism Divided* (1968), pp 58-9.

14 A W Fox, *The Todmorden Unitarian Congregation, a centennial sketch* (Todmorden, 1924), pp 1-29; S A Weaver, *John Fielden and the Politics of Popular Radicalism* (Oxford, 1987), pp 30-5.

15 H P Kendall, *The Origin and History of the Primitive Methodist Church* (nd, c1905), pp 488-92; Walker, pp 250, 274; Stell, pp 28, 33; HO 129/495-6.

16 A Taylor, *History of the English General Baptists* (1818), pp 386-94; Wilson and Davies, pp 21, 30; HO 129/495-6; Shore Baptist Church Minute Book; J Wilson, *A Short Memoir of the Late Mrs Alice Wilson* (Manchester, 1877), pp 14-16.

17 G Lawton, *Collections relative to the Dioceses of York and Ripon* (1842), pp 129-36; HO 129/495-6; Heptonstall Church, terriers and accounts.

18 HO 129/495-6; *Census of Religious Worship 1851* (1853).

19 Stell; K Powell, *The Fall of Zion* (1980), pp 12, 31.

20 E G Thomas, *Heptonstall Slack Baptist Church 1807-1907* (1907), pp 116-7.

21 Ibid, pp 139-40; Fox, pp 65, 70-1; Wilson and Davies, p 16.

22 Thomas, pp 119-24.

23 Ibid, pp 56, 94; Wilson and Davies, p 24.

24 J S Purvis, *Tudor Parish Documents of the Diocese of York* (Cambridge, 1948), pp 104-6; *Charity Commission Reports*, Vol 18, 1828, pp 586-7, Vol 19, 1828, pp 291-2; Ramshaw, *Concerning Todmorden Parish*, pp 28-9.

25 *1833 Education Enquiry Abstract* (1835).

26 Ibid; HO 129/495-6 (Ed); Wilson and Davies, p 25.

27 *PP 1840 Vol X*, p 199; HO 129/495-6 (Ed).

28 Ibid; *PP 1846 Vol XX*, p 631, *1849 Vol XXII*, p 326; Ramshaw, pp 117-20; Holden, *Short History of Todmorden*, p 200.

29 HO 129/495-6 (Ed); *PP 1846 Vol XX*, p 588.

30 HO 129/495-6 (Ed).

31 The account of the mechanics institutes is based upon Yorkshire Union of Mechanics Institutes, *Annual Reports* 1840-48.

32 J W Hudson, *A History of Adult Education* (1851), p 234.

33 Factory Inspectors Reports, in *PP* Irish University Press series 1848-61.

34 Ibid, 30 April 1858, p 39.

35 Ibid, 31 Oct 1868, pp 7-8, 64.

36 Ibid, 30 April 1876, pp 25-6.

37 Spencer, *The History of Hebden Bridge*, pp 92-3, 110.

38 Ibid, pp 90-4; E M Savage, *The Development of Todmorden from 1700 to 1896* (Todmorden Antiquarian Society, 1971), p 15.

39 Minutes of School Boards, Calderdale Archives T/ED.

40 E and R Frow, *A Survey of the Half-time System in Education* (Manchester, 1970), pp 56-67.

41 P H J H Gosden and P R Sharp, *The Development of an Education Service: The West Riding 1889-1974* (Oxford, 1978), pp 17-22; Spencer, pp 103-4; R Birch, *Todmorden Album*, Vol 2 (Todmorden, 1987), p 28.

Chapter 12

1 E P Thompson, *The Making of the English Working Class* (1963), pp 276-7, 526-45, 586-7.
2 Ibid, pp 572-87, 602; HO 40/2/3, 8, 9; M I Thomis, *The Luddites* (Newton Abbot, 1970), pp 92-4.
3 Holden, p 184; Thomis, pp 169-70; HO 40/19, 41/7; Todmorden Political Union minutes, in the public library, Todmorden.
4 *FIC*, pp 26-37, 64-6, 71-5.
5 Crabtree, *Tour through Calderdale*, p 19.
6 Fielden, *Curse of the Factory System*. pp 31-5.
7 The information about poor law administration in 1831-32 is based upon *Poor Law Commission 1832-34*, Report Appx. A. Pt I, *PP 1834*, Vol 28/1, pp 797-9, Appx B, *PP 1834*, Vols 31-34, pp 614-33 in each volume.
8 MH 12/6272.
9 Ibid.
10 *Hansard 3rd Series, XXXVI*, 1016.
11 The account of the new poor law is based, unless otherwise stated, upon the following Poor Law Commission (MH) and Home Office (HO) files: MH 12/ 6272, 6273, 6274, 14974, 14975, HO 40/ 37, 38, 43, 51, 57, 41/13, 14, 45/43, 46.
12 Stansfield Township Order Book.
13 M E Rose, 'The Allowance System under the New Poor Law', *Economic History Review*, 2nd series, Vol XIX, pp 607-20.
14 The account of Chartism is based, unless otherwise stated, upon the files of *Northern Star* and *Halifax Guardian*, and HO 40/37, 43, 51, 53, 57, 41/13, 14, 16, 17, 45/43, 46, 249, 264.
15 J T Ward, *Chartism* (1973), pp 100-5.
16 F Peel, *The Risings of the Luddites, Chartists and Plug-Drawers* (Heckmondwike, 1888), Chapter 38.
17 Ward, pp 137-8.
18 PL 27/11 Pt 2/ERD 1418.
19 Ward, p 163.
20 Hanson, *Story of Old Halifax*, p 255.
21 J T Ward, *The Factory Movement 1830-1855* (1962), p 292.
22 G J Holyoake, *History of Co-operation in Halifax* (1866), p 16; G R Dalby, 'The Chartist Movement in Halifax and District' *HAS 1956*, p 102.
23 Weaver, *John Fielden*, pp 133-5, 268-71.
24 B Wilson, *The Struggle of an Old Chartist* (Halifax, 1887), p 18.
25 *Halifax Reformer* 31 May 1848.
26 Ward, *Factory Movement*, pp 346, 389.
27 Fielden, pp xxxvi-xxxix.

Chapter 13

1 J Marshall, *The Lancashire and Yorkshire Railway* Vol 1 (Newton Abbot, 1969), pp 24-52, 65, 71; Directors' minutes, Manchester and Leeds Railway, Rochdale Reference Library; *A Companion to the Manchester and Leeds Railway* (Halifax, 1841).
2 T Normington, *The Lancashire and Yorkshire Railway* (Heywood, 1898), passim.
3 H Clarkson, *Memories of Merry Wakefield* (Wakefield, 1889), pp 134-6; Marshall, pp 117-9.
4 Ibid, Vol 2 (1970), pp 104-13.
5 *Todmorden and Hebden Bridge Almanac 1897-99*.
6 See Chapter 10, reference 9.
7 *HG* 14 Mar 1840, 13 May 1843.
8 See Chapter 10, reference 9.
9 The Census Returns 1851-81, on microfilm in Calderdale Reference Library, Halifax.
10 *FIC*.
11 J Burnley, *The History of Wool and Wool Combing* (1889), Chapter X; E M Sigsworth, *Black Dyke Mills* (Liverpool, 1958), pp 38-43.
12 Travis, *Chapters of Todmorden History*, passim.
13 Ibid.
14 *TAHBT* 26 June 1901.
15 W O Henderson, *The Lancashire Cotton Famine 1861-65* (2nd ed, Manchester, 1969); N Longmate, *The Hungry Mills* (1978), pp 242-71, 290; *HC* Oct 1861 – Jan 1862; *HG* Jan – March 1962.
16 Henderson, pp 35-41; *HC* 20 Sep 1862; *THBA* Aug – Nov 1862.
17 Henderson, pp 75-80; *THBA* Aug 1862 – May 1863; *HC* 27 Sep, 8 Nov 1862.
18 *HC* Jan – June 12, 12 Sep 1863; *THBA* Oct – Dec 1863.
19 Fielden Brothers Letter Books, 1864-7; J Kelly in N B Harte and K G Ponting (eds), *Textile History and Economic History* (Manchester, 1973), pp 354-86.
20 *Sowerby Bridge Industrial Co-operative Society Jubilee History 1860-1910* (Sowerby Bridge, 1910).
21 Murgatroyd MSS.
22 *HG* and *HC*, passim 1879-82.
23 See Chapter 10, reference 9.
24 *William Edleston Ltd Sowerby Bridge 1848–1948* (Sowerby Bridge, 1948).
25 Rivers Pollution Commission, 3rd Report, Vol II, Part 2, *PP 1871 Vol XXVI*, p 148.
26 H Ling Roth, *Hand Card Making* (Halifax, no date), p 12.
27 Patent Office, 27 patents in the names of the Lord family, 1847-70.
28 *HG* 9 Mar 1850–52.
29 Holden, p 173; Wilson Brothers Centenary Booklet, *One Hundred Years 1823-1923* (Cornholme, Todmorden, 1923).
30 See Chapter 10, reference 9.
31 Agricultural Returns for 1866, 1874, 1880, 1894, 1900: MAF 68/81-2, 383, 725, 1523, 1865.
32 W B Crump, *The Little Hill Farm* (Halifax, 1938), pp 127-30.
33 English, *The Textile Industry*, p 172; the account of the fustian trade is based, unless otherwise stated, upon an unpublished paper by S C Moore, 'An Industrial Study of Hebden Bridge', the substance of which appeared in two articles

in *The Economic Journal*, 'The Industrial
Evolution of a Manufacturing Village', Vol XXI,
1911, pp 613–24, and 'The Trades Board Act at
work', Vol XXIII, 1913, pp 442-7. A copy of
Moore's paper is in HBLHS.

34 *HG* 11 July 1868, 6 Jan 1872.
35 Worralls' *Directories of Cotton Spinners and
    Manufacturers* 1893-1913.
36 Ibid, 1901-13.
37 Holden, p 207.
38 Binns, 'Water Wheels in the Upper Calder
    Valley'; T Gledhill (ed), *Sowerby Bridge Chamber
    of Trade and Commerce Tourist Guide* (Sowerby
    Bridge, no date), p 12.
39 A E Jones, *Roads and Railways of West Yorkshire
    1890-1950* (1984), pp 13-14, 39-44, 54, 56.

Chapter 14

1   N H Gregory, *A Century's Progress: 100 Years of
    Co-operation in Hebden Bridge* (Hebden Bridge,
    1948); *CN* 16 May 1903, 30 Jan 1937; MH 13/
    6274.
2   Gregory; F Pickles, *Jubilee History of the Bridge
    End Equitable Progressionists Society Ltd*
    (Todmorden, 1901); *CN* 16 May 1903 and
    passim.
3   Pickles.
4   *HBT* July 1910 – Feb 1911.
5   Yorkshire Union of Mechanics Institutes,
    Annual Reports 1856-58; Fox, *Todmorden
    Unitarian Congregation*, p 54; *Luddenden Foot
    Industrial Co-operative Society Jubilee History
    1860-1910* (Luddenden Foot, 1910).
6   J Greenwood, *A Brief Sketch of Twenty-one Years
    Work in Co-operative Production* (Hebden Bridge,
    1891), and 'The Story of the Formation of the
    Hebden Bridge Fustian Manufacturing Society
    Ltd', 1888, paper in the records of the Fustian
    Society, CWS Library, Manchester.
7   *CN* 4 April 1903, 8 Aug 1908 and passim.
8   Pickles; *Sowerby Bridge Co-operative History*; *HC*
    and *HG* passim 1859-77.
9   Pickles; Gregory.
10 Pickles; Gregory.
11 *CN* 26 July 1900.
12 Pickles; Gregory; *CN* 12 June, 31 July 1897, 16
    May 1903; *Annual Report of Co-operative
    Congress 1898*, pp 21-3.
13 N A Jepson, *The Beginnings of English University
    Extension* (1973), Chapter 19; B Jennings, *Albert
    Mansbridge* (Leeds, 1973), pp 1-3.
14 Greenwood, *Brief Sketch*; Rewley House,
    Oxford, Extension Delegacy Annual Reports.
15 *OUEG* Nov 1890, Jan – Feb 1891.
16 Ibid, Feb 1894; *The Parnassian* Vol 1, 1925.
17 *CN* 18 Oct 1930; B Jennings, 'Robert Halstead',
    in J M Bellamy and J Savile (eds), *Dictionary of
    Labour Biography* Vol 2, 1974, pp 154-9.
18 *CN* 1897-8 passim; *Annual Reports of Co-
    operative Congresses 1896-8*; *UEJ* Oct 1894, May
    1897, Oct, Dec 1900; R Halstead, 'Working
    Men and University Extension', *OUEG* May

1893, 'The Stress of Competition from the
    Workman's Point of View', *Economic Review*,
    Jan 1894, 'Some Thoughts of a Workman
    Concerning the Plea for a Living Wage', Ibid,
    July 1895, 'Labour Copartnership',
    Commonwealth Vol 4 No 3, 1899.
19 *CN* 19, 26 Aug 1899, 27 Oct 1900;
    A Mansbridge, *Adventure in Working-Class
    Education* (1920), p 13; B Jennings, *Knowledge
    is Power: A Short History of the WEA 1903-78*
    (Hull, 1979), pp 1-7.
20 P Thomas, The Origin and Early Ideals of the
    Hebden Bridge WEA, Leeds MA Dissertation,
    1974; Central Joint Advisory Committee for
    Tutorial Classes, *Annual Reports 1909-14*; J F C
    Harrison, *Learning and Living 1790-1960* (1961),
    p 270; Hebden Bridge WEA Minute Book 1909-
    36; Rewley House MSS C3.
21 R Howard, *History of the Typhus of Heptonstall
    Slack* (Hebden Bridge, 1844), pp 7-14.
22 Hanson, *Story of Old Halifax*, pp 262-5;
    Sowerby Bridge WEA, *Sowerby Bridge, Our
    Memories, Our History* (Halifax, 1988), pp 2-3.
23 Holden, pp 210-1; Savage, *Development of
    Todmorden*, pp 13-16.
24 Spencer, *History of Hebden Bridge*, pp 84-9;
    Luddenden Foot Co-operative History; D
    Warrington, 'From Sorebi to Calderdale', *HAS*
    1974.
25 Spencer, pp 33-6.
26 Ibid, p 89; Holden, p 214; Savage, p 16; H W
    Harwood, article in *HC* Aug 1954.
27 *Annual Report of Co-operative Congress 1925*, pp
    9-10; *HBT* 25 April, 7 Dec 1879, 19 Oct 1880,
    19 Aug 1910, 29 June 1912; Spencer, pp 138-41.
28 *HBT* July 1906 – Jan 1909; *CN* 16 Nov, 14 Dec
    1907.
29 Ibid; *HBT* May 1907 – May 1911; *TA* 18 Nov
    1910.
30 S C Moore, 'The Trades Board Act at Work',
    Economic Journal Vol XXIII, 1913, pp 442-7.
31 W Greenwood, 'Fifty Years of British Industry
    from the Workman's Point of View', *Economic
    Review*, July 1900, pp 323-32.
32 Howard, pp 55-9.
33 Moore, unpublished paper.
34 *CN* 2 Aug 1902, 18 May 1918; Spencer, p 140.

Chapter 15

1   W H Long, *A Survey of the Agriculture of
    Yorkshire* (1969), pp 67-8.
2   Fox, *Todmorden Unitarian Congregation*, p 100.
3   Wilson and Davies, *History of the Halifax and
    Calder Valley District of Baptist Churches*, pp 12-
    21.
4   Todmorden Unitarian Church, *Centenary
    Booklet*, 1969.
5   Calder Civic Trust, *The Case for a Pennine Park*
    (1972); *Pennine Magazine*, Vol 1, No 1, 1979.
6   G Hughes, *Millstone Grit, a Pennine Journey* (Pan
    ed 1987), pp 78, 130.

Index

Note: This is a comprehensive index of topics and major place-names. Churches and chapels, mills, houses, etc, have been indexed selectively, to facilitate cross-referencing. Names of people mentioned once only in illustrative extracts from documents have in most cases been omitted.